THE STORY
OF AUSTRALIA

THE STORY OF
AUSTRALIA

by

A. G. L. SHAW

FABER AND FABER
London · Boston

First published in 1955
by Faber and Faber Limited
3 Queen Square London WC1N 3AU
Second impression 1956
Third impression 1958
Second edition (revised) 1961
Reprinted 1962
Third edition (revised) 1967
Fourth edition (revised) 1972
Reprinted 1975
Fifth edition (revised) 1983
Printed in Great Britain by
Whitstable Litho Ltd Whitstable Kent
All rights reserved

© A. G. L. Shaw, 1955, 1961, 1967, 1972, 1983

British Library Cataloguing in Publication Data

Shaw, A. G. L.
The story of Australia.—5th ed.
1. Australia—History
I. Title
994   DU110

ISBN 0-571-18074-4

CONTENTS

PREFACE TO THE FIFTH EDITION   *page* II

1. THE LAND AND ITS PEOPLE   17
2. FOUNDING A COLONY   31
3. SETTLEMENTS AND TENSIONS   44
4. EXPLORATION BY SEA AND LAND   61
5. SQUATTING   74
6. GOVERNMENT AND SOCIETY   88
7. VARIATIONS ON A THEME   105
8. THE GOLD RUSH AND ITS AFTERMATH   123
9. THE CALM BEFORE THE STORM   137
10. THE STORM BREWS   151
11. THE STORM BREAKS   168
12. FEDERATION   182
13. DEVELOPMENT RENEWED   197
14. THE FIRST WORLD WAR AND AFTER   218
15. BETWEEN THE WARS   233
16. WORLD WAR II   253
17. POST-WAR ECONOMIC PROGRESS   268
18. CONTEMPORARY AUSTRALIA, ABROAD AND AT HOME   286

FURTHER READING   313
INDEX   315

ILLUSTRATIONS

Map of Australia today   *pages* 12, 13
When Welsh meets Welsh (*by courtesy of David Low*)   223
White Australia (*by courtesy of the* Bulletin, *Sydney*) 231

9

PREFACE TO THE FIFTH EDITION

★

This book, originally written in 1954, was intended to give in reasonably popular form the story of Australian development. At that time there were many gaps in our knowledge, for all too little historical research had been done in the past; since the end of World War II, there has been a great advance, and many projects which shed light in dark places have been completed. Some traditional interpretations have been shown to be not wholly true and today we are much better informed about past events than thirty years ago.

In successive editions, I have made a number of changes in detail and in emphasis, though the structure of the book remains the same; for this edition, the last chapters have been completely rewritten to bring the story down to 1982.

Since the bulk of the book is not based on my own original research, my indebtedness to previous writers is naturally enormous, but I wish to thank specifically a number of scholars who have particularly influenced my work one way or another—Emeritus Professors Sir Keith Hancock and R.M. Crawford, Professors John Ward, Michael Roe, Geoffrey Blainey, the late Professors James Auchmuty and Douglas Pike, the late Dr. Charles Currey, Drs. R. M. Hartwell and Allan Martin, Miss A. Thompson (Zain u'ddin) and S. M. Ingham, among others—though indeed the list could be almost endless, embracing almost the whole 'profession'.

Mrs. Eleanor Dark kindly granted permission to publish the quotation from *No Barrier*, and Miss Marjorie Barnard that from *My Australia*.

A. G. L. Shaw, November 1982

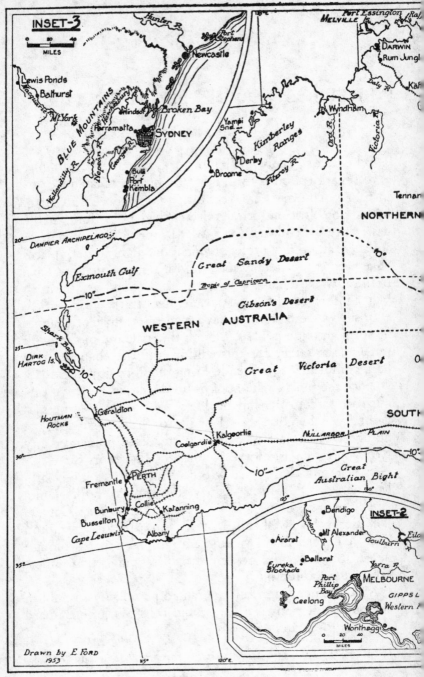

AUSTRALIA

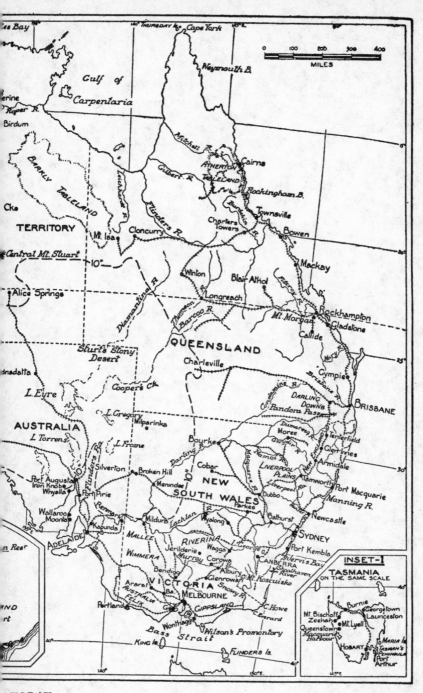

TODAY

THE STORY
OF AUSTRALIA

Chapter One

THE LAND AND ITS PEOPLE

D uring the greater part of the history of so-called
civilized man, Australia remained a land unknown
to the rest of the world, even to its nearest neighbours. To Europeans, it seems the newest of the continents,
only discovered in 1606 by the Dutch when Captain Jansz
sailed the yacht *Duyfken* from the East Indies to the Gulf of
Carpentaria, and developed in the nineteenth century at a
time when steam power and industry were revolutionizing
society in Europe. Yet geologically it is the oldest continent
in the world, for in the north-west is a shield of land that has
probably been above water for 1,600 million years. In another sense too, it is the oldest, since its only inhabitants before 1788 were Stone Age people, said to be the only race
which could serve as a common ancestor for all mankind.
Some of them may have been living in Tasmania in the Ice
Age 30,000 years ago, but the first European settlement was
not made until 1788, eighteen years after the discovery of
the fertile east coast by Captain Cook.

In India, South Africa and New Zealand English colonists
were opposed by native peoples, vigorous and often highly
civilized; in Australia there could be no serious resistance
from the aborigines with their primitive culture. But there
was resistance of a different kind, which formed an experience unlike that of the United States of America, resistance
from the land itself and its climate, from the scanty and un-
reliable rainfall and from the vast semi-arid plain merging
into the trackless desert which covers more than one-third
of the continent.

In the end this resistance was overcome; but the struggle was long and often painful, and it was made more difficult at first by the easy, if natural, assumption that English customs and English standards could be applied, unmodified, to this strange new country. For to Englishmen it was very strange—hot, dry and often drought-stricken, with its clear blue skies, its soils badly starved for manure, and its strange evergreen trees, heavy and hard, so often warped and useless for building, and so difficult to clear from the land. Everywhere there seemed to be something wrong.

On the eastern coast, the site of the first settlements, there was good rainfall but poor washed-out soil except on the river flats, and these seemed so often to be flooded by the short, fast-flowing streams, rushing down their narrow valleys from the mountains, rarely more than fifty miles from the coast. Behind this narrow plain rose a mountain barrier, the rugged 'Great Divide', stretching the entire length of the continent. It was not crossed for twenty-five years, until 1813; then appeared the best land of Australia—now the wheat belt and good sheep and cattle country. This is 'the bush', not parched, like the desert of the interior, but dry, and liable to droughts that may reduce the wheat harvest by more than half, or wipe out a quarter of the sheep and cattle population of the continent. On the western slopes of the mountains the rainfall is moderate and reasonably reliable for wheat-growing and mixed farming; but farther west, on the plains of New South Wales, where the rain is scantier, the sheep rules supreme, giving place to cattle farther north in Queensland. With irregular alternation good and bad seasons may bring rich grasses, or lay the paddocks almost bare; but where in the best of times only some fifty merino sheep can graze to the square mile only large properties can survive.

Beyond the Darling, in far western New South Wales, is the real 'outback', leading to the desert. The Darling itself, in flood a raging torrent, and carrying considerable river traffic in the nineteenth century, often runs salt or becomes merely a series of water-holes; as far as the Indian Ocean there is not another river properly so-called. Dry creek-beds may run for a few days after the infrequent rains and look impressive on a map. They are of no more use for cultivation than are the salt lakes Frome, Gregory and Eyre, with their six-inch rainfall, amid the sea of salt-bush, spinifex, mulga and nothingness.

South-east of the desert the country gradually improves, as the rainfall increases; its temperate climate brings to western Victoria that lusciousness that made its discoverer, Mitchell, write with joy of *Australia Felix*. But to the West the desert stretches on and on, with the transcontinental railway like a ruled line bisecting the Nullarbor Plain, and not a single stream breaking the southern coastline for more than a thousand miles. Only approaching the south-west corner, do we find once more gold and cattle, then sheep, then wheat-lands, timber, orchards and dairy cows.

The north of Australia lies in the tropics. On the narrow coastal belt of eastern Queensland heavy monsoon rains encourage the growth of sugar and tropical fruits. But over the mountains there is the same old story of lack of water. For a space the great artesian basin makes reasonable cattle country; but farther west, on the Barkly Tableland and Victoria River and in the Kimberleys, the monsoons, though heavy, are quickly over. The rest of the year is a long dry spell, with feed only enough for very sparse grazing, with cattle often infected by tick and the buffalo-fly, while men contend with heat and drought, dust, ants, termites, scorpions and centipedes, with 'willy-willies' thrown in for good measure.

For Australians to-day it is perhaps fortunate that the west and north-west coast was so unattractive, since this was the most likely point of contact with the teeming civilizations of south-east Asia. This western and north-western coast would have repelled any chance Chinese[1] visitors who

[1] There is considerable doubt whether the Chinese actually arrived at this time. That they embarked on major expeditions is clear, and a hard stone

might have arrived from their exploring expeditions of the
sixteenth century, just as it repelled the Dutch when in a
series of voyages they landed on and charted parts of the
coast between 1606 and 1644. It repelled the buccaneering
Dampier, in 1688, when he found a land with little water,
no food except turtle, no trees bearing fruit or berries, and
inhabited by 'the miserablest people in the world. The
Hodmadods of Monomatapa, tho' a nasty people, yet are as
gentlemen to these . . . who, setting aside their human shape,
differ but little from brutes.'

It was probably here, in the north between Cape York
and the Kimberleys, that the Australian Aborigines entered
the continent, driven by stronger races from Malaya and
India across the disintegrating land bridge of Indonesia.
When they came the ocean crossing was probably shorter
than it is to-day; but as the extensive continental shelf off
these coasts became covered by the sea, they were protected
by the widening ocean, and by the repellent, dreary land,
from the wilder and fiercer tribes that had driven them
from their homeland. The first comers, a negroid people
with frizzy hair, were slowly driven south to Tasmania,
probably before the formation, by subsidence, of Bass
Strait. There followed a second wave of people with straight
or wavy hair, not quite so dark as their predecessors; they
are probably of Dravidian origin, linked with the hill tribes
of southern India. Some moved south by the west coast,
others went eastwards through the Gulf of Carpentaria
country. Becoming somewhat tinctured with Papuan influences, the majority remained in what is now Queensland,
but a number of tribes continued south to New South
Wales and Victoria, occupying the coastal districts and river
valleys.

figure of the Chinese deity Shou Lao, undoubtedly of Chinese manufacture,
has been found at Darwin. The circumstances of its discovery very strongly
suggest that it must have reached the site not earlier than the late 17th or early
18th century; but there is no other evidence that Chinese seamen reached
Australia then.

Any estimate of their numbers at the time of the first British settlement can only be approximate, but probably there were about 300,000 on the mainland and 5,000 in Tasmania. Today there are little more than half that number, of whom about two-thirds are of mixed blood. In 1788 the Aboriginals were a semi nomadic people. They knew nothing of agriculture, had no permanent settlements, lived in huts of mud or branches, the bark mia-mia or gunyah, and had no domestic animal but the dog. Perhaps this is not surprising, for sailing across the sea in primitive canoes they could bring little with them, and Australia offered them no native animals that could be domesticated and no native plants that could be cultivated for food. Perforce the Aborigine had to hunt, which he did with surprising skill, spearing kangaroos or fish or goannas, and to collect grass seeds for flour, and witchetty grubs, wild honey, turtle eggs, mangrove-fruit pulp or yams.

This scarcity of food affected much of the tribal life and customs. There was the ritualistic sharing of food; the birth control practised by the giving of young wives to old men, and the very long initiation period for young men, during which it was death to touch a woman. There was little fighting, for there was no time for it. To a nomad, who had to travel light, clothing was usually an encumbrance in the mild dry climate, though a few made use of skins. Skilled trackers and keen observers, they did not use the bow in the chase, the weapons of hunting being the boomerang, the throwing stick and the club. A bark tray, a wooden coolamon or drinking vessel, a primitive bucket—these comprised almost their whole equipment.

But material backwardness was not everything. 'They may appear to some to be the most wretched people upon Earth, but in reality they are far happier than we Europeans,' wrote Cook. They 'are naked and are not ashamed; they live chiefly on Fish and wild Fowl and such other articles as the land naturally produceth . . . they may truly be said to be in the pure state of Nature . . . They live in a

Tranquillity which is not disturbed by the Inequality of Condition . . . They covet not Magnificent Houses, Household staff, etc.; they sleep as sound in a small hovel or even in the open as the King in His Pallace on a Bed of Down'. In fact, they had a well-wrought theory of life. Beliefs about the nature of man and the nature of the world were preserved in many complicated myths, legends and rituals. The whole countryside was thought to be infested with spirits living in caves, or in river-beds or water-holes. Over all was the system of totem, usually an animal thought to be an actual ancestor, who was often transformed into the sacred form of the *tjurunga*, commonly an oval of wood or stone, engraved with a geometrical design emblematic of the totem itself, and having its *mana*, or spiritual power and virtue.

Through the totem we see the ancestors governing the whole life of the tribe. Not only were they its direct progenitors, but by means of increase ceremonies the totem was responsible for the growth of the plants and animals on which it depended for its living. As is usual in such a system of ancestor-worship, the old men were the respected guardians of tribal lore and the protectors of tribal society. Only gradually were the youths initiated into its mysteries, after a long training and many awe-inspiring and frequently painful ceremonies. It was at about the age of eight that the boys were commonly taken from the women. Soon might come the first ceremony of the nose-piercing; at twelve the major rite of initiation, accompanied by great feasting and dancing, and with many variations from tribe to tribe. Typical of these was the tree ceremony, jumping down into the arms of the waiting men below; or the ceremony of blood-drinking, to the accompaniment of the swinging of the sacred bull-roarer, and the knocking out of two teeth. In all there might be as many as nine ceremonials in a full initiation spread over many years, with long periods of silence and fasting, before the boy was admitted a full member of the tribe and permitted to take a wife—though curi-

ously enough the aboriginals appear to have had no knowledge of man's share in reproduction and recognized descent
only through the mother. The child was thought to be conceived simply through the child spirit, helped perhaps by
the totem.

Creatively, the chief outlet was the corroboree. The corroboree meant not only the sacred dance for ceremonies
initiating the youth or welcoming strangers, or even for the
hunt or the battle; there were also the play corroborees,
with chorus and dancers, reminding us of the embryo of
Greek drama, and the historical corroboree recording
notable events in the history of the tribe, including even
some of the early encounters with the white men.

These encounters were at first peaceful. The English
government had excellent intentions and wanted to civilize
the aborigines and 'live in amity and kindness with them'.
Philanthropic and missionary zeal kept this aim steadily before the Colonial Office, but 'on the frontier' it was easier
said than achieved. The first accounts of 'New Holland' are
filled with long stories of the 'Indians'; but what most impressed the newcomers were the externals of dirt, disease,
poverty and ignorance. 'It is hardly possible to see anything
in human shape more ugly', wrote Captain Tench. 'They
never clean their skin,' said Hunter. As settlement began to
spread other problems appeared. How could the nomadic
food-gathering tribes be protected 'in the full enjoyment of
their possessions', when they had no land but all the land,
and every new arrival was likely to impinge upon some ancient hunting ground? The land was seized by the Crown
and distributed among the settlers; none was reserved for
the natives, 'driven back into the interior as if they were dogs
or kangaroos'. The totemic shrines were not respected; cere-
monial gatherings became impossible. Hunting and food
gathering became trespass, often stealing. There would be
bloodshed and retaliation. Then the natives had 'to be
taught a lesson', and the punitive expedition followed. The
'battle' of Pinjarra in West Australia in 1833, though offi-

cially disapproved of in Great Britain, showed the inevitable outcome. White violence in New South Wales was virtually unchecked and unpunished until the infamous Myall Creek massacre in 1838; then seven men were hanged for the murder of twenty-eight friendly natives of both sexes and various ages, in retaliation for an alleged 'outrage'. 'We were not aware that in killing the blacks we were violating the law . . . as it has been so frequently done before,' argued the defence. Certainly it was frequently done again, and the Aboriginals were soon driven from the more fertile parts of the continent. Probably few more than 1,000 Europeans were killed by Aboriginals in the whole of Australia; on the other side the death toll seems to have been 20,000 or even more. But much more fatal was sickness (smallpox, influenza, tuberculosis, venereal disease), the effects of alcohol and occasionally of poison, and the occupation of hunting grounds causing loss of food. In the Port Phillip district, where the Aboriginal population fell from about 10,000 to 1,900 between 1835 and 1853, it has been estimated that more than 5,000 died from disease and about 1,000 from settlers' violence; but whatever the cause of their decline, clearly the Aboriginals were not in a position to obstruct white settlement.

Nor were the native animals, like the humans shut in this island continent and cut off from the rest of the world for thousands of years, any menace to the newcomers. But they too were 'interesting'. Grass-eating, they did not prey on each other; and protected by the sea from their carnivorous rivals, they had been able to live on, an almost prehistoric collection, with the marsupials the most peculiar and the most representative. The kangaroos and wallabies, quick-moving, grass-eating, have been compared with the deer and the antelope of other lands and different development, while the tree-living, leaf-eating opossum (strictly speaking the phalanger) and koalas correspond to the more normal monkey, the wombats to pigs and the bandicoots to rodents. To these natives, more damaging immigrants have been added—the dingo or wild dog, probably brought by the Aborigines, the fox and the rabbit, brought by white men, destined to prey upon sheep and to eat up the pastures. These were man-created obstacles to settlement.

Others were the product of nature—water, distance, trees. The greater part of Australia lies in the latitudes of the desert zone which encircles the world, the latitudes of North Africa, Arabia, Persia, Turkestan and the Punjab in the northern hemisphere and the Kalahari desert in South Africa. Forty per cent of the country lies in the tropics, and receives the summer monsoon; but it lasts only about three months, is confined fairly close to the coast and is far lighter and less reliable than farther north, in Indonesia and New Guinea. The east coast receives rain from on-shore winds throughout the year, but it rapidly decreases as one moves inland, so that in the comparison made by Professor Griffith Taylor 'the Australian reached an arid environment rather like that of Arizona, when only 450 miles from the coast, while an American, going west on a similar journey, was just reaching the best section of the United States in Eastern Ohio'. Across southern Australia there passes a great 'westerly drift' of atmosphere, arising originally at the Equator and bringing rain as it moves south and east. But in summer it reaches sea-level far south of the continent. In winter, when the sun has moved northward, the 'drift' and the rains follow it; but they are heavier and more regular south of the fortieth parallel; they strike only the coastal fringe and all too often fail and cause drought. In Central Queensland, north-east South Australia and northern New South Wales the water of the Great Artesian Basin, derived from the rain on the north-east coast, is drinkable by stock and offers a valuable substitute for rain water in an area where the intense heat and high evaporation would make surface conservation difficult. Though too strongly alkaline for agriculture, it has made over half a million square miles of the interior available for grazing.

Valuable though the artesian bores are, they do not solve

the problem of distance, aggravated as it is by lack of water. The bore, it is true, might help stock travelling on the hoof. But the cheapest form of inland transport is by navigable river, and such rivers are almost non-existent in Australia. Only the Murray has a reliable flow, and even it is too shallow in summer. Moreover it goes in the wrong direction, not to the cities and harbours of Melbourne and Sydney, but to a bar-blocked lagoon, inaccessible to shipping, in a desolate part of the coast of South Australia. The coastal mountains blocked early railway building; even after the lines had been laid, railroad mountaineering involved extra expense in fuel and locomotives, not to mention long stretches of route through unprofitable country. It was the relative ease of transporting wool rather than wheat that helped, and still helps, the pastoralist to achieve his economic strength, although in the last seventy years the railway has greatly increased the area of Australia's wheat lands. But long-distance transport through sparsely settled country whether by road or rail is a costly business, which perhaps helps to explain why Australian inland roads are so bad, and why the annual number of air journeys per head is the second highest in the world.

To the first settlers, the Australian landscape was heavily forested. Here was another obstacle. 'We shall close over them like the sea,' says the Chorus of the Trees of the approaching white men.[1] 'Stem to stem, with our narrow leaves turned edge on to the sun, conserving the moisture, we will stand our ground. They come at their peril.... And when we are gone the land will erode and waste, the rains will not come.' Near parts of the coast is a dense evergreen forest of tall cedars and creeping vines. Elsewhere the three hundred and fifty species of eucalyptus reign supreme, from the giant ash, growing more than two hundred and fifty feet high with a girth up to twenty feet, to the dismal

[1] 'A Mask of Australia', in M. B. Eldershaw: *My Australia* (Jarrolds, 1939), p. 15.

and monotonous 'scrub', found almost everywhere in the interior.

There is nothing like the great wide grassy prairie or Canada and the United States to be found in Australia. The 'pastures' of the interior are sparse—spinifex, saltbush and mulga; in the heavier rainfall areas, before cultivation or even extensive pasturage becomes possible, the eucalyptus must first be cleared away. The tree is ring-barked by cutting a ring of bark from the trunk to prevent it from feeding. It slowly loses its leaves and branches and dies, leaving the trunk standing, dry, white and ghostly, until eventually it is felled or blown down or burnt. Clearing was hard work in pioneering days, but often, through ignorance, or greed for land and timber, it was overdone, and soil erosion has been one result; however it had to be done if the land was to be cultivated, and mistakes were probably inevitable. More disastrous have been the great bushfires which in the past have so often brought death to man and beast. Now they are somewhat checked by 'aerial spotting' and the use of bulldozers to make fire-breaks; but they are still a great menace, and 'bush-fire danger high' is an all too common feature of weather forecasts in the summertime.

As in the case of the animals, the most destructive form of vegetation now in Australia was brought by settlers, the cactus known as prickly pear. At one time it covered an area greater than that of England and Wales; now it is controlled by the appetite of the *cactoblastis* caterpillar. But apart from scrub and forest much of the natural vegetation is of great beauty, with the yellow blossoms of more than five hundred species of wattle, the vivid scarlet of the flame-tree, with its flowers sufficiently conspicuous to be seen on the mountains from ships miles out to sea, or the vast mass of colourful wild flowers which grow almost everywhere after rain, and which in their temporary, but most brilliant, luxuriance sometimes give a false impression of the fertility of the countryside. Nor should one overlook the six hundred and sixteen species of Australian birds, of which four hundred

and thirty-one are unique. Here is colour and song in plenty
—the brilliant paroquets, the budgerigars, lorikeets, cocka-
toos, rosellas and galahs, kingfishers, mistletoe- and rain-
bow-birds, the lyre-bird, the mimicking bower-bird, the
stockwhip-bird, the bell-bird and the mopoke, apart from
the universally known trio of magpie, emu and kooka-
burra. This is an essential part of the 'bush' which is known
to all Australians whether country people or not, known
because visited, seen, heard and wondered at even by the
city-dwellers, who can travel or camp in the forest mountain
districts or the national parks within a few hours' drive of
all the great Australian cities.

For Australia to-day, despite its size, larger than all
Europe excluding Soviet Russia, almost the same size as the
U.S.A., is an urban country, with two-thirds of the population in the six state capitals and only one-sixth 'truly rural'.
This division is the result of the difficulties of inland development and is not due to any want of trying to settle outback.
The population of the less distant interior and of the rural
coastline is still growing and will continue to grow; but the
vast empty spaces of the continent are likely to remain, except for scattered mining centres, because they are desert and
semi-arid. They comprise what has been described as a
'fascinating, a tantalizing region' whose history has been a
series of 'promise and hope followed by bitter failure and
ruin. In its good seasons, its miles of waving grasses lure
men to their destruction. . . . Then the grassy plains change
to a burning stony desert, the stock gradually die out, the
sand drifts over the pitiful fences and stockyards. . . . Month
after month the brazen sky is watched, heavy clouds form,
only to clear away again. But some day the cooling torrents
will fall, and the country will wave with grass again.'[1]

Meanwhile the great coastal cities continue to grow, filled
by a population until 1945 more than ninety-five per cent
British, employed in their thriving industries, nourished

[1] C. T. Madigan: *Central Australia* (Cambridge University Press, 1936),
p. 140.

a little, perhaps, by their distance from overseas competition and by sundry advantages drawn from a good and cheap supply of certain basic raw materials. Many publicists deplore this concentration, yet it seems to a great degree determined by geography. For the Australian coastline, with its many attractions of surf and sand of a type undreamed of by most Europeans, has the disadvantage of possessing very few natural harbours, and of these quite a number lack access to a prosperous hinterland. The railway, the roads, the harbours, the governments combine to concentrate the people; and against these forces, the cries of uneconomically minded, unthinking social theorists, with arguments based only on a sentimental feeling, are but voices crying in the Australian wilderness.

But that is no reason for despair, or even for valid criticism. The men who came to Australia, as to the United States, came, as Sir Keith Hancock has said, 'not in despair but in hope', seeking a better life, free from the worst of the grinding poverty of the old world. While they could, they preferred, as a rule, to go to America; it was nearer and therefore cheaper. But when they came to Australia, assisted by government, or seeking gold, or responding to some other attraction, they generally found what they sought, though they still lived in cities, as in England. Even in the cities the sun shone, and though there were slums and poverty and distress the standard of living was higher than that of the old world; and despite initial handicaps and later mistakes, the record of the Australian people, in a century and three quarters, compares favourably with that of an equal, if not a longer period, in South Africa, New Zealand, Canada or even the United States of America.

'Said the Voice of the Continent:

These newcomers will destroy the cycle of life; the dry spells will become droughts, sand will eat up the good lands, fire and floods will wipe him out. If they do not know the secret of life, the secret of the trees, how can they survive?

'Said the Herald of the Future:
   They will bring knowledge and engines from overseas;
   new animals and new plants.
'Said the Voice of the Continent:
   I shall turn their inventions against them. . . . I am old,
   and they are frail and new. I have conquered one race,
   I shall conquer another.
'Said the Herald of the Future:
   Nevertheless, they shall survive. And they will come
   to you at last in love, and will honour and serve you.
   They will take your strength and secret power and
   raise it to another plane. You will be a hearth and home
   to a new race.'[1]

The hearth and home of a new race, or at least a new
nation, of 'independent Australian Britons', as Hancock has
described them, such has this strange Australian continent
become, a nation proud of its connection with Britain—
'home' as it is still so commonly called—but proud too of
itself, its heritage and its traditions, well bearing out the
prophetic hopes of Governor Phillip on his first landing on
the shores of Port Jackson, 'I have no doubt that the country
will hereafter prove a most valuable acquisition to Great
Britain.'

---

[1] 'A Mask of Australia', in M. B. Eldershaw, op. cit., p. 16.

Chapter Two

FOUNDING A COLONY

hy did the British decide to settle in this strange southern land of which early reports spoke so badly? The Dutch had touched on the northern, western and south-western coasts several times after 1606, had reported unfavourably and done little more. They were, in fact, somewhat afraid that settlement in Australia might interfere with their profitable trading monopoly with the East Indies. In 1642–3 Tasman sailed round the continent, landing in Tasmania and sighting New Zealand, but when the reports of this voyage reached Holland in 1645, the directors of the Dutch East India Company resolved that 'it were to be wished that the said land continued still unknown and never explored, so as not to tell foreigners the way to the Company's overthrow.' The only important Dutch voyage made subsequently was that of Roggeveen in 1721–2, under the auspices of a rival concern, the Dutch West India Company. Setting out from America this resulted in the discovery of the Easter Islands in mid-Pacific, with their great figures of basaltic stone which more than two centuries later were to become famous as part cause of the Kon Tiki expedition. But this was not Australia, and to Roggeveen as to Drake, Magellan, Torres and other circumnavigators the great southern continent remained unknown.

In the first half of the eighteenth century interest in the Pacific was kept alive, not only by Swift and the travels of Gulliver, but by accounts of voyages there, especially that of Anson (1740–4), and by the commercial speculations

associated with the notorious South Sea Company and its
'bubble', even though its main concern was trade with
Spanish America. In 1748 an enthusiastic propagandist, John
Campbell, painted in glowing colours the prospects of gain
from 'New Holland', and he was echoed in France in 1756
by Charles de Brosses, who thought not only of the profits
of commerce but also of the glory of scientific discovery.
Unfortunately the Seven Years' War intervened to check
such glory, despite Brosses' appeal for it in preference to 'the
conquest of some little ravaged province, of two or three
cannon-sheltered fortresses acquired by massacre, ruin, deso-
lation'.

After the war, it was the British who once more took up
the task. There was more propaganda, and in 1769, Alexander Dalrymple, a former employee of the East India Company, deduced from earlier reports the existence of an enormous continent of 'greater extent than the whole civilised
part of Asia', with a population of fifty millions; trade here,
he argued, would assuredly 'maintain the power, dominion
and sovereignty of Britain', whatever might be the outcome
of the trouble brewing in North America. More practical
were the voyages of the 'sixties, by the English, Byron,
Wallis and Carteret and by the Frenchman, Bougainville;
these explorers found more Pacific islands, but unfortunately they all returned too far north to sight the Australian
coast. Next came Captain James Cook, who sailed from
Plymouth on 26th August 1768. Ostensibly on a scientific
expedition to observe the transit of Venus from the Pacific,
he carried secret instructions from the Admiralty. Since
'there is reason to imagine that a continent, or land of great
extent, may be found to the southward of the track . . . of
former navigators', he was to sail to the latitude of 40°
south in search of it and, if successful, to explore the coast,
and the nature of the people, of the soil and of its products.
He spent six months on the coasts of New Zealand, and
found it was no part of the great unknown continent; then
he sailed westward once more. On 19th April 1770, he

sighted the east coast of Australia. Ten days later he landed at Botany Bay. From there he sailed up the coast, ran into great danger on the Barrier Reef, proved that 'New Holland' and New Guinea were two separate islands, and after refitting in Batavia reached England again on 13 July 1771. He had not discovered any great continent in the south Pacific; but he had virtually proved that it did not exist. He had not discovered New Zealand; but he had correctly reduced its dimensions from fiction to fact. He had not discovered 'New Holland'; but he had discovered the eastern coast of the mainland, which he charted for five thousand miles. And he was not the first to sail through Torres Strait between Australia and New Guinea; but he had emphasized the separation of the two islands. It remained to be seen what use Great Britain would make of these lands now better known and more fully reported on.

For fifteen years the government did nothing. Involved in the difficulties of the American War of Independence, it had no time to consider any possibilities of settlement in the remote antipodes. Yet it was this American war that finally gave the stimulus to action; for the loss of the American colonies raised a number of problems for British statesmen. What was now to be done with the convicts hitherto transported to America? What could be done, if anything, for the American 'loyalists'? And for British trade?

The imagination of James Matra, a former midshipman on Cook's *Endeavour*, was seized by the possible advantages of founding a colony in New South Wales. It would 'afford an asylum' for the loyalists; it would be good for trade with China, Japan and the Spice Islands; it would make an excellent naval station in the Pacific, of great benefit should Britain again be at war with Spain or Holland. Unfortunately ministers were only lukewarm. The loyalists were far away; the commercial advantages seemed somewhat hypothetical, and in any event the East India Company had a legal monopoly of eastern trade; as so often at the end of a war, disarmament seemed more economical than the build-

ing of naval bases. But there was another factor to be considered—the problem of the gaols.

English criminal law in the late eighteenth century was in
a fantastic state. A primitive police system left the detection
of criminals almost entirely to the activities of an unpaid
magistracy or private societies for the prevention of crime.
Obviously both these means, though partially effective in
country villages where the small population was fairly well
known, were ludicrously inefficient in London and the
growing industrial towns. There the watchmen paid by the
parish were normally so old and infirm as to be useless, even
if they had not warned any evildoers of their approach by
crying the hour. Only in London did the Bow Street Run-
ners provide anything remotely resembling an efficient organization. There were no public prosecutors; any criminal
who did happen to be caught could only be prosecuted by
his victim, a proceeding always expensive and sometimes
dangerous. Hence many a thief, even if arrested, got off un-
scathed, especially if he or his friends were able to make a
timely composition with the injured party. The result was,
as the Solicitor General said in 1785, 'nobody could feel himself unapprehensive of danger to his person or property if he
walked in the street after dark, nor could any man promise
himself security in his bed.'

In these circumstances the only method of checking crime
that Parliament could devise was that of prescribing heavy
penalties to deter offenders. Though the chances of capture
were slight, at least the criminal who was successfully prosecuted should be severely punished so that his fate might be
an example to others. Following this policy, Parliament had
made some two hundred crimes punishable by death. They
ranged from treason, murder, arson and rape, to picking
pockets of more than one shilling, cutting hop-binds, destroying turnpikes or impersonating Egyptians. Needless to
say, there were few if any prosecutions for numbers of these
offences, and acquittals were numerous; even so, more than
fifty persons per year were publicly executed in London

alone between 1780 and 1790, the executions themselves being popular spectacles of entertainment which provided opportunities for further crime. But many sentenced to execution were reprieved, on condition of their being transported to the colonies, while many were sentenced to transportation in the first place, so that before the American War of Independence about a thousand criminals were sent to Virginia and Maryland every year.

No wonder, then, that the war caused an overcrowding of the gaols, which had never been intended to hold large numbers of *convicted* prisoners for long terms of imprisonment. No wonder either, that the hulks, fitted out on the Thames as a temporary, emergency measure to hold the convicts until they could again be transported, were soon overcrowded also. What could be done with these criminals, who were not only being confined in most unhealthy conditions, but were, at the end of their sentences, being released 'in the vicinity of the metropolis', where they would indubitably 'renew their depredation on the public'?

One suggestion put forward by criminal-law reformers like John Howard, the famous investigator of the *State of the Prisons*, and Jeremy Bentham, was that convicts should henceforward be confined in a new-style penitentiary. Here, by a regime of solitary confinement, instruction and well-regulated labour, the criminal would be reformed, and restored to society a changed man, though his experience, especially of solitude and hard labour, would still be such as to act as a strong deterrent to crime. An act of 1779 authorized the construction of two such institutions as an experiment, but, for better or worse, this was never done. There were difficulties. Would the convict really be reformed? Sceptics took leave to doubt it. More serious was the expense. Even if, as their advocates hoped, penitentiaries would yield profits eventually from the produce of their convicts' labour, they would certainly be expensive to build, and Parliament was loath to vote the money for such a 'visionary' project. Moreover it would take a long time, and many penitentiaries, to house those four thousand convicts crowding the hulks and the county gaols.[1] Quicker and cheaper to transport them again.

But where to? After the American war, the erstwhile colonists refused to accept any more felons from England, as they promptly showed by their reception of a trial shipment. Some convicts had been sent in the past to garrison Cape Coast Castle, in Africa. Now the African Company refused to accept them. Perhaps a penal colony could be established. Investigations were made on the River Gambia and farther south between Angola and the Cape; but the reports on both were unfavourable. Why not Botany Bay? Lord Sydney, the Home Secretary, thinking of Matra's proposals, 'observed that New South Wales would be a very proper region for the reception of criminals condemned to transportation'; whereupon Matra in 1784 amended his plan so as to include convicts as well as free settlers. Next year, Admiral Sir George Young wrote on the same theme. A colony of American loyalists, convicts and settlers 'from the Friendly Islands and China' could be formed 'without robbing Great Britain of her inhabitants, and with only a small part of the expense our government are at in their present ineffectual attempts to punish the felons'. Young sounded again the Imperial note, stressing the advantages of a naval station, of Far Eastern trade, and the local possibilities of timber, flax and various other products.

'To what end are all the discoveries of our great forefathers, and lately those of the wonderful Cook! Shall so wide, so noble a field for the exercise of enterprising spirits, be relinquished by this nation? . . . Cook's discoveries were not given in vain; and a very small beginning on this plan is sufficient to promote the general good

[1] In fact the first penitentiary at Millbank was not completed until 1821. It should be noted that the number of prisoners was *not* 100,000 as has so often been stated, following a rhetorical exaggeration by Edmund Burke in the House of Commons. In fact there were, according to Howard, 7,482 prisoners in the whole of England and Wales, including 2,011 debtors and 1,412 petty offenders, leaving 4,050 who were liable to be transported.

of the human race. . . . A territory so happily situated must be superior to all others for establishing a very extensive commerce, and of consequence greatly increase our shipping and number of seamen.'

But Ministers seemed little concerned with such imperial speculations. The settlement of the loyalists was ignored. The expert view of Admiral Howe was that 'the length of the navigation . . . does not . . . encourage me to hope for a return of the many advantages in Commerce and War which Mr. Matra has in contemplation.' The trade of New South Wales might interfere with the monopoly rights of the East India Company. The Committee of the House of Commons which examined the proposal in 1785 discussed it solely in regard to its penal aspects, and the King's speech in 1787 announced simply that 'a plan has been formed . . . for transporting a number of convicts in order to remove the inconvenience which arose from the crowded state of the gaols'.

Naturally, Ministers hoped that the settlement would be profitable. Sir Joseph Banks, who had accompanied Cook and on the strength of a few days at Botany Bay was ever after regarded as an expert on Australia (and it must be admitted he always took a great interest in the colony), thought not only that the escape of convicts from here would be difficult, but that the good soil and abundance of timber would make it possible to 'furnish matter of advantageous return'. In any case it was expected that the settlement would quickly become self-subsistent, so that the expense compared with the hulks would not be very great— 'too trivial to be a matter of consideration to government', in the view of Lord Sydney, which is hardly surprising when we remember that the cost of keeping a convict in the hulks was nearly £27 a year.

And so, in May 1787, the First Fleet set sail from Portsmouth, and on 26 January 1788 Governor Phillip, with his party of 1030, including 736 convicts, landed at Sydney Cove, in Port Jackson, New South Wales. He was optimistic about the future prospects of the settlement. Here was 'the finest harbour in the world, in which a thousand ship of the line might ride in the most perfect security'; although 'no country offers less assistance to the first settlers than this does . . . time will remove all difficulties'. But for the moment the difficulties were immense, and it was perhaps natural that to many of his officers, sent on such an expedition so far from home, the prospects of the colony looked gloomy, 'a country and a place so forbidding and so hateful as only to merit execration and curses'. There were mosquitoes, 'very troublesome', and ants 'whose bite is attended with most acute pain'; there was 'nothing deserving the name of fruit', and the wood was useless 'except for firewood'. Though 'nothing can be conceived more picturesque than the appearance of the country', it was 'greatly to be wished these appearances were not so delusive as they are'. There was no sign of the 'meadows' reported by Cook. On the contrary the land near Sydney was not fertile—'the soil to a great depth is nothing but a black sand which when exposed to the intense heat of the sun by removing the surrounding trees is not fit for the vegetation of anything, even the grass itself then dying away'. It was so very different from England. There might be 'gently swelling hills' and 'vales with every beauty that verdure of trees and form can produce', but where were 'those murmuring rills and refreshing streams which fructify and embellish more happy lands'? The officers of the First Fleet suffered from nostalgia, as have so many more new arrivals from England since their time.

It was not only the men who preferred the conditions of 'the mother country'. The English cereals did not receive the rain which they had been led 'by generations of evolution to expect'. Such knowledge of agriculture as any members of the expedition possessed, and it was slight, was suited to English, not Australian, conditions. How should one cope with the summer heat, or the drought? Little would grow without manure. But with practically no livestock, there was no manure. Phillip had but one bull, one cow, four calves, one stallion and three mares, three colts, and forty-four sheep and a few pigs and poultry; but in six months only one sheep remained, 'owing to the rank grass', and the cattle had been lost in the bush. Indeed, all provisions and equipment sent out were sadly deficient, with the government blandly assuming that 'the settlement will be amply supplied with vegetable production and most likely with fish'. 'I am sorry to say', reported Phillip, 'that not only a great part of the clothing, particularly the women's, is very bad, but most of the axes, spades and shovels the worst that ever was seen. . . . The wooden ware sent out were too small; they are called bowls and platters but are not larger than pint basons.' There was no plough in the settlement till 1803. Even if one had arrived, it would have been almost impossible to use, on land so littered with stumps. As late as 1820 the Society for the Encouragement of Arts, Manufactures and Commerce was offering a prize for 'the best method, verified by actual experience, of raising out of the earth and removing the stumps and roots of trees, so as to clear the land for cultivation'. Consequently the settlement had to rely on a primitive 'hoe husbandry' which did little more than scratch the surface of the ground.

But if equipment and knowledge were scanty, there were even greater shortcomings in the human element. Of the convicts, it is true that the majority had been convicted for relatively minor offences; for the most part, however, they represented the sweepings of London and the provincial cities. Selected from the hulks almost at random, few had any knowledge of agriculture, and there were barely a dozen mechanics with any knowledge of building. Some forty died on the voyage out, and another seventy-eight within six months of landing. Many were sick, especially from scurvy, and lack of proper food, clothing and shelter rapidly increased the number who were a 'burthen' on the community, apart from the fifty-two who were 'unfit for labour from old-age and infirmities', and the women who mostly 'lived in a state of total idleness'. Of those who were well, the majority were unwilling workers, relying on government to keep them from actual starvation (though in this respect their faith was not entirely justified). 'Experience has taught me', said Phillip, 'how difficult it is to make men industrious who have passed their lives in habits of vice and indolence. . . . And though I can say that the convicts in general behave well . . . those who have not been brought up to hard work, which are by far the greatest part, bear it badly.'

Scarcely more helpful were the free men. Phillip had hoped to keep them apart from the criminal element. 'As I would not wish convicts to lay the foundations of an Empire,' he had written before sailing, 'I think they should ever remain separate from the garrison and other settlers that may come from Europe, and not be allowed to mix with them.' But this was not easy to arrange, even though the 'other settlers' were so few. All were confounded into one mass struggling for existence. The officers of the marines tried to keep apart and 'declined any interference with the convicts, except when they are employed for their particular service'. This meant that only convicts were available to act as superintendents or overseers, with inevitable effects on the quality of work done. No wonder that within four months the Governor became anxious about his supplies, and wrote to England 'of the necessity of a regular supply of provisions for four or five years, and of clothing, shoes and frocks in the greatest proportion. The necessary implements for husbandry and for clearing the ground brought out will with difficulty be made to serve the time that is necessary for sending out a fresh supply. . . . The crops for two years to come cannot be depended on for more than will be necessary for seed.'

Unfortunately the store ship *Guardian*, which had left England with supplies and provisions in September 1789, nearly two and a half years after the departure of the First Fleet, was wrecked near the Cape of Good Hope. Conse-

quently the only 'relief' experienced in 1790 was the arrival
of the Second Fleet, which had sailed with another thousand
convicts, though 267 died on the way out. The remainder
had to be fed and cared for, and nearly five hundred were
landed sick, many nearly naked, helpless, and without bed
or bedding. This large sick list was partly due to close confinement on board following an attempted revolt, but what
was worse, the gaol authorities had chosen the most useless
prisoners for transportation. 'The sending out of the dis-
ordered and helpless', commented Phillip, 'clears the gaols
and may ease the parishes from which they are sent; but,
Sir, it is obvious that this settlement, instead of being a
Colony which is to support itself, will, if the practice is continued, remain for years a burthen to the mother-country.'
But in 1791, before this protest could be received, another
1,864 convicts were sent, of whom 198 died on the voyage,
and of the rest 'the greatest part are so emaciated, so worn
away by long confinement or want of food, that it will be
long before they recover their strength, which many of
them will never recover'. During 1791, no less than 171
persons died and 621 were receiving medical treatment,
leaving a 'healthy' population, including women and
children, of 3,433. Even these were suffering from lack of
nourishment on a weekly ration which had had to be restricted at one period to two and a half pounds of flour and
'bad worm-eaten rice', and two pounds of salt pork.

Fortunately by 1792 local cultivation was improving. A
thousand acres of ground were being tilled on public account, and over four hundred by 'settlers'. This development followed the discovery of more fertile land about
fifteen miles up the harbour from Sydney, at Rose Hill, the
modern Parramatta, and was made possible by better seasons
after the disastrous drought of 1790. The first 'settlers' were
only time-expired convicts and mariners, men usually with
neither capital nor agricultural experience; but their farms
were better than nothing, and in March 1791 one emancipist
grantee was self-supporting and took himself 'off the store'.

As early as October 1788 Phillip had asked for free settlers to be sent out, in the hope that these, with the help of convicts' labour, could make the country self-supporting; but only some twenty arrived before 1800. A more important contribution was made in 1792 when permission was given to make land grants to the military and civil officers. These were educated men with capital, if not agricultural specialists; when granted convict labour on easy terms they might be able to increase considerably the produce of the colony.

Meanwhile grants to marines and emancipists had also been made on Norfolk Island, some thousand miles northeast of Sydney. Phillip had been instructed to settle here in order to obtain supplies of flax 'which you will find growing spontaneously on the island'. This suggests that, in founding a penal settlement, the British government was not averse to obtaining commercial and naval advantages on the side. Unfortunately British Ministers were mistaken, and the flax, observed 'growing spontaneously' from the windows of Downing Street, was less obvious at close quarters. None the less, the island was fertile and by 1792 there were more than 700 persons there, including over a hundred marine and emancipist settlers.

When Phillip sailed in December 1792 the first dangers of the settlement had been overcome. It would not have to be abandoned to avoid starvation, even though 'the period at which this colony will supply its inhabitants with animal food is distant'. There was now a population of 3,000, cultivating 1,700 acres of land; and more than 4,000 acres had been granted to settlers, to be worked by convict labour. As private establishments became able to employ the convicts and produce food, 'public farming' would be reduced. But, since there was no flax and the timber was poor, 'the scheme of being able to assist the East Indies with naval stores, in case of a war, must fall to the ground'. There was no move to bring out emigrants, American loyalists or otherwise; on the contrary, the government could not meet Phillip's urgent requests for settlers with some knowledge of farming.

No 'matter of advantageous return' was yet apparent. 'The country, my Lord,' wrote an anonymous officer, in April 1790, 'is past all dispute a wretched one. . . . There is no wood fit for naval purposes; no fibrous grass or plant from which cordage can be made; no substance which can aid or improve the labours of the manufacturer; no mineral productions; no succulent vegetables . . . and, which is the most serious consideration, no likelihood that the colony will be able to support itself in grain or animal food for many years to come.' The production of wool was still far off; even the possibilities of whaling and sealing had barely been explored. Critics complained that the colony was costly and it deprived England of population, for even the labour of convicts was of value and it was being 'entirely lost to the country'.

But the government was satisfied, for it had not fully shared the more grandiose designs of some of the publicists. Probably it felt that it was a good thing to anticipate any possible French settlement in the Antipodes, particularly in view of the Anglo-French disputes over Holland in 1786–87, and the French expedition under La Pérouse, and thus to solve its penal difficulties with an eye to international strategy. However, when defending the settlement in the House of Commons in 1791 Pitt stressed that 'it was a necessary and essential point of police to send some of the most incorrigible criminals out of the Kingdom. . . . No cheaper mode of disposing of the convicts could be found.' Now that it was securely established he thought 'the chief expense of the colony was already passed and paid'—an optimistic illusion, but one which persuaded the government to carry on their experiment until a more prosperous future for it was assured.

Chapter Three

SETTLEMENTS AND TENSIONS

As a penal colony, Botany Bay had its advantages. It was far off; return would be difficult. Conditions were hard; transportation there would be an effective deterrent; in the early days several convicts begged to be executed rather than sent to this terrible unknown land, inhabited by 'Indians'. The life might even be reformatory; at least lip service was given to such a suggestion. The emancipist would be given land to cultivate. He would have an opportunity of earning an honest living, or so it was hoped; and while a convict, subject to irksome discipline and hard labour, he would have previously learned habits of 'industrious labour'.

Unfortunately things did not seem to work out according to these expectations. As settlement developed, the worst hardships diminished. When convicts were 'assigned' to settlers as servants, it sometimes happened that their masters were tempted to treat them kindly, in order to encourage them to work; they would even be given 'luxuries' as incentives—tea and sugar, or even tobacco and spirits. This was especially the case where the convict was a mechanic whose labour was particularly valuable. If he was living in Sydney, he could mix with friends, evil companions who would hinder his 'reform'; it was easy for him to obtain illicit liquor, or to find the society of prostitutes. Convicts working for the government were no better; complaints of their idleness and 'depravity' were continually heard. There were no convict barracks till 1815, owing to the shortage of buildings and the desire for economy, apart from a generally haphazard administration. Convicts, surprising as it may seem, lived in private lodgings; they had to be allowed a certain amount of time to 'work on their own' to earn wages to pay for their board, and such wages could be, and often were, spent on 'dissipation'. To encourage work and good behaviour, or as reward for special services, the practice of granting remissions of sentence grew up, either pardons, or more commonly tickets of leave; and the ticketholder, though he had to report to the police and remain in a prescribed district, could work for himself, and accumulate property if he could earn it.

This too had its objections. By saving money a convict could acquire a farm or small business in Sydney, would be so much the less likely to want to return to England, and might even be able to earn an honest living; but if such an honest living was easy to earn in Sydney, transportation would be no punishment. Forgetting the hardships of separation from one's family and friends, or ignoring the fact that it might be a hardship to a 'labouring' man, who was supposed to lack any family feelings anyway, forgetting too the very real severities of convict discipline, with its frequent corporal punishment, English Ministers could only see how, in one way or another, transportation seemed to benefit the criminal. Reports in England were naturally exaggerated. The few cases where emancipists had made fortunes were regarded as typical. Letters describing the attractions of Sydney were quoted while its hardships were conveniently ignored. Crime in England was increasing, particularly in the more depressed economic conditions after the Napoleonic wars. If one ignored the depression, as most contemporaries did, was not this proof that transportation was no longer a deterrent to crime—that it was failing to achieve what to Englishmen seemed the most important aim of punishment? At all events Lord Bathurst, Secretary of State for the Colonies, was beginning to think so, when he wrote of the convicts being subject to 'little more than nominal restraint', and enjoying 'a freedom inconsistent with the object proposed in transporting them. . . . As a place of punishment, it has not answered all the purposes for which it was intended.'

British Ministers, thinking chiefly of their problems, were anxious to stress the *deterrent* aspect of transportation, however much they might pay lip service to the principle of reformation. But in New South Wales, where Governor Macquarie at least was trying to build a colony from chiefly convict material, it was natural that 'reformation' seemed more important, if it could be achieved. And apart from moral reformation, from the colonial point of view it was necessary by hook or by crook to induce the convicts and ex-convicts to work—whether on public buildings or on growing food—and if they became honest in the process so much the better. Hence the necessity of giving rewards and encouragements during sentence, and of granting land to emancipists; hence Macquarie's opinion that 'once a convict has become a free man, he should in all respects be considered on a footing with every other man in the colony, according to his rank in life and character,' on the principle that 'long-tried good conduct should . . . do away, in as far as the case will admit, with all retrospect of former bad conduct. This appears to me to be the greatest inducement that can be held out towards the reformation of the manners of the inhabitants,' concluded the Governor, and at least in 1812, before the post-war increase in crime in England, a committee of the House of Commons agreed.

But the emancipist, even if granted land—usually thirty acres if he was single, fifty if married, with ten extra for children working with him—did not have everything his own way. Though some of the early difficulties of agriculture had been overcome, plenty remained. As the land near Sydney had proved so unfertile, most farms were now some distance off, either around Parramatta, or on the Hawkesbury. Here the soil was better, but technique remained primitive, transport was a problem, and floods were frequent. Although the settler received his land free from the government, he usually had little or no capital, and quickly ran into debt, a process accelerated by the peculiar commercial and financial conditions of the colony.

The only regular market for local produce was the government store; but curiously, either through ignorance, or through their firm intention to have as little to do with commerce as possible, the governors failed to use this institution to help the settlers, but rather the reverse. After a good harvest, supplies would exceed current demand, and the store would be closed. Little or no attempt was made to accumulate reserves, and the unfortunate farmers were forced to sell their surplus crops to speculators for what price they could get; the fact that prices would soar when the harvest failed was of little benefit to those who would then have nothing to sell, though it brought great profit to merchants, expense to government, and hardship to consumers. In the single year 1813, the price of wheat varied from 5s. 9½d. to 20s. 10½d. a bushel, though of course such fluctuations were not peculiar to Australia. It was all very well for Governor Macquarie, when the shortage came at the end of the year, to criticize the earlier 'most shameful' waste and destruction of grain; he had failed to take the only reasonable means of preventing it by buying it for store at a fair price. Macquarie did try to protect the settlers from some of the exploitation they had suffered before his arrival, but although he was able to get rid of the military-trading monopoly of the 'rum' corps, other traders remained to exploit the vagaries of the market.

The 'monopoly' had arisen, quite legitimately, in the early days of the colony. At that time any trading vessel arriving was able to sell its cargo at fantastic prices when supplies of all kinds were so short. To protect themselves against such exploitation, the military officers in Sydney decided to enter trade on their own account and 'with a few others possessed of money or credit to unite together and purchase the cargoes of such vessels as repair to this country'. This arrangement, it was argued, prevented 'monopoly and the impositions which would otherwise be practised by the masters of ships'. Quite true, it did; but though satisfactory for the officers, for the colonists as a whole it was merely an escape from the frying-pan into the fire, since the officers had greater power and more opportunities to coerce their customers. Soldiers' wages were paid in kind—at the officers' prices; so were payments to settlers selling their crops. And what was most demoralizing of all, was the growing tendency to dispose of rum in this way, particularly in part payment of wages, thus encouraging drunkenness in a community already rather lacking in sobriety.[1]

The result was that 'no one could adequately describe the conditions of riot, dissipation and depravity that existed among the lowest class of the inhabitants'; the colony was 'infested with dealers, pedlars and extortioners'; and thanks to its isolation, the neglect of its needs by the British government and the inexperience of the early naval governors in the handling of economic problems, these traders had plenty of scope, though they were no different in kind from those in any small, isolated community. The farmer soon ran into debt and land was transferred from the small settler to the large proprietor; the 'peasant' society of emancipists, envisaged vaguely by the British government and more clearly by Macquarie, could not survive.

Nor was this surprising. Such an agricultural system had failed in Great Britain in the eighteenth century (if not even earlier) as the advantages of a new technique using capitalist methods became apparent. Why then should it succeed in New South Wales, where the character of soil, climate and market made the advantages of capitalist agriculture so much greater? None but 'capitalists' could afford to buy or breed stock, so necessary not only for 'horse-power' but also

---

[1] It is a mistake to imagine, as a number of historians have done, that rum was widely used as 'currency'; but thanks to the demand for it from 'an insatiable Australian thirst' it was a common article of barter, and was widely used for 'incentive payments' to labour, as is explained by Professor S. J. Butlin in *The Foundations of the Australian Monetary System* (1953), chap. 1.

for manure, nor could any farmer successfully combine stock-raising with agriculture on a farm of fifty acres. And without this combination, how could he carry out a proper crop rotation? He could only sow wheat, year after year, on the same land, with a progressive lessening of harvests as the soil became exhausted. Only the 'capitalist' could survive the droughts and floods, the pests and diseases—caterpillars, smut, rust; only a capitalist as a rule could afford, without crippling indebtedness, even to bring his farm into cultivation (or to procure some other means of livelihood during his years of preparation). 'An emancipated convict', said William Cox, J.P., 'had much better remain as a labourer than cultivate his thirty acres, if he be obliged to live on it.' Governor Macquarie was inclined to disagree. 'The best and most useful class of settlers are the emancipated convicts,' he declared. But even he was forced to criticize them, after a visit to the Hawkesbury River farms in 1810. 'The settlers in general [had] not paid that attention to domestic comfort which they ought to do by erecting commodious residences for themselves and suitable housing for the reception of their grain ... nor [could] he refrain from observing on the miser-able clothing of many of the people . . . whose means of providing decent apparel at least [was] sufficiently obvious to leave them no excuse for that neglect. . . . Here the farms, although long in a certain degree of cultivation, still remain totally devoid of fences, whereby the crops of grain are continually exposed to the inroads of the wandering herds and flocks and are frequently thereby destroyed or at least trodden down. . . . The fallen trees and dead stumps still remaining unburned at once disfigure the appearance of the country and present the greatest impediments to everything like neatness or lucrative cultivation; and where these do not prevail the noxious plant called the Cotton Tree extends over large portions of rich soil, which, with a little industry, might be made to yield valuable crops of grain and pastur-age. A very great neglect of manuring and otherwise im-proving these lands is also too evident to be passed over unnoticed; and to all these circumstances may be justly attributed the general deficiency of those comforts the families of the settlers seem commonly to labour under. The wretched mean appearances of the farm-houses and offices in these districts and the inattention to personal cleanliness of the inhabitants had frequently attracted [his] notice and [had] frequently called for his reproof and admonition.'

The 'gentlemen settlers' were much the same. They were often ex-soldiers, arriving with letters of introduction but without means, ignorant, and 'with military habits of idle laziness' making them 'amost universally lazy, dissipated, turbulent, discontented'. 'Nearly the whole of those persons who have arrived here in the character of Settlers', Macquarie wrote, 'have been ignorant of everything in the farming line, and have in consequence generally proved totally inadequate to the Tasks they have undertaken. . . . Gentlemen Settlers come out here miserably poor, depend principally on the indulgences granted them by Government and very seldom attend to cultivating their lands.' When granted a hundred or a hundred and fifty acres of uncleared country, they were in little better plight than the emancipists. All the governors since Phillip had asked for good practical farmers, with respectable families. But they would not come. They could earn a good living in England.

The men who succeeded were men of capital, and, as might have been expected, those who had capital in New South Wales had not always been too scrupulous in the means of acquiring it. The profits of the rum trade and the public house, the profits of efficient farming in the early days, the favours of government in the grants of land or servants, legitimate speculation, money-lending, sometimes force, often fraud, some good luck and enterprise: these were the means by which most of the early fortunes of New South Wales were made. The numbers of the educated community were small, being almost confined to the military and civil officers of the government, plus a few industrious and intelligent emancipists. As early as 1800 the community was virtually in the hands of a score or so of farming officers, holding the small grantees in their power, and continually in process of buying them out. By 1820, nearly 400,000 acres of land had been granted, but only 70,000 to ex-convicts, of whom most were 'in a state of dependence on their creditors or were seeking opportunities of removing themselves', and many of the small grants had fallen into the hands of the capitalists at Sydney.

Some of these remained merely 'landlords', drawing rents without caring for cultivation. But many of them were interested, for their own profit if for no other motive, in improving their farms and their pastures. Of course there were wide differences. Among the emancipists, both Simeon Lord and Samuel Terry, though holding 4,000 and 19,000 acres respectively in 1820, the bulk acquired by purchase, had cleared less than 400 between them, and preferred to continue in trade and speculation. At the same time six other Sydney publicans had bought an average of more than 1,000 acres apiece. Poles apart from the publican-trader-profiteer were such emancipists as Andrew Thompson, publican and trader certainly, but with much land cultivated on the Hawkesbury, and Dr. Redfern with his model estate of some 2,000 acres near Liverpool. Then there were a number of officers and officials like William Cox, army paymaster, defaulter and bankrupt, who had acquired considerable estates by 1813, the surgeons Balmain, Harris and D'Arcy Wentworth, chaplain Marsden, Commissaries Williamson and Palmer, Lieut.-Colonel O'Connell, Captain Piper and many more besides. Less typical perhaps were the Blaxlands, who arrived in 1806 seeking an investment and received a grant of 8,000 acres and eighty convicts. Still less typical was John Macarthur, who came to Sydney as Lieutenant in the New South Wales Corps in 1790.

Macarthur quickly saw the possibilities of the colony for a man of enterprise. He was one of the principals of that group of officers who combined to form the so-called 'rum monopoly'. But he also saw the profits to be made from agriculture. His farm at Rose Hill was one of the best in the colony. After two years he sold produce worth £400 and still had 1,800 bushels of corn in his granaries; he had twenty acres of wheat and eighty acres of Indian corn growing, with the all too rare livestock—a horse, two mares, two cows, over one hundred goats, and hogs and abundant poultry; in 1796 when a cow was worth £80 and a horse over £100, his wife could well write that 'those persons who took early precautions to raise live-stock have at present singular advantages'. Perhaps his military duties suffered; but they were not very arduous, even though the Secretary of State might complain that 'considering Captain Macarthur in the capacity of an officer on duty with his regiment I can by no means account for his being a farmer to the extent he appears to be'.

Not only a farmer, but a grazier also. He first purchased sheep in 1795 though at first, like other colonists, for mutton. In 1797 he bought some of the Spanish merinos which the future Governor King had persuaded Capt. Waterhouse, R.N., to buy at the Cape of Good Hope to bring to Sydney. Next year he had about 1,000 sheep, but it was only after he had bought the flock of Capt. Foveaux of the N.S.W. Corps three years later that he became the largest sheepowner in the colony. His wool was not then markedly different from that of several other colonists who had been making 'every effort . . . to improve the hair into wool by means of the three Spanish rams brought here in 1797'; but when in 1801 he was arrested for duelling and sent to England for trial, he took with him samples of his wool, which were declared to be 'equal to any Spanish wool'. By skilful if inaccurate propaganda, Macarthur created the impression (which remains widespread to this day) that he was the first and only breeder of fine-wooled sheep in the colony, and so he induced the Privy Council and the Secretary of State, Lord Camden, to instruct Governor King to grant him 5,000 acres on the good land of the Cowpastures, with thirty convicts, so that he might 'extend his flocks to such a degree as may promise to supply a sufficiency of animal food for the Colony as well as a lucrative article for export for the support of our manufactures at home'. To help him in these efforts, he bought five pure merino rams from the Royal stud at Kew and obtained special permission to taken them out of England.

In fact, Macarthur was neither the only grazier nor the only man interested in sheep-breeding in New South Wales. That holy man, the Reverend Samuel Marsden, was interested in his animal flock as well as his human one—but he looked for 'Beauty of Make, Strength of Constitution, and Weight of Carcase' as well as 'Fleece'. Governor King noticed widespread interest in sheep, but his successor reported that 'in general, animal food is a greater object to the proprietors of sheep than the Fleece, as there is an immediate demand for it'. To the Governors themselves, food was still all-important, when a drought or a flood might put the colony on reduced rations. 'Sheep will in time increase both in number and quality,' said Bligh, 'but the latter is not an object which everyone can yet entirely attend to. Herdsmen are scarce, and if a few individuals were to have all the Servants they pretend should be allowed them in this pursuit, the Agriculturist should want his Labour and his Inhabitants Grain for their common consumption.'

Herein lay the germ of conflict with the Governor. For Bligh, anxious for the colony's food supplies, anxious to help the poorer settlers against those whom he thought to be exploiting them, was inclined to oppose the pretensions of the Sydney financiers and speculators of whom Macarthur was one of the chief. Bligh, immediately after his arrival in August 1806, had toured the Hawkesbury districts; he found them suffering severely from most disastrous floods, and so took steps to remedy the situation. He distributed meat from the government herds to the starving farmers, and he undertook to buy for the Commissariat all the wheat they wished to sell at 10s. a bushel. Next year, after 'plenty and contentment had been restored', the

Governor gave to the settlers orders to buy necessary articles from the Commissariat, to be paid for after the next harvest. Here was a direct blow at those 'who had grown corpulent in the drunkenness of the Colony', at those like Macarthur himself who had only recently caused a large rise in the price of mutton by withholding his wethers from the market. No wonder the irascible Governor demanded 'What have I to do with your sheep, Sir? Are you to have such flocks as no man ever heard of before?" and when reminded of promises made by the Secretary of State, is said to have exploded, 'Damn the Secretary of State! He commands at home, I command here.'

This of course was the fact, and was at once the strength and weakness of the Governor's position. In the colony he was an autocrat. Responsible only to the British government, from whom it took over a year to receive an answer to a despatch even if by a miracle it were answered promptly, he could ride roughshod over opposition so long as he retained British support. But distance means misunderstanding. Other people in Sydney could write to powerful persons in England, pouring out their complaints and criticisms, which again took an uncomfortably long time for the Governor to answer. Hunter found himself peremptorily 'relieved' in 1800. After only eighteen months in office, Bligh still possessed the confidence of the British government; but his opponents did not wish to wait while he undermined their financial position, so acting through the courts and through the military, the only possible weapons they could use in the colony, in January 1808 they 'deposed' him by revolution.

For if the Governor of New South Wales, by his commission, had 'the most enlarged powers' of administration, with authority to pardon offences, to impose customs and excise duties, to grant lands and to issue Colonial regulations, uncontrolled by any Council (what else would one expect in a gaol?), he was limited by the existence of a court, composed of a Judge Advocate and six officers of

His Majesty's forces in criminal cases, and a Judge Advocate and two other 'fit and proper persons' in civil cases. Here was a chance to make trouble, especially if the military officers, whose support was ultimately necessary to the Governor's authority, could be won over to the opposition and persuaded, by partisan verdicts in the criminal court, to hamper the administration. Macarthur was involved in a number of legal broils with the government. Finally a warrant was issued for his arrest when a schooner of which he was part-owner violated the port regulations maintained to prevent the escape of convicts. Macarthur refused to be arrested. 'You will inform the persons who sent you here with the warrant . . . that I never will submit to this horrid tyranny . . . if you come again, come well armed because I will never submit until there was bloodshed.'

The constable did come again, though for the time there was no bloodshed. But Macarthur, released on bail, persuaded Lieutenant-Colonel Johnston of the New South Wales Corps to lead his men to arrest the Governor. 'I have been deeply engaged all this day in contending for the liberties of this unhappy colony,' wrote Macarthur to his wife a week later, 'and I am happy to say I have succeeded. The Tyrant is now no doubt gnashing his teeth with vexation at his overthrow.' For two years the rebels were virtual rulers of the colony.

This exploit has seemed extraordinary to most Australians then and since, and they have tried to explain it by stressing the peculiar character of the New South Wales Corps, and the inordinate ambition, if not the avarice, of John Macarthur. In fact, strange though it seems to-day, such 'depositions' were by no means unknown in other British colonies at the time; Lord Pigot had suffered a similar fate in Madras in 1776, and in the same year as the 'rum rebellion' in New South Wales, Sir George Barlow, again in Madras, was in the same way overthrown by a military revolt. It was an age of disobedience to authority, often justified by necessity. Nelson's 'blind eye' at the battle of

Copenhagen is generally commended; strictly speaking he deserved a court martial. Sydney Smith's disobedience involved heavy expenditure and extensive military operations. In 1797 Sir Thomas Maitland, against orders from Britain, handed over San Domingo to the negro Toussaint L'Ouverture; in 1807 Cathcart and Sir John Moore disobeyed orders in Scandinavia; and the following year Sir Arthur Wellesley, not yet Duke of Wellington, was urging Moore (though without success) to overthrow his commander-in-chief, Sir Hew Dalrymple. Was then the action of the New South Wales Corps so peculiar, when confronted with what to them was the misgovernment of the irascible Captain Bligh? Despite the strictures of their opponents, whose success as writers suggests that in history at least the pen is mightier than the sword, the officers of the 102nd Regiment, as the 'rum corps' was officially known, seem to have been very similar in character and upbringing to those of other line regiments of the time. In many cases younger sons, in most cases they had to make their way in the world; but they were well educated men of average family who had gained their commissions by the normal contemporary means of purchase and patronage. What was exceptional there was the combination of the lack of serious military duties and excellent opportunities for personal profit through trade, which New South Wales, like India, provided. When Bligh seemed to threaten these, he had to be removed; and following contemporary practice, he was.

However, the British government had to uphold authority. johnston and Macarthur tried to justify their actions in London; but despite a judicious distribution of presents of Australian curiosities, they failed. Johnston was cashiered; not until 1817 was Macarthur permitted to return to New South Wales. The New South Wales Corps, which had been so long in the colony, was relieved, and at least some of the officer-speculators departed. A new governor, Colonel Lachlan Macquarie, was appointed to bring order to the colony; but in New South Wales conflict was the more usual state. It was a 'peculiar' colony, persistently claiming the notice of English Ministers, like a 'troublesome, undisciplined infant', as Eleanor Dark has put it. 'It struggled, it quarrelled, it starved, it recovered to struggle and quarrel again. . . . Never a Governor's despatch arrived which was not loaded with requests . . . food, stores, stoves, stores, clothing, tools, medicines and blankets, beds, stoves, kettles, tubs, ploughs, lanthorns, ropes, handcuffs, leg-irons, paper, paint, candles . . . and still it went on struggling, muddling, working, idling, rebelling, quarrelling, drinking—a distant, uncouth, unpredictable, unresponsive land.'[1]

There was certainly plenty to squabble about in this community full of self-important busybodies and ambitious fortune-seekers. Land, prices, supplies, debts, drink, convicts—all were subjects of dispute. Not least was the question how the 'emancipists' should be treated, and whether 'officers and gentlemen' could hold converse with them, except on business. Macquarie's policy towards them, no less than that of Bligh, seemed in some ways to be dangerous; if fully 'restored to society', the emancipists would be commercial rivals with the 'exclusives'. And just as important was the social question. Ought they to be received at Government House or the Regimental Mess or be appointed to office in the colony? Macquarie, thinking of a few, like Surgeon Redfern, that monster of insurrection who at the age of nineteen had urged the naval mutineers at the Nore to be 'more united', or the erstwhile Irish rebel, Surveyor James Meehan, or Surgeon D'Arcy Wentworth, no convict indeed but acquitted at the Old Bailey, or the blackmailing Oxonian poet, Michael Robinson, or even the architect-forger Francis Howard Greenway, wanted to obliterate the past; but most 'pure merinos', thinking of the mass, of its numbers and of its potential power in the community, were more fastidious. They thought 'association with convicts under any circumstances (even when they had been freed), to be a degradation'; and 'feelings of this kind are not easily

[1] Eleanor Dark: *No Barrier* (Collins, Sydney, 1953), pp. 28-9.

overcome.' At first, Macquarie had the support of the British government; he could pursue his policy in face of local criticism. But gradually, once again, complaints increased; and once again British Ministers listened. Crime was increasing in post-war Britain—obviously due to Macquarie's 'lenient' policy. New South Wales was a sink of iniquity—owing to the Governor's incompetence. The colony's expenses were increasing—thanks to his extravagance. Was it really of any use, this expensive, far-off gaol? In 1819 Commissioner Bigge was sent out to investigate.

The Commissioner found a flourishing settlement. Indeed, it was rapidly becoming a colony rather than remaining a gaol, though in Mr. Bigge's eyes this development was less to be commended than deplored. Life, he thought, was too easy for the exiled criminal; it had almost all the attractions of London—at least for the uncultured—and lacked many of the shortcomings of that city. The climate was good; food now fairly plentiful. The industrious ex-convict might even, with luck and energy, gain some wealth. This opportunity seemed rather unfortunate to those (including Mr. Bigge) who thought it better restricted to men of substance; however, he was able to console himself with the reflection that 'persons of this class had very little chance of success in the cultivation of ordinary quality land in New South Wales without the possession of some capital'.

More important, Mr. Bigge found that there was now some chance of the colony benefiting the mother country, and becoming self-supporting, by increasing the production of fine wool. For this, the recently discovered lands over the Blue Mountains, and to the west and north of Bathurst, were particularly suitable, since for wool and sheep and cattle transport over the mountains seemed practicable. Moreover it was possible that the development of the interior would reduce the growth of Sydney, with its accumulation of disorderly convicts, its vice and its crime.

This was a vain hope, and visitors continued to criticize the size and debauchery of the capital, as well as its unpaved

streets and slab huts, its dirt and dust and mud, which re-
sembled any primitive township in spite of Macquarie's
planning and his buildings—the hospital, the barracks and
St. James' Church. But at least the pastoral industry provided the export 'staple' for which Governors had been
looking for thirty years, to permit the purchase of 'such
articles of import as are absolutely indispensable to civilised
life'. Hemp had been tried; flax had been tried; but there
was no market, despite the suggestion that the need for their
supply for the Royal Navy was one of the motives for
founding the colony. Tobacco was suggested; few could
grow it, notwithstanding Macquarie's experiments at Emu
Plains. 'Manufactories' perhaps? They might be 'desirable'
but how could they be undertaken without capital and raw
materials? Simeon Lord had begun to make hats, coarse
cloths, blankets and woollen stockings; there were also a
tannery in Sydney, a pottery works whose ware was badly
manufactured and very dear, and a salt works whose produce unfortunately was 'tainted' and therefore only used by
the 'lower orders'. But of course, apart from their quality,
it was bad policy to encourage colonial manufactures; not
only would they compete with British industry but the inevitable 'association' would 'always be found to diminish
the effect of penal restraint'. Macarthur had experimented
with the vine and the olive—but more than a century
would elapse before a 'gentleman' would willingly drink
'colonial' wine; even now, he won't in England. Whaling
and sealing had been tried; for a time the sale of oil and seal-
skins was profitable and until 1830 made up the country's
most valuable export, and there was considerable employment in the building and repair of ships. But the East India
Company's monopoly rights, the navigation acts and the
heavy import duties levied in England hampered this
trade—not to mention the reckless rate at which the seals
and whales were taken. The coal-mines at Newcastle were
being worked; but they were rather a place of punishment
than of profit, and the lack of skilled miners made the output

inconsiderable. Good quality timber was scarce near Sydney; cedar-cutting was an occupation of the future. An early sugar mill at Port Macquarie was in ruins within five years, 'a lasting monument of folly'. But now it seemed that wool would provide the answer.

Investment in wool-growing in New South Wales, argued the youthful Wentworth, was the most inviting opportunity for the capitalist existing anywhere in the world at that time; although 'acquaintance with the management of sheep' might be an advantage, even this apparent necessity was 'by no means an indispensable qualification', thanks to the climate which made superfluous precautions necessary in other parts of the world. If the breeder did not possess enough land, all he had to do was to retire with his flocks farther west where the land was uninhabited (except by blacks who did not count). The rude huts and tents of the shepherds could be moved with little difficulty or expense, and the capitalist himself would remain in comfort in Sydney. John Macarthur thought of further advantages. This 'body of proprietors' would become 'an aristocracy'; being 'dependent on the support of Government', because subject to the envy and hatred of the democratic multitude, they would be a natural support of 'authority'. They would employ many servants and many convicts who, at the same time, would have an opportunity to reflect on their past crimes and would be removed from further temptation. Commissioner Bigge agreed. He recommended that wool-growing be encouraged by government making larger land grants to settlers with capital, and reducing the British import duty on wool—both of which were done. New South Wales could remain a 'receptacle for offenders'; but no longer should emancipists be granted land when their sentences should expire. Nor should the free settler, without capital, get land. Bond or free, the 'lower orders' should work for the pastoralists, who were now spreading with their flocks through the interior in the tracks of the explorers.

Chapter Four

EXPLORATION BY SEA AND LAND

For twenty-five years after its foundation, the penal
settlement of New South Wales had been shut in between the Blue Mountains and the sea. Every attempt
to cross the mountain barrier had failed, stopped by its per-
pendicular gorges and rocky precipices. Even closer to Sydney exploration was difficult, as Governor Phillip himself
had quickly found, although he had succeeded in reaching
the Hawkesbury River, Pitt Water and Broken Bay.
Around Port Jackson, the country was 'rugged and un-
kindly' as one contemporary put it; there was thick scrub
and little water. On the sea, Englishmen were more in their
element. Spurred by natural curiosity, a spirit of adventure
and a desire to anticipate the French, they quickly traced the
outlines of the Australian continent, which so far had only
been touched at two or three widely dispersed points. These
seamen solved at least some of the questions posed by Matthew Flinders when he remarked, on his arrival in Australia,
that 'the interior of this new region, in extent nearly equal
to all Europe, strongly excited the curiosity of geographers
and naturalists. . . . Various conjectures were entertained
upon the probable consistence of this extensive space. Was
it a vast desert? Was it occupied by an immense lake—a
second Caspian Sea—or by a Mediterranean to which existed a navigable entrance in some parts hitherto unexplored.
Or was not this new continent rather divided into two or
more islands by straits communicating from the unknown
parts of the south to the imperfectly examined north-west
coast or to the Gulf of Carpentaria or to both?'

The coastal survey was largely the work of Flinders himself and Surgeon George Bass, both of whom came to New South Wales with Governor Hunter in H.M.S. *Reliance* in 1795. Bass had found medical work in his provincial Lincolnshire somewhat tedious, and had therefore enlisted as Surgeon in the Navy. When he reached Australia, after service in the West Indies, he found plenty of opportunity to indulge his preference for sailing. Flinders, a naval midshipman, had served under Bligh on the latter's second expedition (1791–3) when he had explored the treacherous Torres Strait between Australia and New Guinea. So Flinders was used to charting.

Almost as soon as they arrived in Sydney, Bass and Flinders went on an exploring expedition to Botany Bay in the tiny *Tom Thumb*, of eight feet keel and five feet beam. They followed up George's River and reported so favourably on the country as to persuade Governor Hunter to establish a settlement at Bankstown. In the following year, 1796, they went farther south to Port Hacking; then while Flinders was away in South Africa in 1797, Bass achieved a major success. He had failed in March in a land expedition to find a way across the mountains but in June, returning to the sea, he discovered coal seams outcropping on the coastal cliffs twenty miles south of Botany Bay. In December, in a whale-boat, 28 feet 7 inches long, he rounded Cape Howe, and went on to discover Wilson's Promontory and Western Port. He was convinced from the tides and currents that he had found a strait separating Van Diemen's Land from the mainland, but shortage of food forced him to turn back without finally confirming his theory. On this voyage as, Flinders said fifteen years later, '600 miles of coast, mostly in a boisterous climate, was explored, perhaps without its equal in the annals of maritime history. The public will award to its high spirited and able conductor an honourable place in the list of those whose ardour stands most conspicuous for the promotion of useful knowledge.' Next year (1798) in company with Flinders, in a leaky sloop of twenty-five tons, Bass successfully sailed round Van Diemen's Land, and finally settled the question of the strait which is now called after him.

Two years after his return to England, Flinders induced Sir Joseph Banks to persuade the Admiralty to send him back so that he might explore minutely the whole coastline of the continent. He sailed in *Investigator*, a 334 ton sloop, in July 1801, and sighted the Australian coast near Cape Leeuwin, not far from the place where some ten years earlier Captain Vancouver had discovered the fine harbour of King George's Sound, now the site of the town of Albany. Flinders then proceeded to chart the whole of the southern coast, thus linking the knowledge of the west, acquired by the Dutch on their voyages to the East Indies, with that of the British of the eastern half of the continent. Three months after reaching Sydney, in May 1802, he set out again, to explore Torres Strait and the Gulf of Carpentaria. This done he sailed right round the continent, and so virtually accomplished his object of making 'so accurate an investigation of the shores of *Terra Australis* that no future voyage to this country should be necessary. . . . With the blessing of God, nothing of importance should have been left for future discoveries upon any part of these extensive coasts.' In fact, although the state of his ship forced him to curtail his survey of the north-west and to hasten back to Sydney, the essential outlines of Australia were now known.

So much could scarcely be said of the interior. There, the situation was the same as it had been ten years earlier, for no explorer had yet succeeded in crossing the mountain barrier; yet the coastal regions did not seem to offer great prospects of successful settlement. Flinders thought the land round Port Phillip had 'a pleasing and in many places a fertile appearance . . . capable of supporting cattle, though much better adapted for sheep', but both Banks and Cook had been almost as pessimistic about much of the east as Dampier and the Dutch had been about the west; it seemed a country 'doomed to everlasting barrenness . . . not disposed to yield much to the support of man'. Not until 1813 did the crossing of the Blue Mountains and the discovery of the Bathurst plains transform 'the aspect of the colony from a confined insulated tract of land to a rich and extensive continent'.

This all-important success was won by a party led by William Lawson, Gregory Blaxland and W. C. Wentworth, who were anxious to find if there were any good pasture lands beyond the existing limits of settlements. Keeping to the mountain ridges, instead of seeking to follow the valleys, the party in fourteen days reached the western edge of Mount York, and thus opened up an area 'equal to every demand which this country may have for an extension of tillage and pasture lands for a century to come'. But further exploration raised another problem, with Surveyor Evans's expeditions to the 'new country' in 1813 and 1815. He found rivers, which he named the Macquarie and the Lachlan, flowing west, away from the sea into the interior. Whither did they go? Did they reach the ocean to the north, or to the south of the continent? Or did they find their outlet in a great inland sea? Then, of course, there was the question of the nature of the land farther west. Was it this speculative inland sea? Or if not water, was the country fertile, habitable and cultivable? Or was it desert?

In 1817 Surveyor-General Oxley found no answer to these questions. He followed the course of the Lachlan, finding at times deep water, at others a mere trickle; then the river seemed to lose itself in a vast swamp. Was this the inland sea? Next year he tried again, following the Macquarie. He found another river, the Castlereagh, and the Liverpool Plains as well, but failed again to solve his main problem, for after one hundred and twenty miles, just when he was 'sanguine in the expectation of soon entering the longed for lake', the river lost itself again, this time in 'an ocean of reeds'. Disappointed, he concluded that 'for all practical purposes of civilized man the interior of this country, westward of 147th meridian, is uninhabitable, deprived

as it is of wood, water and grass'. It seemed to be an impass-
able bog. And there for the time the matter rested.

Meanwhile the colony was changing. Commissioner
Bigge had discovered how suitable for wool-growing New
South Wales was; government was fulfilling his recom-
mendation to encourage free settlers with capital by giving
them grants of land where they could run their flocks.
Settlers with capital already in New South Wales needed
little official encouragement; but as more arrived, the problem arose where to find land for their sheep. To the north
the Hunter River valley was quickly occupied after being
opened for settlement in 1822; two years later the great
Australian Agricultural Company received its huge grant on
the River Manning. To the south, Lake George, near the
modern Canberra, the high plains of Monaro, the coast near
Jervis Bay, and the valley of the Shoalhaven were soon
filled. What next could be settled? The government, anxious
to prevent its convicts going too far afield and fearful of its
ability to control its territories, thought this was far enough;
in 1829 the boundaries of settlement, the 'nineteen counties',
were laid down—but the limits had barely been proclaimed
when they were passed.

To the south, stockmen 'looking for grass and not for
glory' had found the Murrumbidgee as early as 1821. Three
years later, Hume and Hovell, starting from the former's
station near Lake George, with the 'sanction and protection'
of Governor Brisbane, if nothing else, set off to explore the
country between them and the southern coast. They crossed
the Murrumbidgee, then the Murray near Albury, where
the great Hume Dam stands to-day; they crossed the mountains of north-east Victoria; they finally reached the sea at
Corio Bay, the western arm of Port Phillip, about ten miles
from the modern Geelong. It was the record of this journey
that induced John Batman to form his Port Phillip Association to develop this territory, which in turn resulted in the
settlement at Melbourne in 1835—trespassers though the
settlers might be in the eyes of the government.

But by then far more of the southern country had been opened up, and the 'problem of the rivers' had been solved. In 1828, Captain Charles Sturt followed Oxley's track up the Lachlan, in a year of drought when the swamps were dry. He investigated the marshes of the Macquarie and found the Bogan River (New Year's Creek), but there was no water. 'The space I traversed is unlikely to become the haunt of civilized man,' he wrote. 'We passed hollow after hollow that had successively dried up.... There was scarcely a living creature, even of the feathered race, to be seen to break the stillness of the forest.... Vegetation seemed annihilated; the largest forest trees were drooping and many were dead. The emus with outstretched necks, gasping with thirst, in vain searched the river channels for water, and the native dog, so thin it could hardly walk, seemed to implore some merciful hand to despatch it.' Still he pressed on. At last he reached a 'noble river', the Darling. He found it salt. 'Our hopes were annihilated'; no wonder he thought that 'the country through which it flows holds out little prospect of advantage'. But when Governor Darling agreed with him, and wrote of this country as being 'from the total absence of water altogether unavailable for the purpose of tillage or pasture', Sturt emphasized that in other years the situation might be very different. 'It has borne the appearance of barrenness, where in even moderate rain, it might have shown very differently.... Our animals on the whole, have thriven on the food they have had, which would argue favourably for the herbage,' and he thought that the deep and water-scoured bed of the Darling showed that sometimes at least furious torrents must flow down it. But where to? He was to find the answer in his great expedition of 1829–30.

This time he sailed by boat down the Murrumbidgee. As he went, the current grew faster and faster, the channel of the river narrower and more treacherous. 'The river in its tortuous course swept round to every point of the compass with the greatest irregularity. We were carried at a fearful rate down its gloomy and contracted banks . . . until we were hurried into a broad and noble river. . . . I can only compare the relief we experienced to that which the seaman feels on weathering the rock upon which he expected his vessel would have struck—to the calm which succeeds moments of feverish anxiety, when the dread of danger is succeeded by the certainty of escape.' It was the Murray, previously found, higher up its course, by Hume. Sailing downstream, Sturt reached the junction of the Darling. Here then was the outlet of the great river system of western New South Wales, of all those tributaries whose course and destination had for so long been a puzzle. It only remained to follow the Murray to its mouth—not in an inland sea, but on the south coast of Australia. Unfortunately there was no wide estuary, but a lake whose outlet to the sea was blocked by sand-bars and breakers.

Sturt was disappointed. Here was no river for commerce; and with its entrance barred, and much of the country through which it flowed barren or far from civilization, 'the noble river seemed to have been misplaced'. But though this was partly true, he had discovered much valuable land along its banks, and in 1836 Major Mitchell filled in another important gap. Marching down the Darling to its junction with the Murray, he crossed it and went on to the coast, which he reached at the mouth of the River Glenelg. Here, in the west of Victoria, was what he called Australia Felix, 'the better to distinguish it from the parched deserts of the interior country, where we had wandered so unprofitably and so long. It was most inviting and still without inhabitants. We had at length discovered a country ready for the immediate use of civilized man. Unencumbered by too much wood, it yet possessed enough for all purposes; its soil was exuberant, its climate temperate. It was traversed by mighty rivers and watered by streams innumerable. As I stood, the first European intruder on the sublime solitude of these verdant plains, as yet untouched by flocks and herds, I felt conscious of being the harbinger of mighty changes, and that our steps would soon be followed by the men and animals for which it seemed to have been prepared.' They were, for even on his return journey Mitchell saw the Hentys settled at Portland 'importing sheep and cattle as fast as vessels could be found to bring them over', and the tents of Batman's party at Melbourne; after the middle of 1837 there was a continued rush to the rivers and plains of the Port Phillip district, which had by then been declared open for settlement.

For a time the rugged south-east corner of the continent held settlers and explorers alike at bay, but not for long. By 1839 there were already cattle stations on the lower slopes of the mountains; then Angas McMillan discovered the Nicholson, Mitchell, Avon and Macalister rivers in Gippsland. These 'beautiful rich open plains' between the mountains and the coast were quickly occupied, and next year the Polish Count Strzelecki, crossing the mountains on an almost direct route from Sydney to Westernport, found the highest peak on the continent (7,328 feet) which he named Kosciusko after his famous fellow-countryman.[1]

Meanwhile stockmen and explorers had been moving north as well. As early as 1816 Allan Cunningham, a botanist, had gone out with Oxley to the Lachlan, and thereafter made many journeys to the Blue Mountains. He found that he could 'blend discovery with botanical research tolerably well', and in 1823 discovered the opening which he named Pandora's Pass through the Liverpool Ranges which had hitherto blocked the route from Bathurst to the north. Four years later Governor Darling put him in command of another expedition to follow up this route, and again he was successful in opening up great tracts of good country. Going on from Pandora's Pass, he found the mass of streams and tributaries forming the head-waters of the River Darling— the Condamine, Dumaresq, Gwydir and Macintyre, in the

[1] The story, often recounted, that Strzelecki gave the name Kosciusko to the present Mt. Townsend, and that subsequently the names of the mountains were changed is incorrect. See *Journal of the Royal Aust. Hist. Soc.*, vol. xxvi, (1940), p. 97.

country which later became known as the Darling Downs
on the borders of New South Wales and Queensland and
as one of the richest pastoral areas in Australia. He found a
pass to the coast through Cunningham's Gap, leading from
the Downs to Moreton Bay, the penal settlement established
on the Brisbane River which had been discovered by Oxley
in 1823. In the next ten years the squatters crossed over the
Moonbi mountains to Armidale, occupied the intervening
district of New England and settled the country up to the
Queensland border.

Still the north and the great interior remained unknown
and untraversed. In 1844 Ludwig Leichhardt, a Prussian,
after two years' geological and botanical researches, set out
to travel from Sydney overland to Port Essington on the far
north coast, through the torrid swamps of the country round
the Gulf of Carpentaria. He accomplished this journey,
though more by good luck than good management and
only after great difficulties and hardships due in large part to
his arrogance and poor bush-craft; but two subsequent
expeditions, when he tried to cross the continent to Perth,
were failures, and on the second, in 1848, his whole party
perished. In 1845, Mitchell had discovered good grazing
country in Central Queensland and the Barcoo River system which he thought might join the Victoria River and
flow to the north-west coast; but in 1847 Kennedy, a surveyor who had accompanied Mitchell, had found that he was
wrong; the Barcoo was the same river which Sturt had
called Cooper's Creek when he crossed it farther downstream
and it flowed (if that word may be used) to the salt lakes of
the interior.

For in 1844-5 Sturt had accomplished the greatest journey
of all those of the inland explorers. After his earlier, most
brilliant exploit on the Murray, he had returned to England
where his reports helped to encourage the South Australian
Association in their plans to form a new settlement at Adelaide. This country soon realized, he wrote later, 'the happy
expectations I had formed of it. Its plains and its rich and

lovely valleys . . . were studded over with cottages and corn-
fields; the very river [the Murray] which had appeared to
me so misplaced was made the high road to connect the
eastern and southern shores of a mighty continent; the
superfluous stock of an old colony was poured down its
banks into the new settlement to save it from the trials and
vicissitudes to which other colonies, less favourably situated,
have been exposed; and England throughout her wide domains possessed not for its extent a fairer or more promising
dependency than the province of South Australia.'

But those words were written in 1849; six years earlier,
the colony was in the midst of an acute financial crisis, and
Sturt, at first Surveyor and then Assistant Commissioner for
Lands, found that government economies transferred him
to the poorly paid and quite unsuitable post of Registrar
General. Unhappy here, he resolved to undertake another
expedition to the interior to try to solve 'the most important
and the most interesting geographical problem in the world'.
He had noticed the flight of the birds to and from the north
and thought that the 'regular and systematic migration of
the feathered race' suggested the presence of fertile land, forgetting, perhaps, that it was easier for birds to fly quickly
over the desert, than for man to toil wearily across it. A
previous attempt to go north from Adelaide, by Edward
John Eyre, had found no grazing land or fresh water, only
two bare hills, which he called Mount Hopeless and Mount
Disappointment; nor did Eyre's incredible journey across
the Nullarbor Plain to King George's Sound (Albany) in
1841 suggest a very fertile interior, for as he crossed the
sandy, waterless country at the head of the Great Australian
Bight, some of the most arid territory in the continent, he
'established the startling fact that there is not a single water-
course to be found in the south coast of Australia for 1,500
miles'. Sturt, however, hoped to avoid Eyre's route due
north leading to the spongy salt pan of the Lake Torrens
basin; instead he would travel up the Darling to Menindie
and from there strike out north-west into the unknown.

In August 1844 he set out. He passed near the Barrier
Ranges (Broken Hill) and followed roughly the line of the
present border between New South Wales and South Australia. Much of the soil seemed good—'it only wanted water
to enjoy comparative luxury,' a small thing perhaps. But
elsewhere, near the Barrier, it 'appeared as if McAdam had
emptied every stone he ever broke to be strewed over this
metalled region', and farther north 'sand ridges covered
with spinifex succeeded each other like the waves of the sea.
There was not a blade of grass to be seen.' At last his party
found water and shelter at a 'Rocky Glen' (Milparinka) in
the extreme north-west of New South Wales; here they
were marooned for six months, 'locked up in that desolate
and heated region . . . as effectually as if we had wintered at
the Pole', when for three months the temperature averaged
103 degrees in the shade. In July they were able to move on
and found Strzelecki Creek and Cooper's Creek, and then,
farther west, Sturt's Stony Desert. Just south of the tropic,
near the present border between Queensland and Northern
Territory, they had to turn back. 'Water and feed had both
failed. . . . From the summit of a sandy undulation . . . we
saw that the ridges extended northwards in parallel lines . . .
and appeared as if interminable. To the eastward and westward they succeeded each other like waves of the sea. . . .
"Did ever man see such a country?" '

Not until January 1846 did Sturt reach Adelaide again,
after a frightful journey through the drought-stricken
country, fighting scurvy and privation. His great achievement was that he solved the geographical problem of Central Australia, by finding the outlet of the great unknown
river system in the salt lakes of the interior. He had failed to
cross the continent, or even to reach its centre; he did not
find an inland sea; and now he had 'no hope of any inland
fertile country'. True, conditions were not always the same;
much might depend upon the season. In 1851 two South
Australian pastoralists looking for feeding grounds for their
sheep found fresh water in Lake Eyre, and good grass near

by, and in 1857 the Deputy Surveyor General of South Australia, G. W. Goyder, found 'babbling brooks and succulent grasses'. There was fresh water in Lake Eyre too in 1951; but one swallow, or even two, do not make a summer, and Sturt's reports of the country he crossed would appear to be correct for nine years out of ten.

The continent had not yet been crossed from south to north, and both the Victorian and South Australian governments began to compete for the honour of sending out the first successful expedition. In 1860 McDouall Stuart, starting from Adelaide, reached the centre, but trying to proceed north-west was driven back by hostile natives. Next year he tried again and was foiled by the waterless desert, but in 1862 he at last succeeded and reached Van Diemen Gulf in the extreme north of Australia. He was now enthusiastic. 'If this country is settled it will be one of the finest colonies under the Crown, suitable for the growth of any and everything,' he wrote. It is a verdict which experience has proved to be somewhat over-optimistic.

Meanwhile, the year before, the Victorian expedition, led by Burke and Wills, had gone to its doom. Planned to travel from Melbourne to the Darling and then due north to the Gulf of Carpentaria in the summer of 1860-1, it suffered from the impetuosity of its leader, O'Hara Burke, Inspector of Police, courageous but headstrong and inexperienced. Lacking patience, Burke made a dash for the north from Cooper's Creek with three companions, without waiting for the rest of his party to come up, and without attempting to make the scientific observations which should have been the most valuable fruit of his work. They reached the sea, but when they got back to their camp, more than a month overdue, it was deserted. Instead of making for Menindie, where help would have been at hand, Burke decided to go to Adelaide by way of Mount Hopeless and both he and Wills perished on the way. Next year John McKinlay again reached Carpentaria, this time from Adelaide; he found a few relics of Burke and Wills, and he found also what he hoped would be good pastoral land—'splendid forest and grassed country . . . open plains . . . and gentle undulating country, grass abundant'. But, and it was a very big 'but', what of water? It was no use saying, as McKinlay did, that the area 'only wanted rain to exhibit richness' when there was no rain. Perhaps Sturt was unduly gloomy in his reports, for he travelled in the middle of a terrible drought; but drought is quite a normal feature of this region. It has been suitable only for sparse occupation by cattle, ever subject to recurrent heavy losses, which can only be partially avoided by the hazardous process of 'overlanding'. Settlement was a problem for the future. But by 1861 the explorers, scientists, soldiers and surveyors seeking knowledge, and the stockmen and pastoralists seeking grass and water, had discovered substantially what was the nature and what were the capabilities of the whole of the continent of Australia, though a more detailed examination of the north-west was not completed for another generation.

Chapter Five

SQUATTING

New South Wales, no longer a mere penal settlement, showed signs of becoming John Bull's Greater Woolsack, as the explorers and graziers discovered the 'good country' in what are now the 'eastern states'. Once the threat of famine had been removed by the spread of local cultivation, the local governors could the more readily help to encourage the new 'staple' export of fine wool on the lines recommended by Commissioner Bigge; and the English government, observing the demand for wool at home, was only too willing to help. Here at last seemed some compensation for British expenditure, and a 'matter of advantageous return'; and the extension of wool-growing, as we have observed, meant that the convicts would be more and more distributed as assigned servants in the country, instead of being kept at government expense in town.

True, the early colonial sheep had been of no very fine breed; but John Macarthur, with his imported strains, and his royal merinos, and his careful breeding on his thousands of acres, had long since changed that. Pertinacious in the face of opposition, skilful and tireless in his propaganda and his sales organization, ably abetted by his wife Elizabeth, at Camden Park, now, together with other sheep-breeders, his disciples and his rivals, he was ready to reap a great reward.

In 1817, at the request of Lieutenant-Governor Sorell, he had sent a shipload of his sheep to Van Diemen's Land to improve the breed there. In 1822 he received two medals from the London Society of Arts, for producing 150,000 pounds of fine wool and for successfully rivalling the best wool from Saxony. This was an achievement much to be desired, for not only were the Saxon fleeces at that time the best in Europe, but such was the insatiable demand of the ever-increasing English mills that English wool production could no longer meet it, and new sources of supply were most urgently needed. Here was somebody's opportunity, and exports to England show how successfully the Australian graziers took it. In 1821, 175,000 pounds of Australian wool were sent to England; in 1830, more than two million; in 1840 eight million and in 1850 thirty-nine million pounds, half the total of English imports and five times the amount purchased in Germany.

At first the wool-grower had his land, as well as his servants, granted to him by the government, normally in proportion to the amount of capital he possessed. This was the policy of the 'twenties. Two large-scale land companies, each with a capital of £1,000,000, received charters—the Australian Agricultural Company and the Van Diemen's Land Company; another syndicate on similar lines was formed to settle at Swan River in Western Australia. These companies were to stock and develop their holdings and to bring out settlers in return for their enormous land grants; but they were only doing on a large scale what many individuals were doing on a small. This policy had its advantages. In encouraging the migration of men of substance, the British government seemed to be building up a local squirearchy, who could control and reform their convict servants, act as local magistrates and gentry, and set an example in conduct and morals to the population generally. But the policy also had its drawbacks. There were allegations of favouritism in the making of grants; and even more important, it was argued that too much land was being granted, that there was not enough labour to work it and that settlement was becoming too scattered. Therefore in 1830 it was decided that no more land should be granted for nothing;

instead it was to be sold at a minimum price of five shillings per acre to stop too much being taken up.

The result was the appearance of a new, typically Australian character, the squatter; he was to dominate the local scene for twenty years. Until the gold rushes of the 'fifties brought his more democratic opponent, the 'digger', he was almost without a rival. And even he was a democrat of a sort. He might exploit his convict servants, and he managed to win almost a monopoly of political privilege; yet at least the squatting life was a career open to all. True, the man with capital had advantages, but in what profession does he not? And, with or without capital, caring little for government regulation or land sale, the sheepmen quickly occupied the huge area opened up by the explorers; they 'squatted' there, defying the government to turn them off, and as the nearer lands were filled they went farther and farther afield, with their flocks, to the west, to New England, to the Darling Downs, to the Riverina and to Port Phillip, looking for empty paddocks.

> *The mountains saw them marching by;*
> *They faced the all-consuming drought,*
> *They could not rest in settled land,*
> *Their faces ever westward bent*
> *Beyond the farthest settlement,*
> *Responding to the challenge cry*
> *Of better country farther out.*[1]

The British government might, and did, object. As one Secretary of State wrote:

'It was as unauthorised an act of presumption for an Australian squatter to drive his flocks into the untrodden wilderness without Her Majesty's express sanction being first obtained, as for a Berkshire farmer to feed his oxen, without rent or licence, in the Queen's demesne of Hampton Court.'

[1] Quoted by W. K. Hancock: *Australia* (1945), p. 13.

But the Governors knew that

'not all the armies of England, not 100,000 soldiers scattered throughout the bush, could drive back our herds
within the limits of the nineteen counties. . . . As well
might it be attempted to confine the Arabs of the desert
within a circle drawn on the sands of the desert as to confine the graziers or woolgrowers of New South Wales
within any bounds that can possibly be assigned to
them.'

The sheep were there, the men were there, the land was
there, profits were there; no power on earth could stop men
taking their flocks to the land and earning the profits. A man
with the smallest capital could acquire a flock, either by buying the sheep if he had the means or by going into partnership with a more wealthy city dweller if he had not. Then
he would set forth, with his often scanty rations, driving his
sheep across the trackless plains, scanning the horizon for
unoccupied or unclaimed land, ever on the watch for fires,
natives or native dogs, fighting distance, drought, starvation
and disease, staking everything, perhaps even his life, on
finding a 'run'.

At first the word 'squatter' was a term of abuse for ex-
convicts or vagrants, who had occupied, without authority,
empty lands near the centre of settlement. But it was not
long before the term changed its meaning. After 1829, when
the government refused to authorize settlement beyond the
'nineteen counties', all outside were 'squatters', without legal
title, not only outside the law but actually violating it; and
these included many of the leading citizens of the colony.
In 1836, they were recognized; every stockman outside the
boundary could get a squatting licence for £10 a year.
Within three years, the courts were ready to protect any
squatter's run against all comers save the Crown. Chief
Justice Stephen said:

'A man passed into the interior and took possession of
a tract of country, established his huts, sheep and shepherds in various directions: the tract of country so occu-

pied by himself and his establishments was said to be in his possession, and he could bring an action against any person who would intrude upon him. He was not bound to show his title. He simply said . . . "I had possession before you came in." '

In 1840 there were 673 of these now legal squatting stations in New South Wales, carrying some 350,000 cattle and 1,200,000 sheep, looked after by a population of 6,664, nearly half of whom were convict servants.

Unquestionably the life was hard. First, one must find a 'run', perhaps with the help of some landmark vaguely hinted at by explorer or bushman, perhaps with no such help; when found it had to be protected against invasion by fellow squatters or by natives. Then it must be stocked. A popular method was to buy sheep on 'thirds', with a loan from a Sydney capitalist who would take a third of the profit. Next came the hut—for as yet it could hardly be called a homestead—built of rough slabs with a stringy-bark roof, rough hinged flaps for windows, a mud floor, a sea-chest for table and a rough bed of sheepskins or opossum rugs, costing a matter of £10 in all. Rarely enclosed, hot and dusty in dry weather, muddy in wet, with flies and vermin attracted by the sheep's dung near by, and mosquitoes breeding on the river or dam—such was the squatter's first home, all alone save perhaps for a similar shanty to house his servants, and some shepherds' huts scattered on the run. Even over the years there could be little improvement until he got security of tenure; for so long as the squatter had no legal title to his land, he might build a homestead only to see himself driven away, and while bushrangers or natives might at any time pillage or destroy his property there was little room for luxury or comfort. According to Professor S. H. Roberts, in *The Squatting Age in Australia*, it was a 'sordid, filthy existence, despite all the eulogies of free life in contact with nature and communion with the gums. The only real contact was with a few degraded convicts and the eternal smell of sheep effluvia. Its sole return was

monetary; in itself it was penal servitude of the worst type
—there is no romance in monotony and mutton fat.'
The squatter must 'dispense with all the comforts of civilized
life, from wine and windows to carpets and crockery,' said a
contemporary, Gideon Scott Lang, 'and look to nothing but
making the most of his capital regardless of risk and hardship'.

Labour was scarce, and in the early days more than half
the squatters' servants were convicts. They were given
rations and clothing according to the government-pre-
scribed scale, which was generous enough, though chiefly
flour and meat, with a little soap and sugar. Masters often
added tea or tobacco as 'indulgences'—an incentive to good
behaviour. 'Well fed,' said Bishop Ullathorne, but 'pray,
are not the horses and cattle you see everywhere well fed?
and why so? In order to produce a greater amount of labour,
out of a greater amount of toil and sweat.'

But if well fed, the convict servant was continually subject
to the most rigorous discipline. For any offence, however
trivial, be it merely insolence, laziness, unwillingness to
work or disobedience of orders, he could be hauled before
a magistrate by his master or overseer (often a convict or ex-
convict) and sentenced to flogging, imprisonment, the
treadmill or work in irons on the roads. Flogging was the
punishment preferred; it interfered less with work. Between
1830 and 1837, 42,000 convicts were flogged in New South
Wales, or about one in five, receiving an average sentence of
forty-five lashes.

Despite this treatment, the convicts often served their
masters well. Many employers praised them. They always
had the hope of earning their ticket of leave, and this hope
and 'indulgences' were better incentives than the lash. But
skilled shepherds were rare among them, and many were
the sheep lost owing to ignorance or carelessness in work
that was by no means easy for the inexperienced. For the
shepherd had to see that the sheep fed quietly without scattering too far, that they had water, and shade in summer,

that they did not remain so long in one spot as to 'paddle' the ground; he had to watch for the dingo, or native dog; at night he had to yard his flock behind hurdles, usually five-barred, about seven feet long, which must be moved to fresh ground daily—for there were no permanent fences until after the gold rushes. And if shepherding, droving, timber-splitting and hut-keeping went on all the year round, there were the seasonal additions of lambing and shearing. Certainly for the latter outside help might be obtained; but imagine the work involved in obtaining a high lambing percentage, when this involved 'taking turns to watch the fold each night during the lambing, and placing each ewe, immediately before or after it had lambed, in a separate hurdle-pen. . . . These ewes were kept in their pens till about 10 or 11 o'clock next day, when each lamb would be thoroughly mothered. At night when the flock came home, all lambs that were not well mothered were placed with their mothers in separate pens, and the others in a separate pen by themselves.'

It was an arduous, monotonous and lonely life for the shepherd even though the *Sydney Herald* might argue that 'social sympathies are awakened, interested and amused by the animal creation. The feathered tenants of the grove, the kangaroo bounding across the plains, the opossum scaling the giant trees, the emu pacing with his majestic step, the black swan proudly sailing in the lake, the myriads of gay insects glittering in the air, the flocks committed to his pastoral charge, with the merry lambs frisking and gambolling all day long, and the very dog that crouches at his feet and licks his hand, and obeys his nod and beck, these are the companions of his most sequestered hours, affording constant gratification of his eye, his ear and his imagination, and banishing that oppressive sense of solitude and abstraction which belongs to the inmate of the cell.'

The labouring population were not convinced of these blessings; they preferred when they could to remain in Sydney.

For them the 'bush' seemed more as it did to John Henderson in 1851, when he quoted, in his *Excursions and Adventures
in New South Wales*, the contemporary ballad

> *Black melancholy sits, and round her throws*
> *A death-like silence and a dread repose;*
> *Her gloomy presence saddens every scene,*
> *Shades every flower and darkens every green.*

They were reluctant to go up-country, which held little
profit for them, so the squatters sought for more migrants;
they sought for more convicts; some even for Asiatic coolies.
When transportation to New South Wales ceased, their immediate reaction was to take out a flood of 'bounty-orders',
by which government paid for the passage of immigrants.
In 1842 the labour position was temporarily easier. Since
1830, with the arrival of free immigrants on a large scale,
the numbers of locally born had steadily increased, and in
the 'forties these children were reaching a working age.
Sometimes even the 'bounty migrants', arriving at a time
when expansion was halted by depression, had difficulty in
finding work. But when prosperity returned to the wool-
grower, so did the labour shortage; it remained a chronic
difficulty.

There were many others, often accidental, always more or
less unforeseen, such as bushrangers, petty thieving, native
raids, the mixing or 'boxing' of flocks, scab, footrot, not to
mention drought, flood or the chance of personal accident
far from the possibility of medical aid. A Victorian pioneer,
Alfred Joyce, in his diary, published as *A Homestead History*,
tells how

> 'I suffered from a most excruciating, deep-seated whitlow,
> on one of my fingers, and had to suffer from it for a week
> before [the doctor] could attend me; just before his
> arrival relief was afforded me by a friendly chemist, a
> visitor for the night, who lanced the finger for me; but a
> joint was lost through the delay. On another occasion I
> was thrown from my horse about two miles from home

and dislocated an elbow and both wrists and sprained an ankle. In this state, I crawled home, where I lay for three days before the doctor could reach me, but the dislocations were reduced in a few moments when he did so.'

No wonder that for enduring such hardships and difficulties the squatters wanted good profits. But if many made fortunes, there were many who did not, suffering one type of disaster or another, or perhaps losing their capital through a collapse of prices. The drought of 1828-9, according to the contemporary Scots parson, the fiery John Dunmore Lang, served 'to blast the golden hopes of thousands and to bring many families to poverty and ruin', and the crash of 1841-2 was even worse. 'We have worked hard and lived on salt beef and damper for nearly six years for no purpose,' wrote one who failed, claiming that 'no one can live in this accursed western port.' 'I have no home, no huts, no sheep,' wrote another. No wonder, then, that as a class the squatters were full of complaints, against their luck, against labour and against government. One lamented his fate in verse:

> Of sheep I got a famous lot—
> Some died of hunger, some of rot,
> For the devil a drop of rain they got
> In this flourishing land of Australia.
> My convict men were always drunk,
> They kept me in a constant funk,
> Says I to myself, as to bed I slunk,
> How I wish I was out of Australia.

The popular, anonymous balladist whom Henderson quoted wrote of his multifarious troubles in a very similar strain.

> Now to all who intend to emigrate
> Come listen to the doleful fate
> Which did befall me of late
> When I went to the wilds of Australia.

I sailed across the stormy main
And often wished myself back again,
I really think I was quite insane
When I went to the bush of Australia.

And when I came to look at the land,
Which I got by His Excellency's command,
I found it nothing but burning sand
Like all the rest of Australia.
But I bought a flock of sheep at last,
And thought that all my troubles were past,
You may well believe that I stood aghast
When they died of the rot in Australia.

In 1841 Edmund Curr, later a successful Victorian squatter, paid over £1,000 in current expenses apart from £1,500 for his ragged run with two thousand scabby sheep. With two and a half pounds of wool per sheep, selling at one shilling per pound, he earned less than £300; at the end of the year he found station property had depreciated by fifty per cent, and he could not sell his lambs. Luckily for him, he succeeded in finding a better run, and was able to retire after ten years a wealthy man. But not all could do this, and a great many squatters felt a grievance. And though they might agree that government could do little or nothing about English wool prices or Australian droughts, it *could* help with labour and land. It seemed an outrage to have to pay £1 a week (plus rations) for shepherds and twice that for an overseer, when one thought of the good old days of shepherds a-plenty for £15 a year, or a convict's labour available in return for his keep. By 1841 it was said that ten thousand men were needed in the Central District of New South Wales alone; instead of a thousand sheep, twice that number were being 'looked after' by one man. This was too many. Losses increased as the sheep were damaged and extra daily travel strained the animals and reduced their condition. No wonder, whatever the shortcomings of convict labour, that many squatters were in uproar when assignment and transportation ceased in 1840. Free immigration, though encouraged by the government, had not yet brought nearly enough men to replace the convicts; besides too many of the immigrants were useless 'paupers' whom the English Poor Law Authorities had been only too anxious to get rid of.

Too often the squatters had begun with exaggerated hopes of easy wealth. Inevitably their disappointments bred bitterness, and this increased with the depression of the early 'forties. Up to 1837, the price of wool was high and seasons were good: there was a good demand for the 'increase' of the flocks, convict labour was available and land was free for the taking. But even 'under the best management and the most favourable circumstances', said a squatter giving evidence to a Committee of the Legislative Council in 1842, 'while wool would pay for expenses, profits would come only from the sale of the increase, and this depended on the industry continuing to expand.' In 1838 and 1839 there was a severe drought and the price of wool fell by about twenty per cent; at the same time wages were rising as the labour shortage became more acute; and it was made still worse in 1840 when transportation ceased, and with it a considerable amount of government expenditure in New South Wales. There were thus good reasons to check the expansion of the wool industry, apart from the fact that the best land had by now been taken up; and once expansion was checked, there was no demand for sheep as stock for new squatters. There was only a small meat market; all that remained was to boil down the animals for tallow. Naturally British investors began to take alarm; by 1842 a first-class slump had developed; by 1844 wool prices had fallen a further twenty per cent. And it was at this moment that the government decided to ask the squatters to pay for their land.

Actually, the land question had been brewing for some years. The squatters wanted security of tenure, so that they could improve their runs and build homes on them without the fear of being displaced. They could not afford to buy their runs outright at the government price, raised in 1842, in the depth of the depression, to £1 per acre; yet, they argued, it was only in the hands of private owners that the land would be properly developed and made most useful to the community at large.

The Governor, Sir George Gipps, disagreed. He sympathized with the squatters' demand for security, and was ready to concede them much so that they might obtain it; but he did not approve of selling cheaply to private individuals, however meritorious, Crown lands which were certain in course of time to become much more valuable. He did not argue that Australian land was at that time *worth* £1 an acre; but he thought it a mistake for the Crown to sell its lands until they reached that value, which they would do as the colony grew and prospered. He thought that the squatting system permitted the profitable *use* of the land without the Crown actually disposing of it, so he proposed to give the squatter security against eviction if he would buy at £1 an acre 320 acres of his run every eight years; or in other words he was to pay £40 a year, for security of tenure on the whole run.

The squatters were furious. This was 'taxation without representation'. Wentworth denounced it as a tribute 'fit for Tunis and Tripoli—worthy of the Bey of Algiers'. The colony would be ruined. Rebellion was spoken of, and Wentworth threatened to impeach Ministers. A Pastoral Association was formed. A Parliamentary Agent was appointed. The British press supported the squatters; business associations and private influence were used to bring pressure to bear on the British government; propagandists threatened an increase in the price of textiles for 'Manchester and Leeds are more formidable antagonists than New England and Monaro'.

To these forces the government yielded; the Waste Lands Occupation Act, 1846, and the Order-in-Council issued under it in March 1847, gave the squatters what they wanted. They could get leases, with pre-emptive right to buy the land, for one year in 'settled' districts, up to eight years in intermediate districts and up to fourteen years in 'unsettled' districts, at a rent of £2 10s. per thousand head of sheep. This meant security for the squatters until someone else would pay £1 an acre for the land; in the meantime they could purchase key-points on their runs—the water-holes, the river-beds, the site of the homestead and so forth. The squatters had won the day. Now they could improve their runs and build comfortable dwellings: the pioneering days were over. As the stately mansions of the grazier appeared throughout the country, and as the loneliness decreased with improved communications and a growing population, the squatters frequently became a target for the criticism of the land-hungry miners and the poor in the cities, for in securing their land they had gained a monopoly. As time went on the squatter often led a leisured life, giving perhaps some justification to his detractors, in the bitter fight between Australian democracy and the 'squattocracy' in the next half century. But in the early days many 'squatting' fortunes were earned by the hard labour of men who started with nothing and worked their way upwards by enterprise, skill, a little luck, a great deal of tenacity and sometimes a little cattle-duffing.

The squatters' struggles had an important incidental effect on Australian society. They did not, and could not, form a leisured, cultured class of landed gentry, like that which played such an important part in local government in Great Britain. This lack, and the relative weakness of the 'official' Church of England, shattered any idea of creating in the antipodes a replica of English society. Wealthy landowners and government officials were too few, and the Anglican Church too much opposed by Roman Catholics, Presbyterians and Dissenters alike, for these groups to reproduce a ruling class like that of England; the strength of the combined 'opposition', Irish, Catholic, non-conformist, Chartist, emancipist and radical, was such as to encourage the building up of a democratic, anti-government ideology. The squatters, though men of means, were almost forced into association with this opposition during much of the crucial twenty years following the arrival of the 'Whig' governor, Sir Richard Bourke, in 1832, owing to their dislike of the government's land policy; hence the largest class of wealthy men in the community, instead of being predominantly conservative and anxious to support the governors, became their bitterest critics.

But economically, in establishing and developing the wool industry, the squatters were primarily responsible for the prosperity of Australia up to 1851, and Wentworth exaggerated only a little when he told the electors of Sydney in that year:

'If it had not been for the squatting class, when transportation was discontinued to the colony, it must have dwindled into insignificance, they would have had the grass now growing in their streets; if it had not been for this class their magnificent city would have shrunk into a small fishing town, unfamed, and disregarded by European nations. Their sixty thousand inhabitants, if it had not been for this class, would not have exceeded one-third of that number. It was to this class that they were indebted for the tall ships within their harbour. It was this class that had caused the lofty warehouses to rise on their quays; it was this class that provided the splendid equipages that rolled through their streets, and afforded the means for all those appliances of wealth and splendour which abounded in their dwellings. It was to him and to to this much-abused class that they were indebted for all their greatness, all the comforts, all the luxuries, that they possessed.'

Chapter Six

GOVERNMENT AND SOCIETY

The squatters were not only the backbone of the Australian economy in the second quarter of the nineteenth century, they were also the most important political group in the community. It was largely they who fought for, and won, colonial political rights; it was chiefly their agitation that gained the very considerable degree of local self-government in Australia in the next fifty years, although by the 'forties the Colonial Office was quite ready to listen to such demands, as had appeared from its policy in Canada and other parts of the Empire. Yet twenty years earlier the pastoralists of New South Wales had feared any advance towards 'democracy' in a community of former felons; they were nervous about local political rights, and strongly opposed both the political and economic claims of the emancipists. In consequence they had tended to shelter behind the authority of the Governor, at least for as long as their interests coincided with the policy he was adopting on instructions from Great Britain, which was the case at least until about 1835. But the policy of the British government, decided in essentials in London, by no means always followed the advice of the Governor, its local representative, and it frequently ignored popular opinion in the colony; and although it would be untrue to say Australian interests were ignored in administration and policy making, it is equally certain they were not paramount.

As has been said, the power of the early Governor was limited only by the existence of the courts. He could, and did, issue regulations which often controlled the minutest details of civil life; he could impose taxation; he had the right of pardon for nearly all offences; he had extensive local patronage, especially regarding appointments, grants of land and the distribution of convict labour. Even after the rebellion against Bligh in 1808, no change was made until 1814, when a Supreme Court was set up with a professional judge to preside, to supplement the somewhat unsatisfactory Judge Advocate's Court. In 1823, after Bigge had reported, courts of Quarter Sessions replaced altogether the military jurisdiction of the Judge Advocate. But seven military officers continued to act as 'jury' in criminal cases, although they could be challenged for 'interest or affection'; only in civil cases could the parties, if they chose, have a jury of freeholders. By the same Imperial Act, the colonies of New South Wales and Van Diemen's Land were to all intents and purposes separated and Legislative Councils were established in both colonies. These first met in 1825; but since they were nominated bodies with no power of initiative, and the Governor could override them if he thought it necessary to do so, it is hardly surprising that they were not a very effective check on his power. On the other hand, the Chief Justice had now to certify that any proposed ordinance was 'consistent with the laws of England, so far as the circumstances of the colony will permit'. This gave him at least a limited power of veto, which was used, for example, by Sir Francis Forbes in New South Wales to prevent Governor Darling imposing a censorship on the press in 1827. Next year, another British Act increased the size and powers of the Legislative Councils. The 'veto' of the Chief Justice was abolished, but the Governors could no longer override the opinions of the Councils. However, since their fifteen members were all nominated by the Crown, since a majority (counting the Governor who presided) were officials, and since no law could be even discussed without the Governor's consent, it was still only rarely that conflict between Executive and Council arose.

This strong, despotic government was essential in the

'penal' days, and even in the free settlements 'ample government' by a paternal administration was necessary to overcome the difficulties of their foundation. Governors often
had to use their powers to protect the interests of the convicts and emancipists, who had no political rights and would
probably have had none, whatever the constitution; for the
free settlers would, if they could, have treated them virtually
as slaves. As late as 1833, we find Bourke commenting on
'the evil of legislating for the whole community by means
of a Council composed of one party . . . only checked by the
power possessed by the Head of the Government'.

It was, of course, natural that there should be criticism of
such a state of things; and colonial political agitation was
marked by the intense bitterness which is common in small
communities where personalities and personal interests play
such a large part. Even after the shock of the 'Rum Rebellion' against Bligh, Macquarie (1810–1821) was attacked by
men like the Reverend Samuel Marsden and Judge Advocate Bent in language neither clerical nor judicial; they were
ably supported by other critics of a policy said to be too
favourable to the emancipists, and the latter naturally replied in kind. There was no widespread popular demand for
representative institutions in 1821, but there was a great deal
of popular criticism of the so-called 'exclusives', 'an aristocratic body, which would monopolise all situations of
power, dignity and emolument' according to the youthful
W. C. Wentworth, whose own parentage placed him for
the time being on the popular side. Wentworth went further than most in his demand for reform and in his fury at
the attitude of Commissioner Bigge. He described Bigge's
report, so critical of the convict element of the colony, as
'nauseous trash . . . collected with mischievous industry
from the very dregs of the people—from the whores, the
rogues and vagabonds of Sydney . . . like a public scavenger
raking together all the dirt and filth, all the scandal, calum-
nies and lies that were ever circulated in the Colony', and
indeed he was already suggesting that people of New South

Wales might look to the United States of America for help, if, as seemed likely, the colony were to be 'goaded into rebellion'. For a time, few seemed to agree, but the arrival of the somewhat authoritarian Governor Darling at the end of 1825 changed the situation.

Darling was worried about a possible convict rising; he claimed that the tone of the press was inflammatory, which it was, and tried to impose a censorship on it. Naturally he opposed the popular party's demands for trial by jury in criminal cases and a representative assembly in such a community as New South Wales. He thought the claim of the 'rights of Englishmen' absurd in a convict colony, and although he retained the support of the exclusives, his attitude tended to intensify the popular agitation rather than allay it. This agitation sometimes sprang from genuine liberal convictions, as in the case of Chief Justice Forbes; but it was often whipped up by more opportunist politicians, lawyers and pressmen, like Wentworth, Wardell and Dr. Bland.

As the number of free immigrants and colonial free-born gradually increased, the danger to society of granting free institutions became less. No longer would a representative assembly be dominated by the votes of ex-convicts, or a jury be composed of former felons; by 1840 the political divisions of New South Wales were tending to follow the more usual groupings of rich and poor, rather than the temporary and particular distinction between bond and free.

By this time there were signs of working-class organization, with political agitation, trade combinations, and occasional strikes. In 1838 an Australian Union Benefit Society was formed. Next year appeared 'delegates of the trades' to speak for the workers at public meetings and to write for them in the press, and, strengthened by the large free immigration after 1835, this group gradually began to put forward a radical programme. A co-operative flour mill in 1839 suggests some contact with contemporary ideas of British labour, but its principal activities were the product of local circumstances. It bitterly opposed the Draconian

'Masters and Servants Act' of 1828, under which servants neglecting their work or spoiling or losing their master's property were liable to six months' imprisonment; even the amending act of 1840 left the penalty at three months. In 1837 it was reported in the *Sydney Gazette* that a single hour's unpermitted absence from work had brought a sentence to the treadmill; 'we hear of repeated instances of examples like these being made, and shall be glad to hear of many more.' No wonder there were references to 'worse than Egyptian Taskmasters', even if employers retaliated with the charge that free servants 'were as vicious in their habits as the convicts and less subject to control'. We read of a convict servant, charged with attempting to form a combination to 'raise wages and increase rations', being sentenced to one month's solitary confinement on bread and water, five hundred lashes and transportation to a penal settlement. It is not surprising that the working class feared the competition of convict labour, demanded the end of transportation, opposed its resumption and attacked projects for the immigration of coolies from Asia.

For a short time, the working class formed a Radical element in the Australian Patriotic Association which had been founded in 1835 to further the popular agitation for liberal reforms in the colony. At that time the 'exclusives' or 'pure merinos' were still dominant in the nominated Council; they opposed political change, and if reform was inevitable, they wanted to limit it as much as possible; in their petition of 1836, they submitted that 'it is still questionable whether the colony is prepared to enjoy the free institutions of Great Britain'. The 'Patriots' disagreed; they demanded 'the establishment of a Representative Legislature on a wide and liberal basis'; but what exactly was meant by a 'wide and liberal basis'? The argument on this question led to further disagreements which brought a re-alignment of parties.

For the Patriotic Association was not a working-class body. The annual subscription was £1, a considerable sum when the unskilled worker was earning no more than £30 a year. Many members were wealthy emancipists, but the Association included free immigrants and native born, like Sir John Jamison and Wentworth himself. It wanted more political privileges, but only for 'men of property'; when in 1838 it protested to the British government against its proposed abolition of transportation, the 'labour' group withdrew. Now the Association was faced with the threat of colonial radicalism as an alternative to British 'authority'; better to ally with the exclusives!—especially when James Macarthur, son of old John, who had died in 1834, announced that he thought 'that the time had arrived when the long agitated emancipist question might be dropped'. That was in 1841, when wealthy men of both parties found much to criticize in British policy, particularly about land, emigration, colonial expenditure and a proposal to divide the colony; they were inclined to agree with Charles Buller, Member of Parliament and agent for the Patriotic Association in England, when he wrote:

'I utterly despair of ever getting an honest and wise management of lands in this country; the wisest course seems to me to be that of confining our exertions to getting you representative government and thereby enabling you to do this as well as other things by yourselves.'

Both wealthy groups now wanted local self-government, with a representative assembly elected on a restricted franchise.

Current British policy on the 'management of lands' was still largely based on the ideas of Edward Gibbon Wakefield. Writing with that great experience of Australian conditions which he had acquired in Newgate gaol, Wakefield had argued in his so-called *Letter from Sydney* (1829) that under the old system of land grants it was too easy to get land and too hard to find labour to cultivate it. He therefore urged that the land should be sold at a 'fixed price', high enough to prevent its being bought by every needy immigrant who arrived; the purchase money should be used to assist migration, but when the immigrants arrived they would be compelled by economic circumstances to work for existing landowners; only after several years' labour would they have saved enough to buy farms for themselves. This would mean that more purchase money would be available to bring out further migrants; in this way a permanent balance between land and labour would be achieved, and the colonies would no longer depend on convicts for their labour supply.

Though Wakefield's ideas were not put into practice in all their details, the policies of land sales and assisted migration were adopted in 1831. Between 1825 and 1850, 200,000 free migrants arrived in Australia, 70,000 in New South Wales between 1832 and 1842; and owing to the high price of land, fixed at five shillings an acre in 1831, and raised to twelve shillings in 1839 and £1 in 1842, these newcomers were rarely able to acquire land of their own. All was well so long as paid work was available; but the depression of 1841-2 caused much unemployment and distress, especially in Sydney. Government made little effort to provide relief; this was left to private philanthropy.

The initiative was taken by Caroline Chisholm, wife of an Indian army officer. Even before the slump she had been particularly concerned with the fate of the girls who arrived and could not find work. For them she organized a 'home' in Sydney, in part of a disused convict barracks, a draughty rat-infested building, without a fireplace, where she was 'dependent on the kindness of a prisoner employed in an adjoining government printing office for a kettle of hot water for tea'. As the depression grew worse, she set up a kind of labour exchange, and later, 'a second Moses in bonnet and shawl', she escorted parties of young women, more than seven hundred in a single year, into the country where she found them positions. She became convinced that migrants should be 'dispersed' from Sydney when they arrived, and to the Legislative Council Committee on Immigration in 1843 she urged the need of settling them on the land. She thought private individuals might lease property to groups of some fifty families for ten to fifteen years. These families would then clear the land and settle on it, and in two or three years they would be self-sufficient. It was the old, old story of the belief that 'peasant', small-scale farming in Australia was an easy road, if not to affluence, at least to subsistence and that it would strengthen social stability.

Yet, even at the very moment when she put forward her scheme, the small farmers who did exist were in difficulties. Technique was still backward, even though the plough had replaced the hoe and the horse was becoming common; but as there was still no proper system of crop rotation, or regular manuring or fallowing, the soil was cropped unremittingly until exhausted. Bad roads and bushrangers made transport expensive; for example, in 1831 it took a team of nine bullocks two weeks to bring fifty bushels of grain about one hundred miles. The market for grain continued to be uncertain, as gluts and scarcities, good seasons, droughts and floods succeeded one another and the New South Wales farmer began to meet competition from Van Diemen's Land and even South America. He asked for tariff protection, but did not get it. In 1831, the *Herald* regretted 'that considerable numbers of our smaller settlers have been compelled to abandon the renting of land from an inability to maintain themselves and their families by the produce of their farms'; in 1840, it commented that 'our agriculture has gone on in *inverse* ratio with our population and wealth,' owing to the difficulties of farming and the greater profits to be made from wool. In fact, in 1836 when the population of New South Wales was 77,000, 51,600 acres were under wheat; in 1842 though the population had grown to 160,000, there were only 57,500 acres under wheat. No wonder then that the Legislative Council was not over-enthusiastic about Mrs. Chisholm's scheme, though some members were also nervous that, if successful, it might deprive the squatters of their labour.

For despite assisted immigration, labour remained the major problem of the mainland colonies up to 1850, especially after transportation to New South Wales had been stopped in 1840. The preceding twenty years had been the heyday of the Australian convict system, though it lasted for another decade in Van Diemen's Land, and until 1868 in Western Australia. In 1840 no less than 56,000 convicts were undergoing punishment in the two eastern colonies, and the 80,000 who had arrived between 1820 and 1840, well over half the total number sent to Australia, naturally comprised an important addition to the labour force. Yet they were not enough. Demands for convict servants continually outstripped the supply, and although Wakefield pointed out that 'if for every acre of land appropriated there should be a conviction for felony in England' all would be well, in fact there were not enough convictions.

While convict labour was insufficient to meet the needs of the colony, the transportation system was coming under fire from other directions. In Britain, critics argued that the punishment was insufficiently severe, so that it was no longer a deterrent to criminals. On the other hand, it was increasingly resented by free labourers in New South Wales who disliked the competition of felons for employment, and by public men, both in England and Australia, who were disturbed by the prevalence of vice and crime in the colony, which was said to be the result of the convicts' presence. Although it is impossible to decide how far contemporary lamentations about the state of society were justified, it seems certain that the convicts of this period were not the heroic martyrs to English injustice so often described by romantic Australian nationalists. Whatever may have been the case of the relatively small numbers transported before 1815, afterwards, as both the criminal law and administration in Great Britain were steadily reformed, most of those sent out were from the 'dregs of Society'. Political offenders were few, though notorious; including the west country rioters of 1831, the 'Tolpuddle Martyrs' of 1834, some

Chartists and Canadian rebels, they comprised far less than a thousand. The vast majority were from the slums of London and the growing industrial cities of Britain, and were convicted of fairly serious offences after a career of crime. The poacher, so often spoken of, was exceedingly rare; even those Irish, who were sometimes convicted only of being out after curfew, were only transported when the government was convinced that they had been implicated in murder or outrage.

For a long time the employing class was willing to accept 'vice' in return for the economic advantage of cheap labour; but when it seemed likely that they would lose this by assigned service being abolished, and when it was realized that continued transportation was incompatible with self-government, the colonial advocates of the system grew fewer, even though a number of employers, led by Wentworth, were still very reluctant to see it go. Nevertheless, it was largely because of English influences that in 1838 the government decided to change its policy, and that in 1840 assignment was abolished and transportation to New South Wales ceased.

The system certainly rid Britain of many of her criminal population. Few ever returned; for the passage was expensive, and as the convict obtained his ticket-of-leave after serving little more than half his sentence with good behaviour, he was often able to spend a considerable time working for himself and establishing roots in the colony, so that when he received his full freedom, he had little wish to leave. Despite much controversy, it would seem that the system was cheap, granted that there was little desire, or even opportunity, to employ prisoners on public works in England. To the colonies in the early days it provided a valuable supply of labour when that was badly needed. And if it did little directly to promote the reformation of the character of the convict, it did remove him from a society where unemployment was common and wages were low, to one where he would readily obtain work and a good living, so that at least the temptation to crime was proportionately reduced.

This is not to say that his character was ignored. By 1820, there were schools held on most convict ships, where reading and writing were taught and religious instruction was strongly emphasized. Prayer-books, Bibles, catechisms and other religious tracts were always loaded on to the transports; even the First Fleet carried 200 copies of *Exercises Against Lying*, 50 of *Caution to Swearers*, 100 *Exhortations to Chastity* and 100 *Dissuasions from Stealing*. Arrived in the colony, the prisoners continued to observe their religious duties; attendance at church was made compulsory wherever possible. As a result the foundations of religion in Australia were closely linked with convict reformation and for thirty years its growth was almost exclusively connected with the work of the Church of England and its official chaplains appointed to the various convict establishments. Other denominations were not encouraged, and the first Roman Catholic priest did not arrive officially until 1820. Only gradually did the Scottish Presbyterians among the emigrants challenge the monopoly of the Anglican establishment, while increasing numbers of Irish convicts swelled the ranks of the Church of Rome. Dissent allied with radicalism fought for equality, and the exclusive privileges of the Church of England slowly gave way to a variety of state-aided religions and state-aided schools where, after the customary amount of theological polemic, religious equality was established by Governor Bourke.

It has been a point of much debate whether or not the Church of England was legally an 'established Church' in the early days of the settlement, although it certainly received official support and its clergy were paid by government. But in 1825 an Archdeaconry was established in Sydney, and Earl Bathurst ordered one-seventh of the land of each county in the colony to be set aside to provide for the support of the Anglican clergy and Anglican education, and a Corporation to be formed to administer this endowment.

This seemed to give to the Church of England rather more control of state-assisted education than it had possessed previously; for the first schools in the colony, starting with Governor King's Orphan School established in 1800, and comprising nearly a dozen establishments by 1820, were government or private institutions rather than Anglican. Now, under the Church and Schools Corporation, it seemed that an 'exclusive and intolerant system of Episcopal domination' might be foisted on the community. The Presbyterian prejudices of the Reverend John Dunmore Lang would have none of it, nor would the Roman Catholic principles of Father J. J. Therry; the radical opponents of Governor Darling seized on the religious issue as another stick to beat him with, and even his usual supporters, the wealthy landowners, were far from enthusiastic in a cause in which the Corporation's land claims might threaten their own expansion. In 1829 it was suspended, and in 1833 dissolved, though less because of colonial opposition to the Church than because of the difficulties of administering its lands and changing opinion in England.

Bourke realized that no one creed could be supreme in a community of many religious persuasions like New South Wales. 'The inclination of these colonies, which keep pace with the spirit of the Age, is decidedly adverse to such an institution', he wrote, 'and I feel the interests of religion would be prejudiced by its establishment.' Instead he urged that support be given 'to every one of the three grand Division of Christians indifferently', and in education he recommended a scheme similar to the National System recently introduced in Ireland, wherein state financial assistance was coupled with separate doctrinal instruction by the clergy of the different faiths. To this suggestion, however, the Anglicans would not agree; instead, state aid was given to schools of all denominations. But the monopoly of the Church of England was broken, on the eve of the creation of the Anglican diocese of Australia in 1836, and the consecration of Archdeacon Broughton as bishop. A Roman Catholic See had been established in 1835, and next year the Church Act extended government assistance to all religious bodies for the building of churches and the salaries of their clergy.

The growth of educational and religious controversy at least showed that some cultural ambitions were stirring in the erstwhile 'gaol'. The 'thirties saw the foundation of the first three permanent secondary schools in Australia, the King's School at Parramatta in 1832, Sydney Grammar School and John Dunmore Lang's Presbyterian Australian School in 1835. A decade earlier there had been a Philosophical Society of Australasia, founded by the astronomically minded Governor Brisbane in 1821; unfortunately it soon expired 'in the baneful atmosphere of distracted politics which unhappily clouded the short administration of its President', but not before a series of papers were read which were subsequently published by Judge Barron Field. The Judge had also tried his hand at poetry:

> *Kangaroo, Kangaroo,*
> *Thou spirit of Australia*
> *That redeems from utter failure,*
> *From perfect desolation*
> *And warrants the creation*
> *Of the fifth part of the Earth,*
> *Which would seem an after-birth,*

but his efforts were little appreciated in the words of one critic:[1]

> *Thy poems, Barron Field, I've read*
> *And thus adjudge their meed,*
> *So poor a crop proclaims thy head*
> *A barren field indeed.*

There were attempts at drama. Theatricals for long were all amateur productions, often provided by the men of visiting regiments or men-of-war; but a regular theatre opened in

[1] Quoted by M. H. Ellis: *Lachlan Macquarie, his life and times* (Sydney, 1952), p. 373, note.

1832 in Sydney, and another in 1834 in Hobart, and that
year saw too the first performance of Grand Opera, and the
first regular musical society. On the other hand, said a visitor, 'literature of every kind is at a very low ebb. . . . John
Dunmore Lang is the only author of eminence.' One may
doubt the last judgement, but it is true that early Australian
writing consisted almost entirely of political or theological
tracts, like those of Lang, Wentworth, Macarthur or Mudie,
plus the virulent, scurrilous, often libellous outpouring of
the press, and the diaries or journals of visitors. Some, like
Lang, deplored local tastes and habits like drink and horse-
racing, 'the signal for the periodical assembly of all the
wealth and beauty of the colony, the concentration of all its
vice and villainy'. He was critical of sport generally.

'Let the reader turn over a file of the colonial newspapers for 1833 and he will find them stuffed almost to
nausea with advertisements and accounts of races, cricket
matches, boxing matches and regattas, with challenges to
fight or to run or to row. The energy of the native mind
of the colony seems of late to have been diverted almost
exclusively into this frivolous channel.'
If this indictment is true—and though the Scottish pastor
is a prejudiced observer there is independent evidence to
support it—it would seem that the Australian climate early
encouraged an outdoor life. What else was there to do? Not
everyone could follow the example of Sturt and, when
bored, go exploring.
Despite the growing number of imposing mansions on the
outskirts of the town, general living conditions indoors were
still somewhat primitive, and in the crowded area of the
'Rocks', especially, many of the houses and their furniture
were little superior to the shanties in the bush. This might
have been expected; there were few 'mod. cons.' a hundred
years ago, and Sydney still 'coincided much with a second
or third class town in England', having also the handicap of
distance and isolation. Was it surprising that it should be
said that there was 'more squalor, misery and vice than in

any other town in the British dominions'? Better, even Lang would agree, to indulge in sport than in the excessive drinking which visitors invariably noted on their arrival, in 'the propensity to gambling, which appears to affect all classes of the community', or even '(we touch upon it with delicacy and reluctance, but the truth must be told) in that illicit intercourse between the sexes which prevails to so great extent throughout the land'. Perhaps these vices are to be expected in a community largely composed of ex-convicts and their children; perhaps they are not unknown elsewhere; perhaps are even in certain conditions a sign of prosperity—for several writers blamed them on to the 'excessive' wages paid to mechanics, and indeed how else would they spend their money?

Certainly labour conditions were good by contemporary standards, in spite of the Masters and Servants Act, for labour was wanted everywhere, and the possibilities of work with the squatters, or of cedar-cutting (highly profitable at this period), kept up wages in town. The large-scale immigration caused a great deal of building and the growth of population was stimulating 'manufactories'. Many were connected with primary production—such as the flour mills, meat-preserving factories and tanneries—many such as Simeon Lord's woollen mills at Botany Bay were producing coarse goods of poor quality used by the 'lower orders'; but five soap works 'commanded the entire local market'; the ship and boat building establishments and the brass and iron foundries were active, not to mention the distilleries and the breweries, of which there were fifty-one in Australia in 1848. Already there were complaints of the size of Sydney, to add to those of drinking habits, vice and crime.

The capital not only attracted a large population; as the centre of government, it was the focus of political activity and agitation through press and public meeting. As in so many small communities, political differences were intensified by personal jealousies and malicious backbiting; but apart from this there was plenty of scope for public controversy over the questions of land, migration, finance and the constitution. The regulations abolishing land grants and substituting sales at five shillings per acre had been introduced in 1831 by the decision of the British government alone. They were not at first unpopular, for the price was low and the proceeds of the sales were to be used to assist immigration; but it was a potential grievance that the British government should have the power to decide how the revenue should be spent, and when the British Treasury decided, in 1834, to charge the expense of the colonial police and gaols on the land fund, criticism increased. Why should the colony contribute to the expense of the British convict establishment? it was asked by men forgetting the various other benefits received as a *quid pro quo*. It was only by his casting vote, supported by all the official members, that Bourke was able to carry this measure through the Council; and every year the opposition grew more bitter. When the stopping of transportation was threatened, the colonists thought it all the more necessary that the *whole* land revenue be spent on immigration; but they were still highly critical of the type of migrants sent out by the English authorities.

The first assisted migrants were not always well chosen, but it was not easy to obtain the able-bodied farm servants that the colonists wanted. Possibly their criticism of the female migrants was better justified. These women were sent out to reduce the inequality of the sexes in New South Wales, but too often were only the sweepings of the streets of London, Dublin and other cities of England and Ireland.

These were grievances that made even colonial conservatives think of demanding a greater amount of local self-government. For a long time, the threat of radicalism had given them pause, but in 1840 greater threats seemed to be appearing from England. The price of land was raised; migration was not yet satisfactory; Lord John Russell proposed to divide the colony; transportation was stopped; yet no concession was made about the land revenue. If this was what could be expected from England, was colonial radicalism likely to be any worse? Better to have a local representative assembly, elected on a limited franchise. Now that New South Wales was no longer a penal colony, the British government was ready to make concessions, for local representative institutions were in the tradition of British colonial government. By the Constitution Act of 1842, the powers of the Legislative Council were increased: it was given considerable, though not complete, control over local finance; it was enlarged to thirty-six members of whom twenty-four were to be elected; of the twelve government nominees not more than six were to be officials; a high property qualification for voting and a gerry-mandered distribution of seats ensured a majority for the squatters. For the time being Great Britain retained control of colonial lands, for these were regarded as a trust for posterity. But this attempt at imperial trusteeship was too much for the self-interest of the squatters. Using their financial powers they threatened to cut down supplies, and in 1852 full control of land policy was handed to the colony. This was one of their last victories, for by now their power was being threatened by 'democracy'. It was largely popular opposition that prevented the revival of transportation in 1849 and 1850, when the anti-transportation leagues thwarted the wishes of some of the squatters in the Council; after 1851, the gold discoveries further weakened their position by attracting free migrants in their thousands. But the social importance of gold can easily be exaggerated. Democracy was growing before 1850; wool and squatting retained their importance long afterwards. The free immigration of the 'thirties and 'forties had changed the character of the Australian colonies before a single nugget had been found, for by 1850 convictism was virtually at an end, prosperous communities, largely self-governing, were winning wealth from the former wilderness, and the cultural and social foundations of a nation had been laid.

Chapter Seven

VARIATIONS ON A THEME

At no time was Botany Bay the only British settlement on or near the Australian continent. Almost as soon as he landed, Phillip sent an expedition to occupy Norfolk Island in the Pacific. His immediate objects were to increase supplies of food and to reduce the number of convicts dependent on the poor soil near Sydney, but he also had hopes that the cultivation of flax and cotton might be profitable for the mother country. The island was fertile, even if it did not grow flax; but it was singularly difficult of access. There was no harbour and ships had to lie off in the swell; in March 1790, H.M.S. *Sirius* was wrecked there. The upkeep of a separate establishment in these conditions was troublesome, so between 1808 and 1813 the settlers, apart from a few who returned to Sydney, were transferred to the New Norfolk district in Van Diemen's Land, some twenty miles up river from Hobart Town, which had been occupied in 1803-4. At that time Governor King was afraid that the French scientific expedition under Baudin, which had arrived in Australia in 1802 during the shortlived truce with Napoleon, indicated an over-zealous French interest in the country, following as it did the earlier voyages of La Pérouse in 1788 and Bruni d'Entrecasteaux in 1791. Baudin's officers complained of their commander's excessive interest in butterflies; but in case the butterflies were a sham, King sent off two parties to Van Diemen's Land to forestall any possible *arrière-pensée*—one to the River Derwent, under Lieutenant Bowen, who landed at Risdon in September 1803, another to the River Tamar in the north in 1804.

Meanwhile, and for the same reason, the British government had sent out David Collins, formerly Phillip's secretary and Judge Advocate and the first historian of New
South Wales, to found a settlement on Port Phillip Bay.
Collins however was nervous of the natives at the north of
the Bay, and near the heads, which were difficult to enter,
he found the soil poor and water short; as a result he concluded, somewhat hastily, that 'when all its disadvantages
are publicly known, it cannot be supposed that commercial
people will ever be desirous of visiting it'. After three
months, unmoved by one of his subordinate's visions of 'a
second Rome rising . . . giving laws to the world, super-
lative in arts and arms', he moved to Van Diemen's Land.
He joined Bowen on the Derwent, but in February 1804
the settlement was transferred across the river to the present
site of Hobart.

Like New South Wales, the new colony went through
various early vicissitudes. Even if it was not so seriously
threatened with famine, there were clashes with the natives,
and the practices of escaped convicts, of whom one Michael
Howe was quickly notorious, soon enriched the language
with the term 'bushranger'. Government was handicapped
by its dependence on Sydney and 'out of sight is out of
mind'. Though Collins was a capable administrator, the
same could hardly be said of his successor 'Mad' Colonel
Davey, appointed Lieutenant-Governor in 1813 after three
years' interregnum, even in the comparatively rare intervals
when this functionary was sober. Even so, by the time
William Sorell arrived as Lieutenant-Governor in 1817,
the local press was established, the first Church, St. David's,
Hobart, wàs building, whaling and sealing were temporarily prosperous and wheat was being exported to New
South Wales. Macquarie had visited the Island in 1811. He
prescribed a plan for Hobart Town and had 'the names of
the Great Square and Principal Streets Painted on Boards
and erected on Posts and the Angles of the Square and
Streets to define . . . them', and he planned to move Launces-

ton nearer the sea, to George Town. Thereafter his interest waned; he had other things to think about in Sydney, and his next visit was one of 'farewell', in 1821. But the seal and whale fisheries, the export of wheat and the development of the pastoral industry with the encouragement of Sorell had increased the number of free settlers, and in consequence Commissioner Bigge recommended the separation of the two colonies. In effect this was carried out when Colonel George Arthur replaced Sorell as Lieutenant-Governor in 1824.

Arthur may perhaps be regarded as the 'Macquarie of Van Diemen's Land' even if his name does not make quite so many appearances on the map as Macquarie's. Each held office for twelve years; under the rule of each a struggling settlement became a flourishing colony. Their problems and policies were by no means identical; but each left a lasting imprint on the colony he ruled.

Arthur's first task was to complete the extermination of the bushrangers, who were a far worse menace in Van Diemen's Land than in New South Wales. Most of Howe's gang had been killed or captured by Sorrell in 1818, but the succeeding quiet was broken by absconders from the penal settlement at Macquarie Harbour, which had been founded in January 1822. Alexander Pierce, one of the first, was soon recaptured; his exploit is notorious only for his cannibalism. Far more troublesome was Brady's gang, which continued at large for more than two years despite frequent arrests. Their life was terrible. In constant fear of capture, but yet in constant need of food, ammunition or female company, they were forced to haunt the settled districts, where murder, pillage and arson grew frequent and those in outlying homesteads lived almost as if in a state of war, with sentinels and loop-holes on their houses. The roads were infested; travel became most dangerous. When Governor Arthur offered a reward for Brady's capture, the bushranger announced his 'concern that a person known as George Arthur is at large. Twenty gallons of rum will be given to any person that will deliver this person to me.' Not for two years was the gang finally broken up.

Next, Arthur had to turn his attention to the natives. Despite unfortunate encounters in the early days of misgovernment, outrages committed by irresponsible settlers and the Aborigines' natural objection to the white men occupying their lands and hunting-grounds, the blacks had been slow to resist. But in time, with the continuous spread of settlement, relations became increasingly bad, as thefts, attacks and reprisals became more and more frequent. After he had tried reconciliation, and failed, Arthur tried to segregate the two races by driving the natives into Tasman's Peninsula; but when a spectacular expedition costing £30,000 brought in only one woman, found with a boy asleep, he was forced to revert once more to peaceful methods. He employed one George Robinson, a missionary who had won the confidence of the blacks, to persuade them to come in, to give up their bush life and to trust the government. Placed on Flinders Island in Bass Strait under Robinson's superintendence, they were well cared for materially, but their spirit was apparently broken, and they slowly pined away. In 1847 only forty-seven were left out of an originally estimated population of about five thousand, but a number of Tasmanians still possess Aboriginal blood.

But Arthur's most important work was with regard to the convicts. Although general policy was the same in New South Wales and Van Diemen's Land, it was more efficiently administered in the latter, thanks to Arthur's long tenure of office, his experience and his energy. An enthusiastic believer in transportation as a punishment, and a vigorous defender of his system in pamphlets and despatches, he regarded everything else as subordinate to his penal administration, and by the end of his term had worked out a highly efficient system of discipline. The normal fate of the convict, thought Arthur, should be assigned service to a settler, which was economical to government, profitable to the master who would obtain cheap labour, and also beneficial to the convict. He would be taught agricultural labour and would thus be able to earn an honest living when his sentence expired; and it would be in the interest of his employer to treat him well and to try to reform his character by moral teaching and religious instruction in order to get the greatest benefit from his service. Thus much could be left to the operation of 'enlightened self-interest'. But should this fail, the Governor was always ready to step in; and no one could have been more vigilantly on the watch for abuses. If a master failed to treat his servants fairly, or if the conditions of his establishment were such as to appear unlikely to promote 'reformation', the servants were withdrawn—on many occasions to the bitter complaints of the settlers. On the other hand, if the conduct of the convicts was unsatisfactory, they could be sent before a magistrate to be punished. In 1829 Arthur brought great improvement by replacing the old 'amateur' settler-magistrates with paid professionals, on whom he could rely for the regular reports on masters and servants in their districts, and who could order convicts brought before them to be flogged, imprisoned, or returned, under various conditions, to government.

These conditions were carefully graduated. At the top of the scale came those ordinarily employed on public works or in the public departments—hospital, shipping, commissariat, surveyor-general, roads and so forth—where conditions were allegedly the same as in private service. None the less most convicts preferred the latter, for though closer supervision might sometimes involve harder work there were usually more 'indulgences' (such as tea, sugar or tobacco) to be gained from a private employer, and on the whole his discipline was less strict. This led the British government to criticize the assignment system, despite its support by Bigge in 1821. At that time, the Commissioner had deplored the cost of the public works on which the convicts were employed, but he also argued that the superintendence in government service was so bad and the discipline so lax, that the convicts were idle and disorderly; only in assigned service would they be properly punished. In time, English opinion changed, and in 1833 Stanley, then Secretary of State, told Arthur that only the need for economy stopped him ordering all convicts to a term of service on the roads before being assigned. Arthur however insisted that 'transportation with assignment', with its loss of liberty and exposure to summary discipline, was itself a very severe punishment. Those convicted of disobedience, idleness, drunkenness or insubordination, apart from any more normal offences, might be sent to the chain gang. Here, as the name suggests, they had to work in irons, discipline was very strict and the work extremely heavy; but an even more severe punishment was sentence to a penal settlement, usually inflicted only for serious colonial crime, violence or continued attempts to escape.

Of the two famous penal settlements of Tasmania, Macquarie Harbour on the west coast was founded in 1822 but abandoned about ten years later because too difficult of access and Port Arthur on Tasman's Peninsula replaced it. Though approached by land only by the narrow isthmus of Eaglehawk Neck, guarded by fierce half-starved dogs, this establishment was in easy communication with Hobart by sea across Storm Bay, and so possessed an almost perfect site for such an institution. Existence in this place, as in those successively used in New South Wales, Newcastle, Port Macquarie, Moreton Bay and Norfolk Island, has often been described as 'worse than death'. Certainly conditions were as severe as the human frame could stand, with primitive living, arduous labour and brutal discipline, and a few men even committed murder in order to get release by execution. Long sentences in the settlements must have been almost unbearable, especially on Norfolk Island, which was the worst, but less than five per cent of all convicts were ever sent there, even for short periods, and their inhabitants were nearly all doubly convicted criminals of the lowest type.

Among the rest of the convicts who were sent to Australia, over 160,000 in all, there were naturally many differ-

ent types. In the early days, the law was harsh and administration was haphazard. But less than a fifth were transported
before 1820; by then, and continuously thereafter, English
criminal law was being reformed and its administration
made more merciful. The bulk of the prisoners, who comprised about one-fifth of those convicted of crime at the
Assizes and Quarter Sessions of England, were the town
thieves, pickpockets and shop lifters, that constituted such a
serious menace to the badly policed English society of the
early nineteenth century. The result, wrote one 'emigrant
mechanic' was the prevalence of

'drunkenness, profanity, dishonesty and unchastity. What
else could be expected? The original stock is the very
lowest; the blood-stained hand and ruthless heart from
the most barbarian parts of Ireland; the professional de-
predator from the vilest haunts of London; the lowest
slaves of profligacy, inebriation, violence and lust.'[1]

Females were always comparatively few—less than 20,000
in all. Their discipline was always a problem owing to the
small number of women in the country. In the early days
they were often given tickets of leave on arrival; later they
were either assigned as domestic servants, or sent to the
female factory—at Parramatta in New South Wales or in
Hobart Town. In neither case were they likely to be very
much 'reformed' in their morals and conduct. The female
factory really meant a gaol where female convicts were
either 'employed' at making clothing, treated for illness or
delivered of their babies.

Many boys were transported, for the problem of juvenile
delinquency is no new one. Frequently they were the vic-
tims of circumstances, orphans, deserted by parents, un-
educated, homeless, friendless, but frequently trained to
'earn a living' by crime. In the days of Fagin and 'the artful
Dodger', the government could not well afford to be too
lenient, ignorant as it was of the penal theories to be put forward by future sociologists; transportation offered a way

[1] A. Harris: *Settlers and Convicts* (1953), p. 230.

of getting rid of these unwanted children and possibly a chance for them to earn an honest living in a new country. Unfortunately, for a long time they were given no special treatment or education on their arrival, and it was argued they were frequently 'hardened' by their associates. At last, in 1835, Arthur established a juvenile reformatory at Point Puer, adjacent to Port Arthur.

Transported boys were sent there directly on arrival, and were taught a trade so that they could be apprenticed to, or employed by settlers. Although discipline was strict, conditions were very different from those in the penal settlements, and considering the state of contemporary English schools, and even the habits of contemporary parents, they cannot be considered very severe. 'It is refreshing to find that kindness and coercion were united in the discipline of Point Puer,' wrote one clerical critic of the system as a whole; 'it is an oasis in the desert of penal government.'

In maintaining his convict system Arthur inevitably came into conflict with the free settlers, just as the early Governors of New South Wales had done. The distribution of servants, dependent on the needs of convict discipline rather than the wants of employers, was naturally criticized; on the occasions when he withdrew servants from unsatisfactory masters the abuse knew no bounds. In his early days he was handicapped by incompetent officials; and as he gradually replaced these by his own nephews, he was attacked for giving jobs to his family. As governor of what he looked on as a gaol, it was natural that he had little time for democratic liberties, and his attempts to control the press inevitably aroused the wrath of the large tribe of Hobart journalists. When news came of his recall in 1836 there was widespread rejoicing, with a special press supplement calling for a day of 'general thanksgiving for the deliverance from the ironhand' of the Governor. REJOICE FOR THE DAY OF RETRIBUTION HAS ARRIVED was the placard. Yet Arthur had deserved well of the colony. If much of its progress and prosperity was due to the influx of population, both free and bond, Arthur had provided what was hitherto absent, a firm foundation of law and order and a reasonably competent administration; he had encouraged religion and provided education; he had successfully opposed the imposition of a tax on convict labour, and though he had been unable to prevent the colony being saddled (as in New South Wales) with the cost of the police and gaols, he had carried out with convict labour many public works of benefit to the colony.

His successors were handicapped by changes in the transportation system. Continued crime in Great Britain had convinced the British government that the normal existing punishment did not sufficiently deter the criminal classes. Therefore, it was argued, the punishment must be made more severe. Some reformers favoured the building of penitentiaries in England; others, increased severity in the penal colonies. Either would be more costly than the existing system, but the latter, being the cheaper of the two, won the day. All convicts were to be employed by government. Assignment to private service was abolished. So much depended on the nature of the master that assignment, it was said, reduced punishment to a 'lottery', and one moreover in which the odds were loaded in favour of lenient treatment as being the best means of inducing one's servant to work well. In vain Arthur described the hardships of the assigned servant, his loss of liberty, his subjection to harsh discipline and summary authority; in vain did visitors in the 'thirties record their surprise at the severity of his treatment. The British government listened to the voices of the past, describing a lax state of affairs which no longer existed; it heeded those propagandists like Archbishop Whately whose fervour and confidence in their own opinions were matched by their ignorance of colonial conditions. It was apparently unaware that the increase of crime in England was caused more by conditions at home than by systems of punishment.

Under the new system all convicts were to work in government gangs for a period which depended on their original sentence and the subsequent behaviour; only after this 'probation' would they be permitted to seek private employment, but when they obtained it they were now to be paid wages. The organization of the probation gangs threw on the convict administration a strain which it could not bear. Discipline relaxed; there were widespread accusations of idleness and vice. To make matters worse the economic depression which began in 1842 reduced the private demand for labour, so that the convicts when due for release from the government gangs found it difficult to obtain work, especially as they had now to be paid; at the same time the stoppage of transportation to New South Wales greatly increased the number of prisoners sent to Van Diemen's Land. Conditions became so bad that in 1846 transportation was suspended for two years. Revived in 1848, it was soon unpopular again. The enthusiasm of employers for convict labour was noticeably cooler now that they had to pay for it. The large influx of 1840–46 had created what was at least alleged to be a threat to society. There were more prisoners in the island than ever before in its history, and 23,000 out of a population of 70,000 were convicts. Troubles arose with the Legislative Council on the question of government finance. The non-official members opposed the estimates, and when these were passed by the Governor's casting vote the 'patriotic six' resigned, leaving the Council without a quorum to conduct its business. They were persuaded to return, but the growing popular feeling against the convict system provided another bone of contention.

In 1846 the British government tried to persuade the mainland colonies to receive 'exiles', that is convicts sent out with tickets of leave after a period of reformatory discipline and hard labour in an English prison. Governor FitzRoy and some of the squatters supported the idea; Wentworth drew up a report for the New South Wales Legislative Council almost lyrical in its praise of the proposal, speaking of

'our boundless interior which seems to have been created the vast solitude that it is and to have been assigned by

Providence to the British nation as the fittest scene for the reformation of her criminals. . . . If the yet untrodden wilds lately discovered by that enterprising traveller Leichhardt and those opened out by previous explorers were made available to these great ends, how many millions now spent for the support of the poor might be saved . . . and how largely might the sum of human misery and crime be reduced? How many happy and smiling countenances, how many prosperous homes might soon brighten up this now lonely but beautiful wilderness? How many souls that may otherwise perish might be turned to salvation? . . . The seeds of a great community would be sown of this continent. . . . A mighty colony would arise, a faithful subject and never-failing customer that would be attached to her in peace, that would not desert her in war, that would consolidate her strength and be the mainstay not only of her supremacy and dominion in these seas, but probably of her continuing supremacy and dominion in the world.'

The Council was not convinced; still less were 'the operative classes', whom Wentworth had correctly expected to give the proposal an 'unhesitating veto'. Their temper could be judged from the reception already given in Melbourne in 1844 to a trial ship-load of convicts sent with conditional pardons—'expatriated villains from the gaols of England, either under the fanciful name of exiles or of any other appellation', as the Mayor described them. In 1849 and 1850 the inhabitants of both Melbourne and Sydney threatened to resist by force the landing of more 'exiles' from the ships *Randolph* and *Hashemy*, and they had to be taken to Moreton Bay for disembarkation. Clearly the policy was impossible. In January 1851, a number of local organizations united to form one Australasian League for the Abolition of Transportation.

Since 1820 Van Diemen's Land had made much progress. Its free population had grown from 2,500 to 49,000; British expenditure on the convict and military establishments had stimulated prosperity and much private capital had been invested in the colony, in agriculture, wool-growing, banking and commerce, whaling and sealing. Apart from the huge Van Diemen's Land Agricultural Company, smaller flock-masters had been constantly expanding their activities; it was their desire for new land that had stimulated settlement at Port Philip. Compared with sheep-farming, agriculture was backward and inefficient, but the area under crop had steadily increased, and wheat exports were regularly sent to New South Wales. As an administrative and commercial centre, Hobart became quite a lively metropolis with theatre, public library, mechanics' institute, church secondary schools, nice terraces, crescents and taverns and many a substantial villa, 'solidly built on the English model'.

This society of convicts, civil servants, soldiers, sailors, emancipists and immigrants suffered severely from depression in the 1840's, owing to the collapse of the wool-market, excessive free immigration and too many convicts. Lieut.-Governor Denison (1847–55) rightly feared that stopping transportation would impoverish the colony further by reducing British expenditure and the supply of cheap labour; but moral considerations triumphed over material, and the colonists insisted on having no more convicts. Its case was greatly strengthened by the gold discoveries—'there are few English criminals who would not regard a free passage to the gold-fields, via Hobart Town, as a great boon.'

In 1852 after a report from the Surveyor General of Prisons the British government gave way and transportation to Van Diemen's Land ceased. Next year the colony turned its back on its past by changing its name to Tasmania and in 1855 received full self-government at the same time as New South Wales.

Yet almost at this moment, transportation to Western Australia was beginning. Here there was no question of responsible government; it was a question of survival—and survival was possible only if labour could be sent, since it refused to come voluntarily. Yet the settlement at Swan

River had been started with high hopes, by a group of wealthy speculators impressed by the reports of Captain James Stirling who had examined the site when on the way to plant a station at Raffles Bay in the north. Healthy climate, good soil, fresh water, safe anchorage, 'not inferior in any natural essential quality to the Plain of Lombardy', a favourable situation either for trade with the East or 'for the equipment of Cruizers'—what more would be needed? The answer was soon apparent—labour and capital. But such prosaic things barely crossed the mind of Thomas Peel, Esq., even though three of his partners withdrew when the British refused to give any help save a grant of land in an area isolated, undeveloped and not as fertile as Stirling had reported. In theory capitalists were to be attracted by the land grants—forty acres (later reduced to twenty) for every £5 invested. In three years a million acres were thus disposed of, but they were unexplored and unsurveyed, and without labour to work them, for the bulk of those who went out in 1829 to found the colony were hopeful employers not labourers, and such labourers as there were soon preferred to move on to the more civilized conditions and better wages of the older settlements in the east. As in the foundation of New South Wales, there were few experienced farmers; no one apparently realized what conditions would be like in a 'new country' without roads or houses or the public facilities one might expect to find in an English country town. For twenty years the settlement was almost static. By 1849 the population was only 5,000, though admittedly its future was then assured, with self-sufficiency in foodstuffs achieved, a steadily expanding pastoral industry, and flourishing out-settlements at Pinjarra, scene of the bloody battle with the natives, Busselton and Bunbury to the south, not to mention Albany on King George's Sound, originally occupied by a military party from Sydney in 1826 to forestall the French. Lack of labour remained a great handicap; indentured servants proved useless, 'idle, disobedient or drunk', and so the colonists swallowed their pride and petitioned for convicts, which the British government was only too glad to send.

But if the experiences of the Swan River settlers showed the difficulties of colonizing uninhabited lands with little government assistance, two almost contemporaneous establishments in the east told a different story, thanks to their better natural resources and their proximity to New South Wales and Van Diemen's Land. The first impetus to settle what was later known as Victoria came from Van Diemen's Land. A number of pastoralists there felt cramped by the confines of their small island and attracted by the favourable reports of the exploring journeys of Hume and Hovell to Port Phillip and Sturt along the Murray. Encouraged by Governor Arthur, who had hopes of expanding his jurisdiction and gaining more room for his convicts, they cast their mind's eye on the fertile lands across Bass Strait. The first to move were the Henty family, disappointed at Swan River and unable to buy land or obtain a grant in Van Diemen's Land, who 'squatted' with their possessions at Portland Bay in 1834. Next year two more groups of enterprising squatters, one led by John Pascoe Fawkner, the other by John Batman, landed on the shores of Port Phillip. Batman took the precaution of acquiring his land—a mere 100,000 acres—by purchase from the blacks in return for a yearly payment of a hundred blankets, fifty knives, fifty tomahawks, fifty pairs of scissors, fifty looking-glasses, twenty suits of clothing and two tons of flour. Arthur thought highly of this treaty, believing it a 'fatal error' that such an arrangement had not been made in Van Diemen's Land; Batman, too, was sure the native 'fully comprehended' his proposals and were 'much delighted with the prospect of having me to live among them', but neither Bourke in Sydney nor Lord Glenelg in London took the same view, and the settlers were denounced as trespassers for settling without government authority. Such an attitude could not of course be maintained, and in 1836 the district of Port Phillip was recognized as part of New South Wales, with that colony's land regulations in force. The town of Melbourne was soon laid out, and when Bourke visited the district in 1837 there were 100,000 sheep in the colony, mainly sent from Van Diemen's Land. But the New South Wales squatters were not slow to follow, especially after Major Mitchell's reports on his journey through 'Australia Felix' and back from Portland to the Murrumbidgee. By 1845 virtually all the grazing land of Victoria was occupied; by 1850 there were 77,000 settlers and over five million sheep in the colony, which succeeded in that year in gaining its 'independence' from New South Wales.

Equally prosperous by this time was South Australia, whose settlement was once again undertaken on the strength of an explorer's reports—this time those of Sturt, on his journey down the Murray—but whose driving force came from England, not Australia. After several abortive schemes had fizzled out, a South Australian Association was formed in 1833. It consisted of a mixture of colonizing enthusiasts, theorists and political radicals with capitalists, speculators and philanthropists. This body had hoped to found and govern the colony by chartered company, but it found the Colonial Office strongly opposed to such an idea. They then agreed to the establishment of a crown colony with the ordinary type of government, except that control of land sales and migration was to be entrusted to a Board of Commissioners, of whom one would be resident in the Colony; Commissioners were to follow broadly the Wakefield System, to sell land at a high price and use the proceeds to subsidize emigration. Ordinary expenses of government were to be met for the time being by loans raised on the security of the future tax revenue of the colony, so that there was to be no charge whatever on the British Treasury. Thus the colony was to get no financial help; and there were to be no convicts.

Unfortunately, on the terms offered few purchasers of land were forthcoming; even when one acre of 'city' land was thrown in with eighty acres of 'country' land, £1 per acre seemed a high price; and a temporary reduction to 12s.,

though obviously offering possibilities of speculation, likewise failed to attract buyers. But help came with the successful flotation by G. F. Angas of a South Australian Company,
which not only bought more than a hundred of the '80-acre'
sections, but with its capital of £320,000, provided a variety
of valuable services in primary production, banking and
commerce. Even so the early period was one of great difficulty for the investors, for the Governor, Hindmarsh, and
for the 546 settlers who arrived in 1836. Again these
'pioneers' had failed, as at Swan River, to realize the difficulties of settlement in a strange land with a strange climate,
with literally no public facilities and not even a reasonable
harbour. Nor was progress helped by the division of authority between governor and commissioners, the greater possibilities of land speculation in the city than of land cultivation
in the country, and the slow progress of surveying estates.
Although by the end of 1838 the population was over 5,000,
when the new Governor, Gawler, arrived, there were only
443 acres under cultivation whereas 170,000 acres had been
sold; all necessaries were brought from Sydney and Hobart,
and exports were negligible.

Gawler at once began a vigorous programme of public
works, drawing bills on England to pay for them to the tune
of some £300,000. The rebellion in Canada stimulated migration to Australia and further land sales. The survey office
was drastically reorganized and expanded so that by 1841
not only were 500,000 acres surveyed, and 7,000 cultivated,
but 5,000 settlers were now in the country districts with
200,000 sheep. But government expense had been heavy and
in 1841 the British Treasury ordered 'retrenchment and
reform'. Sir George Grey replaced Gawler as Governor.
Public works were cut, and unemployment relief reduced;
the general depression in Australia did not help, though it
stopped further land sales and immigration. The population
of the capital drifted to the bush where it was gradually
absorbed by the expanding agriculture as South Australia
became the granary of Australia.

The depression was over by 1846, when the discovery of copper gave a further boost to the colony's fortunes. By 1850 there were 63,000 people in the colony, 60,000 cattle and nearly 1,000,000 sheep; 65,000 acres were under cultivation and exports were worth £570,000. South Australia, like the other Australian colonies in the east, seemed sufficiently advanced for self-government, which was readily granted in 1855.

In the north, progress was more difficult. Despite government assistance in this case, the economic base was lacking. In 1824 Governor Brisbane sent an expedition to Melville Island on the north-west corner of Arnhem Land. Once again the motive was strategic, but it was hoped that a settlement would not only be useful as a military station and 'give security to the East India Company's trade to China', but that it would open a market for British merchants in the Malay Archipelago. These hopes were vain. Malayan traders would not come; the settlement was unhealthy and expensive. A move to Raffles Bay made no difference. After five years the station had to be withdrawn; a little later a settlement at Port Essington had to be abandoned after only eleven years (1838–49), and before 1850 the only thriving establishments north of latitude 29° S. were near the erstwhile penal settlement at Moreton Bay (Brisbane) in southern Queensland and on the Darling Downs behind it, where squatters and convicts were opening up the country.

The successes—and the failures—which by 1850, before any gold had been discovered, had laid the foundations of all the states of the future Australian Commonwealth, had shown the need for 'ample government', as Wakefield put it; for outside assistance in overcoming the hardships and deficiencies of pioneering communities, and collective action in mastering the difficulties of an obstinate environment, were so absolutely essential. Who was to provide this necessary help? Attempts by private individuals or by companies succeeded only with the greatest difficulty until vigorously supported by the state; and if, in the first settlements of Australia, the British government made reception of convicts a condition of help, this penal element was not wholly to be deplored, bringing as it did cheap labour for public and private development alike, and providing the ever parsimonious British Treasury, opposed at this period to colonizing ventures for their own sake, with a motive to justify the expense. If it be argued that in the United States of America progress was achieved without such assistance, the reply must be made that the analogy is a false one. The early American settlers of the seventeenth century demanded English help just as the Australian did, although thanks to the much greater fertility of the country and the shorter distance across the Atlantic they could get more support from colonizing companies, and so had less need to fall back on the state. Thereafter expansion 'west' was steady and regular, from a settled base into fertile country, and did not involve the sudden occupation of an isolated area in the wilderness. Perhaps this contrast is one reason why the Australian has always been ready to look to government for assistance; such an attitude, inbred as it were, has been handed down by tradition and sanctified by necessity. Even so, the squatting occupation of the interior of the eastern states was a staunchly individualistic movement; for in this case conditions did more closely resemble those in America, and the advance was made, not with the help of government, but in spite of it. But the squatters were a minority; their occupation of the sheep-lands created a 'land monopoly', a citadel of privilege to be attacked by those excluded. What wonder then that again, in this attack, state assistance should be sought and won; that true to tradition the new settlers should combine to overcome man-made obstacles as well as those created by nature, that in the second half of the nineteenth century the 'masses', now favoured by democratic institutions, should follow the example of the 'classes' in the first half in their dependence on collective action, on government, for much of their progress and prosperity?

Chapter Eight

THE GOLD RUSH
AND ITS AFTERMATH

Australia in 1850 was an urban and centralized community, in spite of the country's dependence on the pastoral industry. Each colony, except Tasmania, had grown from a single centre, and the close link between administration and trade, helped by the lack of good harbours on the Australian coast, concentrated commercial activity. As a result, although the more highly industrialized countries in Europe had a greater proportion of city dwellers in their population, none had it massed in so few centres. Sydney with 54,000 people, twenty-eight per cent of the population of New South Wales, even at this early period exercised a dominating influence on colonial life, and with its variety of trades and professions, with its press controversies, its public meetings and debates, with its infant labour movement and its growing manufactures, with its religious and educational activities, its mercantile wealth, and above all the character of its population, was already threatening the power of the squatters. Although the Australian population trebled in the decade after the discovery of gold, there had been 120,000 free immigrants between 1832 and 1842; and although the 'diggers' reduced the convict element in the population to negligible proportions, it was already less than fifteen per cent in 1850. The 'diggings' attracted political radicals and ex-chartists to Victoria, but such persons had long been present in New South Wales and Van Diemen's Land; and although the influx of population made it easier for the British government to grant full responsible government in 1855, constitutional reform was already on the way. Only in the newly separated colony of Victoria were the effects of gold decisive. Here the finds were greatest. In ten years 22,000,000 ounces were mined, eighty-eight per cent of Australian output. The population rose from 80,000 to more than half a million, vastly outstripping that of New South Wales, which for forty years had to take second place.

The first discoveries were actually made in the older colony near Bathurst, at Ophir and later Turon, in early 1851. At once there was a 'rush' and wild speculation, with great shortage of labour and disturbance of business elsewhere. The *Sydney Morning Herald* fervently hoped 'that the treasure does not exist in large quantities'; otherwise the colonies would have to be prepared 'for calamities far more terrible than earthquakes or pestilence'. As far as New South Wales was concerned, the paper's hopes were fulfilled, but the far richer and more accessible fields stretching from Ballarat to Bendigo in Victoria discovered before the end of the year partly bore out its forebodings—or at least, if they brought great advantage they also brought considerable trouble. At once there was another 'rush', now on a larger scale, and not only from Melbourne, but from Adelaide, Sydney and Tasmania as well. Again for a time ordinary business was at a standstill, though speculation in land and food supplies or in sly-grog was in most cases a surer road to fortune than the possibly more exciting search for nuggets. Prices sky-rocketed and the wages of unskilled labour trebled within a year. In the first eight months of 1852 the 'rush' was only from the other colonies; but September showed the effect of the news overseas, when 19,000 people landed in Melbourne. The number of immigrants that year was 95,000, seven times that of 1851, and less than 9,000 went to New South Wales. There was no foreign flood. All nationalities were to be found on the goldfields, but the English, Scots and Irish by far predominated. Not even the Chinese were a problem for four or five years.

Government's first problems were to maintain order, and to raise the revenue necessary to meet the cost of the gold-field administration, the police, the courts, the surveys and so forth. At first, observers were surprised and delighted at the absence of 'Judge Lynch' and his committees of vigilance; apart from sly-grog selling, for officially the diggings were 'dry', there seemed little to worry about. Lord Robert Cecil, when in Bendigo in March 1852, found 'that the police commissioner who had to collect licence fees, punish offences and guard the gold, had as his only coffer a tin paper-box secured by a sixpenny padlock; and his coercive force consists of three policemen, two carabines and a sword. Yet his tent has never been robbed nor his authority resisted.'

As time went on conditions changed. The numbers of diggers increased and the chance of a fortune or even a livelihood grew less. Alluvial mining declined, particularly near Ballarat, and as the shafts went deeper, not only did costs increase but so did the irritation of having to come to the surface to show one's licence, sometimes three or four times a day. The police became more and more unpopular as they tried to collect the miner's licence fee of one pound per month. This had to be paid by successful and unsuccessful alike. It was comparatively easy to evade, and the police, inexperienced, often only accustomed to controlling the convicts of Van Diemen's Land, and sometimes ex-convicts themselves, were tactless if not ruthless in their methods. Ill feeling between them and the miners grew, accentuated by corruption, bias and brutality. To these 'valid grounds of complaint too long unredressed', found by the Commission of Inquiry in 1855, was added the constitutional issue of 'taxation without representation', at this very moment being fought about so furiously by the squatters in the New South Wales Legislative Council.

In Victoria, whose separate existence had only begun in 1851, the administration was somewhat inexperienced. Governor La Trobe wished to replace the licence fee by an export tax on gold, but the newly established Victorian

Council would not agree. The fees were slightly reduced, but the resulting fall in revenue caused the new Governor, Captain Sir Charles Hotham, in September 1854, to spur the police to greater activity against evaders, for even in 1853 the £660,000 raised was £136,000 less than the government's goldfield expenses. Unrest increased, and in October the acquittal by corrupt magistrates of an ex-convict publican charged with the murder of a miner led to a riot. After this, the publican was convicted; but three rioters, probably not the ringleaders, were prosecuted and this caused further unrest. The Ballarat Reform League was formed, demanding the release of the rioters, the abolition of licence fees and political reforms including manhood suffrage. After further disorder, at the end of November the miners built a crude stockade at Eureka, which was attacked and destroyed by the police and military on December 5. Twenty-two were killed in the mêlée, of whom seventeen were miners; 120 were arrested but the leaders, tried for high treason, were acquitted. Such was the notorious Eureka affair.

It is often painted as a great fight for Australian liberty and the rights of the working man, but it was not that. Its leaders were themselves small capitalists, many of whom, like Peter Lalor, were very dubious of the virtues of 'democracy'. As Lalor himself said afterwards, 'I would ask these gentlemen what they mean by the term "Democracy". Do they mean Chartism or Communism or Republicanism? If so, I never was, I am not now, nor do I ever intend to be, a Democrat.'[1] The affair was a justified protest, which developed into a riot, against bad administration and tactless, if not corrupt, police. Next year, the justice of the men's complaints was recognized and their principal demands granted. An export duty on gold was imposed to raise revenue. Special local courts were established on the gold-

[1] Quoted R. M. Crawford *Australia* (1952), p. 121. See also *Historical Studies, Australia and New Zealand*, Eureka Centenary Supplement, Dec., 1954; Bruce Kent: Agitations on the Victorian Goldfields, 1850-4, in *Historical Studies*, Nov., 1954; and C. H. Currey *The Irish at Eureka* (1954).

fields to settle disputes. The monthly licences were replaced by an annual 'miner's right' costing only one pound. As this was a qualification for a vote, it was argued that all would willingly pay. But they did not, despite the hopes of the politicians and idealist democrats. Evasion continued, and even after universal suffrage was introduced, without payment, only about a fifth of the miners bothered to vote, although by then fully responsible government had been conceded by Great Britain.

In 1850 the Australian Colonies Government Act had granted considerable independence to New South Wales, Victoria (then separated from New South Wales), South Australia and Van Diemen's Land. Two-thirds of the Legislative Councils in each colony would henceforth be elected, as had been the case of New South Wales since 1843; the franchise qualification was now expanded; and though the British government still insisted on controlling Crown lands in the interests of the Empire as a whole, in other ways the powers of the colonial Councils, including that of New South Wales, were increased. The civil list set aside in 1842 to support the minimum government establishment was maintained, but the Councils were given a limited power to alter it, and also to manage the Customs administration and to impose duties, so long as these were uniform—a limitation which later handicapped intercolonial Customs agreements. In most details the Councils could even propose amendments to the constitution act itself, though these had to be laid before the Imperial Parliament before receiving the royal assent. For the moment self-government was denied. 'A responsible executive', commented The Times, 'would throw all Australia into the hands of political agitators, and rob it of that tranquillity so needful to infant colonies.' Consequently colonial officials were still responsible to colonial governors from England, and not to the local Legislature. The latter could not directly control policy; it could only try to influence it through the power of the purse.

This power, under the leadership of Wentworth, the New

South Wales Council threatened to use in order to achieve the grant of full self-government. Remonstrance followed petition. Wentworth, referring to the acts of the Long Parliament in the seventeenth century and the North American colonies in the eighteenth, declared 'that if they were not prepared to levy war against the Queen, they had better submit to be the laughing stock of Europe and become the opprobium of the world'; he demanded that the Council at once refuse to grant supplies to the government. This was going too far for the majority; but they resolved in August 1852 not to grant them in the future unless 'the grievances complained of . . . be completely redressed'. This was sufficient indication of their temper, and in December a new Colonial Secretary, Sir John Pakington, abandoned the British claim to control colonial lands and authorized the Council to draw up a new constitution. Similar concessions were made to the other colonies.

In New South Wales, Wentworth dominated the constitutional debates. He had fought vigorously for local self-government, and for colonial control of land policy. Having defeated his opponents in Britain, he had now to tackle his critics in the colony. They wanted to wrest political control from the squatters, whom Wentworth represented and admired, and hand it to the people; they wanted to establish that democracy which he regretted to find 'was almost daily extending its limits'. He feared that if this was allowed 'all property and intelligence' would leave the colony, for 'who would stay, while selfishness, ignorance and democracy hold sway?' To check it, he proposed that the distribution of seats should be weighted heavily against the radical towns, and that there should be an hereditary upper house. The latter was rejected, but he secured a chamber nominated by the Governor and so, he hoped, removed from popular influence, and the provision that a two-thirds majority in each house should be necessary to amend the constitution or to alter the distribution of seats. Here he thought were safeguards against the relatively wide franchise of the Legislative

Assembly, the British statute authorized the deletion of the 'two-thirds' clauses by a simple majority of each house in the New South Wales Parliament, and this was done immediately.

Victoria, South Australia and Tasmania were granted similar constitutions at the same time, excepting that in these colonies the upper house, instead of being nominated, was to be elected on a restricted franchise. This procedure was thought to be more 'democratic' than nomination, but in practice it has been less so; for it was always possible to 'influence' a nominated assembly by the threat or the actual appointment of new members, while the elected councils were immune from such an attack. Simultaneously in all the colonies the executive became 'responsible' to the local Parliament, not to the Colonial Office. Governors were henceforth to act on the advice of their Ministers chosen from those supported by majorities in the various Legislative Assemblies. By 1860 most of the Assemblies were elected by universal male suffrage through a secret ballot (for long described overseas as the 'Victorian' or 'Australian' ballot).

Unfortunately when these democratic governments were set up no provision was made for any form of co-operation between them on matters of common concern. Earl Grey had suggested such machinery in 1847 when the separation of Victoria from New South Wales was being considered. Grey feared the consequences of intercolonial tariffs with customs houses on the border, and in 1849, following a report from a committee of the Privy Council, he urged that a federal authority consisting of delegates from the various colonies in proportion to their population be set up to supervise a commercial union, intercolonial communications and other minor matters.

These suggestions were ill-received. At that moment the colonies thought badly of Grey on so many subjects—self-government, lands and transportation—that even when he did propose something to their interest they would have none of it, though Wentworth, to do him justice, supported the idea. Jealousy of New South Wales was at its height;

Port Phillip was agitating vehemently for separation; although some Tasmanian merchants wanted intercolonial free trade, Governor Denison was afraid that Van Diemen's Land would be swamped by imports, and asserted the need for different tariffs for each colony rather than a customs union; in England the welcome was no warmer. In deference to general criticism Grey abandoned his scheme. The colonies were left completely independent of each other, free to raise hostile tariff walls and to build railways with different gauges which would plague the traveller for a century, for the supervisory powers given to the Governor of New South Wales as 'Governor-General' in 1851 were too vague. Thus the separate colonies, freed from immediate British control, unhampered by any national feelings, were able to go their own way in tackling the urgent problems that beset them; of these, like the parts of ancient Gaul and the theological virtues, there appeared to be three—intensified by the effect of the gold discoveries—land, immigration and employment; and the greatest of these was land.

Here, the squatter had a 'monopoly'. This was not, as so many believed, because of the 1847 leasing regulations, but because of the now long-hallowed principle of the minimum price—no Crown land was sold for less than £1 per acre. This high price had been introduced on purpose to control settlement by restricting excessive purchases; it was now violently attacked for doing this very thing. True, the squatters were entitled to take up pastoral leases which gave them security for a term and limited pre-emptive purchase rights. But thanks to almost incredible delays in the surveyor general's office the amount of land actually leased in New South Wales was negligible, and in Victoria La Trobe had in practice modified the regulations. Almost no land had been 'pre-emptively purchased', and yet by 1855 the land question was giving no end of trouble.

Migrants who had flocked to the goldfields now wanted to buy and cultivate farms. Successful diggers or successful tradesmen had the urge to obtain 'an interest' in the country.

Those who were unsuccessful were also interested when they found work scarce on the goldfields, even though they lacked the necessary capital to acquire and cultivate a farm. The fact that none had any training as farmers appeared of little import; they wanted land and seemed to imagine that agricultural skill was either unnecessary or would come spontaneously. The 'Eureka' commission in Victoria had reported the land grievance as a major source of discontent. The survey department had put up for sale only 80,000 acres in four years; in 1854 nearly half a million were offered, but this would only provide for about a thousand families—and the population was 300,000. And how many could afford to buy a farm at £1 per acre? How many would spend their money before the land they wanted was surveyed—a process which in New South Wales took anything from six months to a year? No wonder, even when the survey departments did increase their staffs and could work quicker, that the demand was for 'selection before survey' and for a lower purchase price—like the five shillings per acre in the United States—which in reality had nothing to do with the squatting leases. But naturally the squatters feared the low selling price. They thought the farmers would invade their domains, even though it was pointed out that the graziers could then afford to buy considerable portions of their runs themselves.

Depression and unemployment, plus popular agitation backed by universal suffrage, forced the government's hands, and after much controversy land acts were passed in all the colonies. In New South Wales the famous Robertson Acts of 1861 allowed any selector to take up from 40 to 320 acres of crown land, before survey, still for £1 per acre, but paying only five shillings cash, and without interest on the balance for three years; he had to reside on his land and make improvements worth £1 per acre. The squatters could still lease unoccupied lands, at a higher rent; but now the squatting runs were open to selection at any time, though the squatter was given a pre-emptive right to purchase an area proportional to the sums he had spent on improvements. The Acts were intended to hold the balance even between grazier and farmer by giving to both what Robertson and his supporters thought were 'reasonable' rights to acquire and to occupy land. They were not intended merely to expropriate the squatter, but to make it possible for every man to buy a reasonably cheap homestead; he was then left, without knowledge or experience, with little capital, in a country with a difficult climate and bad transport facilities, to try to make farming pay.

Similar acts, varying in their details, were passed in Victoria, allowing selections to be made on relatively easy terms, though with more stringent provisions to enforce residence and cultivation. In South Australia, with no ex-miners agitating and in natural conditions more suitable to agriculture, settlement proceeded satisfactorily under the old terms for a few years. In Queensland, in effect, payment for purchase could be deferred for eight years. In Western Australia and Tasmania the minimum price was reduced from £1 to ten shillings per acre, and in the latter colony payment on credit was allowed. All the colonies continued the system of squatting leases, essential as they were if the huge areas of the interior were to be occupied at all, but the fight against the squatter was by no means ended. To conservatives it appeared that a revolution had taken place. The *Sydney Morning Herald* saw 'democracy in its fullest import determined to destroy the pastoral tenure of land by capitalists'; numbers were supreme; they governed property and would transfer capital from the few to the many.

Immigration provided another subject of dispute between the 'classes and masses'. Originally one of the chief reasons for introducing the system of land sales in 1831 had been to raise revenue to subsidize the passage of migrants for the relief of the labour shortage in the colonies. But the quality of migrants caused criticism. The squatters and others in the colonies wanted skilled tradesmen and agricultural labourers, if possible in families, conveniently ignoring the fact that such people were usually reasonably well off in the

British Isles and so had no great incentive to leave; if they did leave, America was nearer than Australia, the voyage cheaper, shorter and more comfortable. Consequently Australians had to take what they could get. In 1835 Governor Bourke had introduced the 'bounty' system, whereby private persons, would-be employers, could select migrants and receive a government bounty for each approved person landed. Between 1838 and 1841 nearly 40,000 'bounty migrants' landed in Sydney and rather more came with government assistance. The 1842 depression halted land sales and created unemployment, so assisted migration of both types was stopped, but it was not long before the labour shortage reappeared. Some squatters asked for Asian coolies or more convicts, but the British government forbade the one and popular agitation prevented the other.

In 1847 large-scale government-subsidized immigration was resumed, again financed from the land revenue. The migrants were again mainly selected by the English commissioners for emigration and were again criticized in the colony as 'people unsuited to our wants and in many instances the outpourings of the United Kingdom'. In New South Wales an Act of 1852 made it easier for colonists to nominate government migrants, and all immigrants whether assisted by government or by private individuals could be indentured to employers for five years while they repaid their passage-money from their wages. In practice these contracts could not be enforced. Indentured servants were often unsatisfactory and the refusal or neglect to repay passage-money either to government, migration societies or private individuals was almost universal, and it was equally difficult to enforce contracts of service. Still some 70,000 migrants were assisted to New South Wales in the 'fifties, and about the same number arrived without help, attracted in the main by one or other of the various gold rushes. But in the 'sixties popular hostility to immigration increased and Victoria, South Australia and New South Wales all refused to vote money to assist it.

The inconsistencies and fits and starts of the various immigration policies show the conflicting feelings of Australians. Employers wanted cheap labour; but they wanted able-bodied and willing workers, which they often did not get, and in fact the poor quality of much of the human material sent to Australia frequently gave them cause to wonder whether spending money in this way was worth while. The wage-earner, seeing in the newcomer a competitor for work was at best indifferent and frequently hostile, if it seemed that the migrant was bringing with him a low standard of living. Nor were his fears groundless; for after the first rush to the goldfields was over, unemployment was frequent, and living conditions in parts of Sydney and Melbourne were such that no one would want to make them worse. Certainly in most occupations wages had risen sharply after the gold rushes, outstripping the rise in prices. The ordinary mechanic who was paid 4s. 6d. per day in Melbourne and Sydney in 1850 could earn at least 25s. a day in Melbourne, 12s. 6d. a day in Sydney in 1853. But unskilled workmen were much worse off, except when close to the diggings. The normal earnings of farm labourers and shepherds—£18 to £24 a year, plus rations, in 1850—had risen only to £26 to £40 plus rations in 1853, and after 1855 wages fell again. Industry was hit by the gold rushes and even the manufacturing of woollen cloth, soap and candles in Sydney, all of which had been fairly well established, failed to survive. In Victoria in 1861 there were only 403 factories employing 3,830 people; by then the very considerable distress in all the colonies had caused agitation for relief works such as railway building, for tariff protection for local manufacturers, for stopping assisted immigration and for unlocking of the land.

Lack of capital delayed the building of any major railway line: less than 200 miles were open in 1859, the greater part being in Victoria; the principles of free trade were as yet too firmly fixed in the public mind to be seriously criticized; and land settlement remained difficult. It was, of course, a sturdy myth, especially strongly held by politicians and pressmen, that if only men would leave the capital cities, all would be well, but those who did so found it as hard to find work in the country as in town. Witnesses before the New South Wales committee inquiring into unemployment in 1860 reported that the frequent complaints of a rural labour shortage were due chiefly to employers being unable to find reapers or shearers at hand wherever and whenever they wanted them, and that many countrymen were coming to Sydney in a vain effort to find work. In fact, the distress was general, and it was due to trade depression following the unhealthy expansion of the gold rush.

Conditions in the Sydney slums were described by the visiting English economist, Stanley Jevons, as being worse than anything he had seen in London, Liverpool or Paris. In this opinion he was not alone: the city health officer, not to be outdone, described them as 'worse than in any other part of the world'. The Australian cities had to pass through a 'shanty-town' stage, and although they were 'new' towns, Sydney and Melbourne did not escape the sanitary horrors of early nineteenth century England which are retailed with such delight and yet so little understanding by sentimentalists who judge all things by the standards of to-day. Even contemporary witnesses described the housing as 'deplorably bad', and pointed out that many buildings, though new, had their 'drainage and ventilation almost entirely neglected'. Houses built on the steep slopes of the town had filth and refuse from above pouring in their front doors, not to mention rain through the roof. Narrow courts, badly constructed, unpaved, uncleansed and undrained, abounded, with privies few, dilapidated and overflowing. Despite the land available, overcrowding was as bad as in Europe (as was almost inevitable through the lack of any efficient transport system) and the suburbs were as bad as the city, thanks to the very rapid increase of population during the gold rush.

'In the short space of a life-time', reported the committee of inquiry, 'we have reproduced here all the enormities which have grown up through centuries of ignorance, pesti-

lence, arbitrary government and civil wars in the old world.'
All the more surprising then, in view of the past, was the
lack of crime, and the good order of the streets at night, even
though Jevons harboured the suspicion that 'vice in secret'
might still exist. This was doubtless true; for in what society
does it not? But his comments contrast markedly with the
descriptions of the vice of Sydney some twenty-five years
earlier, and certainly there had been a great change.

Later generations, in their anxiety to cast off the taint of
convictism, have been anxious to exaggerate the importance
of the 'diggers', viewing them, as Professor Hancock has put
it, 'as their Pilgrim Fathers, the first authentic Australians,
the founders of the self-respecting independent strenuous
national life'. But though this is sheer idealism, and though
nearly all the future problems and characteristics of the
Australian colonies were present before 1850, no country
can have its population almost trebled in a decade without
obvious effects; and though it was the rate rather than the
nature of development that the gold discoveries influenced,
none the less, thanks to them, in ten years the eastern states
at least had undergone a transformation little dreamed of in
1850.

Chapter Nine

THE CALM BEFORE THE STORM

Australian development has tended to be a thing of fits and starts. At one moment there is a vigorous programme of expansion, undertaken with over-optimistic enthusiasm and carefree abandon; then comes a crisis of greater or less severity, in turn followed by a phase of caution. In the 'sixties the Australian colonies were passing through one of these hangovers. The dreams of a Utopia founded on gold, democracy and self-government had vanished. In practice it was found that even self-governing democracies had problems; that it was not easy for the horde of restless gold-seekers to be absorbed into the economy, given work, and transformed into ordinary colonists after perhaps ten years of 'unsettlement'; that economic problems produced political tensions which at times severely strained the working of the newly created democratic constitutions. It took fifteen to twenty years for the colonies to achieve a satisfactory re-adjustment before beginning another vigorous advance. But even in this period of quiescence, the problems of government and the nature of development remained the same; only in degree did they change.

In 1860, one colony had still to experience its boom. Queensland had been separated from New South Wales only the year before, with a ready-made constitution and the right of immediate self-government, despite its scanty population of 25,000. Its 668,000 square miles of vast territories—bigger than New South Wales and Victoria combined—were virtually unoccupied, save by the aborigines who have so rarely counted in Australian history. The first need was obviously men, and these Governor Sir George Bowen and Premier Herbert set about attracting. No obstacles were put in the way of the squatters, who, given a fourteen-year lease provided their runs were stocked within a year, quickly spread into the interior. At the same time Herbert wanted to encourage closer settlement on the coast, in the so-called 'agricultural reserves'. 'Land orders' were given to any immigrant or any person who brought out an immigrant, who could then buy £18 worth of Crown land immediately and £12 more after two years. By this ingenious device migrants were brought out to the colony at no cost to the government, but in most cases the orders were given to shipowners or speculators, who sold them to the squatters. After six years more than 50,000 migrants had arrived, and five million acres had been sold; but the small farmer remained conspicuous by his absence. It was the same old problem—what also could be expected when the immigrant had no capital and no agricultural experience?

Needless to say the migrants had helped to promote a temporary boom. Certainly the government had little revenue; but this was the usual experience of the governments of each successive settlement in its infancy. Money could be, and was, borrowed for carrying out many necessary and some unnecessary public works, so that if the migrants could not become farmers, they could easily find work, at least so long as the government could find money. In fact, the colony seemed so flourishing that some of the northern districts of New South Wales, like the Clarence River, began an agitation to join it.

Like most good things it could not last. In 1866 the London banking firm of Overend and Gurney failed, and in the ensuing panic so did the Agra and Masterman's Bank, at this time the colony's financial agent. British investors, caught by the Southern States of the U.S.A., by South American republics and by Spain, Turkey and Egypt, were becoming nervous even of one of their own colonies. Brassey, Peto and

Betts, the principal railway contractors, were in difficulties. The local banks, notably the Union Bank of Australia, virtually refused to help, so the government found itself without even enough funds to pay civil service salaries. In this emergency, Premier MacAlister proposed to issue inconvertible legal tender notes, but the Governor announced that he would veto the measure, thus adding a serious constitutional crisis to the existing financial one. The cabinet resigned, unemployment increased, bankruptcies were numerous and even the Bank of Queensland failed. From the north, west and centre came complaints of neglect, and of the favours shown to the south-east, near Brisbane, and the Legislative Assembly in 1867 passed a resolution of 'Principles of Government' demanding that government expenditure to be more equally distributed. But by this time the government had succeeded in raising a loan in London; relief works were started, and the discovery of gold at Gympie, 100 miles from Brisbane, saw the end of the crisis.

Parliament could now go back to the land, even if no one else did. In September 1866, the coalition government passed the Land Leasing Act providing that certain areas after being leased for eight years at 2s. 6d. a year should be regarded as 'sold' to the lessee—which was useful to the capitalist who could buy his land on time payment, but of little value to the moneyless selector. In 1868, after an electoral victory by the squatters' party, another act gave easier terms to purchasers of agricultural and pastoral land alike; but despite the attempt to prevent 'dummying' and the enlargement of the defined agricultural districts, its principal effect was to enable the squatter to buy up more of his holding.

In its land legislation, Queensland like the other Australian colonies was trying vainly to discover how land could be made easily accessible to the poor, without at the same time being made even more easily accessible to the rich—and this at a time when natural conditions were favouring the wool-growing activities of the wealthy squatter, rather than the agricultural operations of the poor selector. It was inevitable, then, that the land acts failed of their purpose. In Queensland between 1868 and 1884, despite frequent changes of the law, over six million acres were sold and only 120,000 acres brought under crop. In New South Wales, by 1884, 39,000,000 acres had been sold; only 550,000 were under crop. Drought or flood in every year from 1862 to 1870 caused difficulties; lack of transport caused greater difficulties; The squatters could 'select' on easy terms the 'eyes' of their run through 'dummies'[1]—friend, wife or child, for anyone of any age or sex could get their 320 acres, and Victorian families were large. If need be, the squatters could still buy on the old system at £1 per acre; for they could afford to make some purchases at this price, obtaining bank advances, if need be, on the security of their land, their stock or their wool.[2] As a result many grazing properties became mortgaged to banks and other big companies; but the individual pastoralist survived, and if his freedom was sometimes limited, he at least secured funds to meet his difficulties and to expand his assets.

For the grazing industry underwent a technical revolution in the days after the gold rushes. For years it had needed cheap labour—even convicts and Asians would do at a pinch—anything to keep wages down to a payable level and keep the shepherds and shearers in their place. In 1849 a squatter magistrate noted that 'it will take a great many more immigrants to force upon these scoundrels the practice of propriety or common honesty'. The immigrants came, but they all went gold-digging and the labour situation seemed worse than ever. The number working in the industry fell from 27,000 to 20,000 between 1851 and 1857; even in 1861 it was only back to 27,000. Here was the check

[1] Sometimes a pastoralist's dummy might turn nasty. See, for example, the pamphlet, *Dummies and Mediums, Plain Directions and Hints to*, by Doodledum Dummy (1865), explaining the various ways in which a Dummy might exact money from his 'principal'.

[2] Advances of this type were legal in the Australian colonies, though disapproved of by orthodox English banking opinion.

to the increase of flocks, which rose only from 17,500,000 to 21,000,000 in the decade. But salvation came—from the fence.

Hitherto flocks had been as carefully watched as in Europe, and brought to shelter at night. It was strange that it took so long to find out that this was not necessary in the Australian climate, and that when the sheep were not driven back and forth over bare and dusty ground every day their health and their fleeces improved, and the labour of the shepherd could be dispensed with. The gain quickly repaid the heavy initial expense. Paddocks grew larger and larger; and as wire replaced the post-and-rail while the fence was spreading from Victoria in the 'fifties through New South Wales in the 'sixties to Queensland in the 'seventies, the cost grew less. By 1890 there were over one hundred million sheep on the continent, more than half of them in New South Wales, with a clip of six pounds per sheep, nearly double that of thirty years before. No wonder that the small selector could not compete with such a user of the land, and that 'democracy's benevolent intention to temper the wind to the farmer's shorn lamb could not endow the tender creature with the vigour that enabled the pastoral ram to survive and fatten. So it came to pass that demagogues dispersed the public estate and pastoralists gathered up the freehold thereof.'[1]

Demagogues—such indeed the local politicians seemed to be as in every colony ministry after ministry succeeded one another with bewildering rapidity, and parties and coalitions formed and reformed in patterns comprehensible to none. There were twenty-three ministries under eight different Premiers in South Australia between 1861 and 1876, while in Victoria and New South Wales, respectively, there were eighteen and seventeen changes of government between 1855 and 1877. Party organization was almost negligible and discipline therefore impossible. Since a number of

[1] E. O. G. Shann: *The Economic History of Australia* (Cambridge University Press, 1930), p. 233.

different controversial matters were being dealt with, groups could rarely find a common policy on all of them and even on any single topic there were so many shades of opinion that 'breakaways' were frequent. Land, tariff policies, the sectarian issue, education and temperance reform, all played a part in the confusion. Obviously in such a situation there was ample scope for intriguers and self-seekers; and these seem to have utilized their opportunities to the full 'The curse of Australian politics is that . . . there are no parties in the strict sense of the term, but merely cliques or groups,' said Sir John Young, Governor of New South Wales in the 'sixties. This affected the working of 'democracy'. The conservatives were helped by the lack of strong working-class political organizations; the effective power of the masses, so much feared by 'men of property', was limited by the absence of strong and stable party government; though universal male franchise was the rule in most colonies, so was plural voting, and the distribution of seats usually favoured the country districts. In the result, although the political institutions of the Australian colonies were very much more democratic than those of Great Britain, government policies were perhaps less radical than might have been expected. In most political controversies there was no clear-cut division between rich and poor, but a series of alliances between groups. The squatters were almost universally defeated, despite their strength in the various Legislative Councils, for they had neither the ability, tradition, education nor the sense of public spirit to copy successfully the English landed gentry whom they vainly strove to emulate; but their conquerors were not extremists, but usually a combination of artisans with other propertied interests that were always able to prevent what would have been called the 'dangerous excesses' of radicalism.

Naturally enough, it was in Victoria, where the number of ex-miners was the greatest, that the radical party was most successful. As elsewhere, its first aim was land reform. Under the 1862 Land Act, many selectors sold their holdings to the pastoralists, who thus soon bought on easy terms the best areas of 'Australia Felix'; but the act of 1865 stopped this practice by insisting that the selector should settle on his land before he received his title to it; after three years of 'improvement' he was less anxious to sell. Fifteen million acres were sold between 1860 and 1880; at least 1,500,000 were cultivated. Railway building brought about a particularly rapid development of the Wimmera in the 'seventies. But this progress, though better than in New South Wales, was not good enough. Many miners were emigrating; others who stayed still wanted work. Their demand for protection for local industries was backed by David Syme, proprietor of the *Age*, a newspaper whose power in the colony later almost equalled that of *The Times* in London. His propaganda was vigorous and sustained, though he was by no means the only preacher of this 'heresy' and the first Tariff Leagues anticipated his support. There was much popular agitation by 'artisans'; conditions were favourable; free trade had never been so universally accepted as in Great Britain, and even John Stuart Mill, whose *Principles of Political Economy* was the accepted Bible of contemporary economic thinking, was willing to countenance duties for 'infant industries'. Manufacturers supported the idea, whatever the merchants of Collins Street might say; the farmers were not directly concerned, but were willing to support the protectionists in return for a radical land policy; to politicians the urgent need for increased revenue was an important consideration. In 1861 came the first 'protective' tariff, though many of its duties were avowedly imposed only to raise revenue; in 1865 it was raised further by the McCulloch Ministry, despite the fact that the Premier and his Attorney-General, George Higinbotham, were allegedly free-traders. Protection had come to stay; thereafter it was only a question of increases and variations of detail. By 1875, when those employed in factories had risen from 7,000 (in 1864) to 28,000, every serious politician supported it as a national policy. But in origin it had been essentially 'democratic', popularly supported, and imposed after a bitter struggle with the allegedly 'reactionary' influences of the Legislative Council and Great Britain.

In 1865 the Council had rejected an Appropriation Bill on the ground that the government's tariff proposals were unfairly tacked on to it. Notwithstanding this, the government levied the unauthorized duties. Legally it was unable to spend any money; but it borrowed funds from a bank of which Premier McCulloch was the sole local director, and then repaid them on being sued for the debt. Eventually, after the government parties had won a general election, the Council gave way; but meanwhile the British Colonial Secretary had criticized the policy of the government and reprimanded the Governor, Sir Charles Darling, for allowing such illegal proceedings. Higinbotham was furious at such 'foreign' intervention, and argued that the Governor had to accept the advice of his Ministers, otherwise 'what becomes of self-government?' This view was reiterated in 1868. The Legislative Council rejected a proposal to grant £20,000 to Darling who had by now been recalled; the Colonial Office again intervened and Ministers once more declared 'that the interference of the Crown in a matter so completely within the discretion of the Assembly as the form of a bill of supply threatens the existence of responsible government'.

In truth the Governor was in the awkward position of serving two masters, and though the Colonial Office did not often interfere, on occasions it did and then there might be trouble. The Governor was not responsible for local policy, and though occasionally he might be able to 'influence' it, Sir William Denison wrote from New South Wales that 'one is powerless to do good, or to prevent it'. The Duke of Newcastle admitted from London that the powers of colonial governments 'might occasionally be used amiss' but trusted that the 'errors of a free government would cure themselves. . . . The general principle is . . . that in matters of purely local politics [the Governor] is bound, excepting in extreme cases, to follow the advice of a ministry which appears to possess the confidence of the Legislature.' But what of the 'extreme cases'? They were only likely to occur at a time of acute political crisis, and then the interference of the Governor would be especially resented. Even so, said Lord Granville in 1870, 'it would be better to be in collision with your advisers than with the law'—possibly a doubtful dictum if such a collision were serious. Fortunately in practice one side or other was always willing to abate its claims, although criticism of the Governors' powers continued. By 1875 the Governor of New South Wales had abandoned any desire to exercise independently of his Ministers the 'prerogative of mercy'; and by 1885 he had virtually abandoned his 'recognised independent discretion' in making appointments to the Legislative Council. But all Governors still claimed the right to decide whether or not to dissolve their Legislative Assemblies when asked to do so by a ministry defeated in the House, and of course it was their duty to safeguard 'imperial' interests. If necessary, for this purpose, the Governors could even disallow legislation; but they were instructed 'to leave the local authority as free as possible' and between 1856 and 1900 only five acts from the Australian colonies were vetoed.

One of these was a Tasmanian Act in 1867 imposing 'differential' customs duties on imports from the other colonies, and discriminating particularly against Victoria for her high tariff policy. The Australian Colonies Government Act of 1850, though permitting customs duties to be levied, forbade discrimination, for at that time it was argued that the United Kingdom still controlled the commercial policy of the Empire and that the 'common interest' required that such policy should be the same. The British government had hoped indeed that all colonies would follow a free trade policy, but on the ground that 'the principle of self-government was even more important than the principle of free trade' it had long accepted colonial tariffs. To remove conflicting trade barriers an attempt was made in 1863 to draw up a uniform tariff. After this failed, the colonies hoped at least to make mutual concessions by intercolonial agreements, but before the British government had considered a request from New South Wales for permission to do so, the Tasmanian parliament passed its Act. Its disallowance was due to the British fear that differential duties might create difficulties with foreign countries, but the Australians were not impressed. In a series of intercolonial conferences they held to their view, and in 1873, after vainly trying to persuade them to form a complete customs union, the British government gave way. It was then too late. Tariff policies growing increasingly diverse had ended all hope of agreement, even on the limited scale at first proposed; the result was nearly thirty years' tariff war, especially severe between Victoria and New South Wales. The latter clung firmly to her free trade policy. She had a smaller population and fewer ex-diggers to find work for, despite much unemployment and distress between 1865 and 1872; labour was therefore weaker, and the pastoralists were stronger; moreover there was an abundant revenue from the sale of crown lands, whose alleged 'unlocking' by the Robertson Acts in 1861 together with railway building and coal mining was thought to provide sufficient outlet for the working man. The liberal leader, Sir Henry Parkes, had been completely converted to free trade during his visit to England in 1860 and to his dying day he was reluctant to abandon a policy of *laissez-faire*.

His main preoccupation seems to have been to combine the difficult tasks of keeping in office and out of the bankruptcy court, but he managed incidentally to spare a thought for educational reform; for in his view, 'education will make people acquainted with their rights and mindful of their duties. . . . It is equally hostile to anarchy and despotism. . . . It alone has the power to awaken the humble classes to a true sense of the dignity of humanity, and inspire them with a true love of equality and order combined, which is the true foundation of freedom.' In this he agreed with his old antagonist W. C. Wentworth who had successfully urged the establishment of the University of Sydney in 1852. Now, following the contemporary liberal opinions of Europe the feeling was growing that education should be not only free but 'secular'. New South Wales schools had originally been controlled by the various religious denominations, but in 1848 'national schools' had been set up in those areas where the church schools were inadequate—which meant chiefly in the sparsely populated country areas. Unfortunately this dual control, with one board allocating funds to religious schools and another to the national schools, was inefficient; a committee of inquiry in 1855 found that in both systems many schools were in need of repair, attendance was poor, discipline was lax and teaching unsatisfactory. After prolonged controversy between the supporters of the denominational and secular systems, Parkes's government in 1866 set up a single council of education and refused government aid to new church schools. The effect of the measure was to destroy the church schools as possible rivals to the 'national system'; their future expansion was impossible. The Roman Catholics strongly opposed such restriction, and so did most of the Anglican bishops and clergy; but the laity were in the main indifferent, and many supported Parkes. The church schools were short of money; inspection by members of a number of different denominations involved duplication, waste and inefficiency. The nonconformists generally preferred the national system; anti-Catholic feeling and growing opposition to 'ritualism' in the Church of England gradually changed Anglican opinion. Victoria in 1872, Queensland in 1875 and South Australia in 1878 had all ceased to recognize or assist denominational education. The doctrines of materialism were criticizing the foundations of religion; growing nationalist feeling was critical of control of education by other than state authorities. 'In a couple of generations,' it was asserted, 'through the missionary influence of the State schools, a new body of state doctrine and theology will grow up. . . . Let our children be sent to the same schools irrespective of creed and let them be brought up in that creed of kindliness which will make them forget that other creeds divide them . . . and create a united community, the fit germ of a nation.' Almost alone, Roman Catholics remained bitterly hostile to secular education. As a result many argued that state aid to church schools was equivalent to state aid for the propagation of Roman Catholicism; and the newly defined dogma of Papal infallibility, and the contemporary attitude of the Catholic Church in European politics, weakened her position among liberals. In 1880 Parkes withdrew state aid from the denominational schools, leaving the children of New South Wales to the tender mercies of 'the seed-plots of future immorality, infidelity and lawlessness', as Roman Catholic Archbishop Vaughan described the national schools, 'calculated to debase the standard of human excellence and to corrupt the political, social and individual life of future citizens'.

Perhaps Archbishop Vaughan had good cause to lament the standards of conduct of the time, whether or not they were due to national schools. 'Larrikin gangs' were a conspicuous feature of Sydney; and as a result of the selection acts, it was said, in the country perjury became a commonplace in the lives of all. The countryside was studded with dens in which horse-thieves and highwaymen found shelter and sympathy. There was a great revival of bushranging, helped inevitably by primitive communications, scattered settlements and the carrying of considerable wealth on the roads. Frank Gardiner 'the king of the roads' robbed the Eugowra Gold Escort of £28,000 in 1862; three years later Ben Hall and his gang 'robbed the up and down mail from Gundagai in each of two successive weeks, while at the same time Captain Thunderbolt 'worked' the main northern road, defying the police for seven years, and the Clarkes operating in the vicinity of present-day Canberra kept the countryside in a state of terror. Yet all these gangs enjoyed much popular sympathy. They represented pluck and daring; they were the 'under-dogs' fighting the law, which is rarely highly respected in pioneer communities and attacking property, often looked on as 'fair game' by those who have none. They were helped by the 'bush telegraph'; juries frequently refused to convict; 15,000 people signed the petition for the reprieve of members of Gardiner's gang. Many still retain this attitude towards the Kelly gang who operated chiefly in north-eastern Victoria in the 'seventies. From being cattle duffers (an occupation admittedly that several now highly respected and respectable pastoral families formerly indulged in), the Kellys developed into a major menace to society. Sometimes they made expeditions into New South Wales, once holding up the town of Jerilderie which they 'occupied' for three days; at Euroa in Victoria they took £2,000 from the bank and booty from fifty prisoners whom they bundled into the police station. They were finally laid low at Glenrowan, Victoria, in 1880, after failing to derail the special police train sent with reinforcements against them; three of the gang were killed in the fight but Ned, the leader, was captured, tried and hanged.

The day of the bushranger ended with the coming of the railway and the electric telegraph, but these had been slow in appearing. By 1875 there were only about 10,000 miles of telegraph, very little in a country the size of Australia. Little over a thousand miles of railway were open, nowhere more than one hundred and eighty miles from the sea. But in a land of great distances and a small population, railways were uneconomic; the time of 'developmental works' had not yet come; capital was scarce and there were great engineering difficulties involved in crossing the precipitous mountain ranges close to the coast. The major achievement in railway construction had been made in the decision of the different states to adopt different gauges, so as effectively to prevent the eventual construction of a genuine through service. But this was a problem for the future, for up to 1875 Australian transport was by road—the bullock wagon for goods, and Cobb and Co.'s coaches for passengers. These were travelling 28,000 miles a week by 1870, and certainly provided fast (for the time) and regular services, even if their coaches running over bad roads could be described as 'instruments of torture'. The lack of rail transport was a serious obstacle to the opening-up of the country. It was partly for this reason that up to the mid-'seventies development had been relatively slow. Large-scale capital investment was necessary, and at this period not only were British capitalists somewhat reluctant to lend to the Australian colonies while investment opportunities were so good in England, but colonial statesmen brought up in the English *laissez-faire* tradition had not yet fully realized the extent to which *government* investment was necessary. They still thought mainly in terms of making opportunities for the individual, whether by tariff protection or land sales on relatively easy terms. These were not enough, without public works; though it should also be remembered that during the 'sixties the eastern colonies were plagued with one of those periodical successions of bad seasons which have ever since been the bugbear of the primary producer, and which had all the greater influence at this time because of the country's dependence on primary production.

As a result then of the climate and of a considerable amount of economic conservatism, the years 1865 to 1872 were a time of stagnation; immigration dwindled, unemployment was heavy, agriculture lagged and mining decayed; only the wool industry continued its triumphant career, checked but a little by land laws which ignored economic realities. It was only after 1873 that progress was resumed, though then at such a pace, as if in an attempt to make up for lost time, that it carried the seeds of disaster which would be reaped in due season in the calamitous crisis of the early 'nineties.

Chapter Ten

THE STORM BREWS

Following the fifteen years spent on readjustment after the gold rush, the Australian economy entered on another period of rapid development, ushered in by the successful advocacy of a 'vigorous policy of public works', especially railway building. Rapid immigration, a spell of good seasons, further protection, and mining discoveries all combined to stimulate the boom, which in turn encouraged the growth of a vigorous labour movement, and a strong nationalist feeling, apparent both in politics and literature. Almost until 1890 there seemed to many to be no limit to Australia's progress though in fact it was a case of sowing the wind to reap the whirlwind.

Not that some awakening from past lethargy was undesirable in the mid-'seventies. Australia like any other 'new' country needed to be opened up, and as private enterprise was able (or willing) only to undertake part of the burden, it was all the more necessary for goverment to shoulder the rest, particularly in extending communications. Sir Hercules Robinson began to urge the need as soon as he arrived as Governor of New South Wales in 1872. He thought the government should build at least fifty miles of railway every year, and the politicians agreed. The necessity was great; many of the proposed lines were badly wanted. It was not Sir Hercules' fault that the policy was later extended so much as to become a 'riot of extravagance'. In accordance with the maxim that what 'America had done, Australia would and could do', expansion in America was thought to justify expansion in Australia, despite the differences between the two countries in nearly everything except size. Railways were not always built because they were economically desirable but to win parliamentary votes. Between 1871 and 1891 nearly 10,000 miles of track were added to the thousand in existence in the Australian colonies. Sir Hercules Robinson's fifty miles a year became one hundred and seventy in New South Wales and one hundred in Victoria in the 'eighties, and the total public debt rose from £39,000,000 to £194,000,000, or from £20 to £50 per head of population.

Not all this money was spent on railways. Telegraphic lines were quadrupled, reaching 40,000 miles. Victoria started to irrigate the drier parts of the colony, in response to the urgent pleas of Alfred Deakin, an enthusiastic advocate of social services, public works, national development and federation, who was now beginning his long and distinguished political career. To irrigate a million acres would be to double the population of the colony by establishing a 'prosperous and intelligent class of farming citizens . . . obtaining its wealth by the surest possible means, from the soil, delivered from the risks of rainfall'; he had a vision of the 'triumphal march of water . . . bringing life to the grass and flower, to the loaded tree, to man and the city of men whose homesteads and harvests follow in its wake. . . . No price is too high for the promise of such progress.'

Such ideas of course meant disaster. Later Deakin himself admitted that 'we constructed railways and waterworks that ought not to have been constructed'; but for the time being, even allowing for political rhetoric, the prevailing philosophy was reflected in the phrase , 'no price is too high'. Capital poured into the country, for British investors, faced with a depression at home, were as anxious to lend to Australia as local politicians and others were to borrow. £150 million of British capital was invested in Australia in the 'eighties alone, two-thirds of it directed to government loans, and £50 million to individuals and companies, particularly in mining and in land. Gold production had fallen by half since 1860 and many diggers had emigrated; despite important finds at Charters Towers and Cooktown in Queensland in 1872. But in 1882 and 1883 two veritable hills of metal were laid bare, one containing over five million ounces of gold, with 100,000 tons of copper added for good measure, at Mount Morgan near Rockhampton in Queensland; the other of silver, lead and zinc at Broken Hill near the south-west corner of New South Wales. At the same time silver-lead, copper and tin were found in Tasmania, while the old established coal trade of New South Wales, receiving a great impetus from the railway and the steamship, more than tripled its output in less than twenty years.

There was also much investment in land, and in wool, stimulated by the general boom. Much of this was healthy and justified; some was not. Australian bankers had long been accustomed to lend on the security of the pastoralists' wool and stock, though such a thing was frowned on by their more conservative colleagues in England. In 1870 the Privy Council upheld the legality of bank loans made on the security of land, whatsoever might be the terms of the banks' charter. This too was heresy according to orthodox banking practice. Was not land singularly 'illiquid' as an asset? Would not repayment inevitably have to be extended over many years? Were not land values highly speculative? Possibly so, but what a help to the squatter anxious to buy his freehold! And how much more anxious was he to do so now that the railway was making his land accessible to the selector! The desire of the banks to 'lay out' their funds so profitably led to a great extension of this type of business and sometimes the borrowers' financial standing was not too closely scrutinized. By 1880 a Victorian banker thought that what was strictly 'legitimate banking business' bore but 'a very diminutive relation' to total bank advances, but he was not worried—there was no danger unless there should develop 'a hitherto undiscovered combination of circumstances'. Unfortunately this combination was coming; but for the time being everything in the Australian garden seemed to be growing nicely.

To the improvements in the flocks brought by paddocking and fencing in the 'sixties were added the practice of marketing the wool 'in the grease' and the invention of the shearing machine in the 'eighties; the average fleece improved by more than fifty per cent between 1861 and 1891, while the land laws of New South Wales, pasturing half the sheep in Australia in 1891, were enabling the graziers with the banks' help to buy their lands. But the pastoralist was now producing and exporting meat as well as wool One James Harrison of Geelong, Victoria, had been experimenting with refrigeration since the 'fifties, and, according to his epitaph, 'was the first man in the world to produce ice in commercial quantities for commercial purposes by mechanical means. His discovery paved the way for the entire transoceanic traffic in perishable articles: the reward for his discovery was financial ruin.' This was regrettably true, for after he had successfully kept meat for six months in 1873 before serving it at a public banquet, his first consignment by ship went bad. However, T. S. Mort, a wool auctioneer and one of the founders of the famous pastoral company of Goldsbrough Mort, continued to experiment, and in 1880 forty tons of frozen beef and mutton were successfully shipped to London on the *Strathleven*, paving the way for exports of frozen meat which were worth more than £1,000,000 by 1890.

Refrigeration not only allowed the wool grower to export frozen mutton if he so desired; it also gave a stimulus to large-scale cattle grazing in the north. Here, in the very hot climate where high evaporation makes dry seasons drier, and where feed is coarse, sheep find life hard; but cattle can go farther to water, and the discovery and tapping of artesian supplies considerably extended the grazing possibilities of the interior. Meanwhile on the thousand miles' coast of Queensland, with its rich soil and regular rains brought by the south-east trade wind, there were high hopes of 'tropical agriculture'. Cotton had had a temporary boom during the American Civil War, but sugar showed more lasting qualities. Thomas Scott, who came from Antigua in the West Indies, had begun experimental cane growing in 1819 near Port Macquarie, but ran into trouble through fire, high labour costs, and his own inefficiency.[1] In the sixties, pioneer planters in Queensland, chiefly around Mackay, were having more success, and twenty years later more than 30,000 tons of sugar were being manufactured for the 'sweetest-toothed community in the world'.

The Queensland sugar planters had solved their labour problem in the way the New South Wales squatters had been forbidden to do—by the importation of coloured labour: not Asian coolies but Kanakas from the South Sea Islands, of whom nearly 50,000 were 'imported' before 1890. This 'black birding' was really a thinly veneered slave trade; its regulations, though well-intentioned, were continually broken or evaded. Here was deceit, treachery, kidnapping and murder. The Queensland Parliament tried to control recruitment in 1868; the British Parliament passed a Polynesian Protection Act in 1875; the German Foreign Office seized the opportunity to take a high moral tone in 1884; for twenty years the British Admiralty tried to police the laws, but in vain. The trade went on, and the death rate of the Kanakas rose to five times that of the white man. Only stricter control in Queensland could end the abuse; and though liberals and the growing labour movement in the south demanded it, the northern planters threatened to secede if what they claimed to be the prerequisite of their tropical plantations were to be denied. At last stricter regulations were enacted in 1883 and the secessionists' petition to England was rejected by the Colonial Office in 1887; but as we shall see in later chapters the battle was not yet ended.

Meanwhile agriculture was booming in the south, as farmers slowly began to modify their practices to suit Aus-

[1] See Colin Roderick: T. A. Scott and his work at Port Macquarie, 1823-8, in the *Journal of the Royal Aust. Hist. Soc.*, 1958, vol. 44, part 1, pp. 1-48.

tralian conditions, and to adopt a series of labour-saving devices. The Ridley stripper, said to be copied from the ancient Gauls, was the first. Invented in the 'forties, it replaced the ancient reaping hook. It was a great economy when reapers were demanding 40s. an acre, but, even more important, by its speed it made less likely the scattering of the ripe ears by the hot, burning sirocco-like winds of the Australian summer. Next came cheaper methods of clearing; then the 'stump-jump' plough, soon doing 'multiple furrows', followed by seed drills and finally in 1884 by the H. V. McKay 'complete harvester', capable of stripping and winnowing in one operation. Even so, there were problems over the horizon. Australian soil lacks phosphates, and the farmer would not yet apply any artificially; the wheat strains used were very prone to 'rust'. A succession of good years made men forget the dangers of the climate, but they were not thereby removed—especially as farmers had been moving into the drier parts of the interior. If wheat acreage doubled, output did not; in fact yields per acre were steadily declining, so that a bad season or a fall in price would bring disaster. The Australian farmer still had much to learn.

Meanwhile the expansionist mood had extended to the city populations and was there reflected in a growing radical nationalism which was already exhibiting those features that have become so characteristic of the Australian tradition. 'There is perhaps no town in the world in which an ordinary working man can do better for himself than he can in Melbourne,' wrote the visiting English novelist, Anthony Trollope; 'he not only lives better with more comfortable appurtenances around him, but he fills a higher position in regard to those about him and has greater consideration paid to him than would have fallen to his lot at home.' Here are the signs of a society with a high standard of living, and a strongly egalitarian outlook, lacking that respect for birth, wealth and intellect which was usual in nineteenth-century England. In this sense, the Australian colonies were in the van of progress, and had successfully pioneered a radical democratic political system, part cause and part result of the high status in the community of the 'common man'.

In Victoria, radical nationalism was less extreme than in New South Wales and Queensland, though it appeared there first and its early manifestations in Melbourne caused conservatives to tremble and even forced the attention of the far-off Colonial Office. But the Radical politics of the late 'seventies were the product of a temporary but unstable alliance of conflicting groups, bound in time to break up. Manufacturers, who had been given an initial dose of protection in 1865, were threatened with tariff reductions ten years later. Naturally, they flew to arms, and the United Manufacturers' Association of 1874 was followed by the Protection League of 1875. More support was necessary; so an alliance was made with the National Reform League, advocating a land tax and political reform, to form the National Reform and Protection League of 1877, which was the basis of radical-liberal organization in the ensuing political crisis. Protection and a land tax on big estates were the major issues linking city manufacturers and artisans with country selectors against the squatter and mercantile-financial interests; the by-products were the usual 'liberal' reforms of 'chartist' vintage—payment of members, reform of the Legislative Council and the abolition of plural voting. The election of 1877 was a landslide for the League led by Graham Berry, after excitement had been worked up to fever heat in the masses of the towns. Possibly however the party zealots exaggerated its importance; for since two-thirds of the voters were ratepayers, it is hard to visualize any intended destruction of property or class war, or even to agree that this was a 'turning point in the history of the country'. The merchants in the Legislative Council deserted their squatting allies to pass a land tax on estates over 640 acres, and the battle was joined on the relatively minor issue of payment of members.

Of greater constitutional importance, however, were the means which the Berry ministry used to carry out their policy. Following the precedent of 1865, they resorted to the device of tacking, which had the incidental advantage of provoking the conservatives and so helping a popular agitation. Appropriations for members' salaries were included in the estimates, which the Council could not amend, so it could not oppose this provision without rejecting the appropriation bill as a whole and thus throwing all administration into confusion. None the less, in defence of its position, and in opposition to the 'tack', this was done. The Governor, Sir George Bowen, had foreseen the trouble but had been advised from England that to avert an otherwise 'inevitable' collision between the Assembly and the Imperial Government he must follow the advice of his Ministers, 'half-educated' though they might be, and even if they had won power by 'lavish expenditure on public works and in new employment in the Civil Service'. Consequently, when the Council rejected the appropriation bill (for the fourth time in twelve years) Bowen agreed to the dismissal of nearly four hundred public servants, including magistrates and departmental officials. This famous 'Black Wednesday', 8 January 1878, was an attack on the opposition rather than a genuine measure of economy; it got rid of nearly all Berry's political opponents in the Civil Service and allowed him to appoint his supporters to the vacancies in the best American tradition; and though temporarily paralysing administration, it was effective in showing how far the ministry was prepared to go.

Both sides tried to justify their position, sending addresses and deputations to Governor and Colonial Office. For the moment the Council triumphed, when in 1879 it accepted an Appropriation Bill but without the 'tack' and with payment of members only until 1880. But many of the dismissed public servants were not reinstated; and the Council's action intensified the popular demand for its reform. In 1881 its membership was increased, the franchise qualification lowered and its electoral term reduced; but even more important for the time being was the lesson learned by all

parties of the dangers of pushing political passions too far.
The Colonial Office had given some sound advice on these
lines in 1879; by 1883 the moderates on both sides had
joined forces in the coalition that ruled for the next seven
years, and which by its financial extravagance did so much
to bring about the crash of 1890. But this apparent 'revolution' in party alignments was less extraordinary than it
seemed at the time. The alliance of manufacturer and working man always had its difficulties, once protection was assured, despite the current acceptance (at least by employers)
of the theory of the harmony of interest between labour
and capital. The 'selector', too, had no very deeply ingrained
radical ideals. On the other hand, with the acceptance of
protection as the 'settled' policy of the colony, the merchants
found alliance with industry in the struggle for interstate
trade more to their interest than blind allegiance to an out-
worn shibboleth; and the prosperity of the 'eighties, artificial though it largely was, tended to reduce the intensity
of political warfare. Bowen in 1879 had contrasted the 'extreme violence' of Victorian parties, where 'democratic feeling' was so strong, with the 'more moderate principles and
feelings of the adjacent colonies'. At the time this was true.
But the influence of the Victorian 'diggers' was waning and
now a more radical philosophy was beginning to appear in
Sydney.

By 1880 the Australian colonies, and particularly New
South Wales and Victoria, were no longer 'immigrant communities'. Two-thirds of the population was native-born;
even the rest were there to stay. Labour was hostile to assisted immigration; and although prosperity brought many
migrants in the 'eighties, since 1860 their numbers had been
small. There was growing hostility to the old world with
its hereditary privileges, its landlordism, class distinctions
and alleged oppression, not to mention its national rivalries
and militarism. With these things, Australia should have
nothing to do; she should turn her attention to her own
problems and continue her already bold experiments in

social reform, develop her labour movement, extend the eight-hour day and encourage the small farmer. Here, said the *Bulletin* in 1887, defending its policy of 'Australia for the Australians', 'vested interests of wealth and caste are less potent than in other countries. . . . The intellect of the people is freer, stronger and more original than in the age-old states of Europe.' 'We have little in common with the English people except our language,' wrote Henry Lawson. 'We are more liberal and more progressive than England is.' Of course many Australians managed to combine an intense local patriotism with allegiance to Britain; but in the 'eighties, in Australia (as in the United States) the part played by the Royal Navy in keeping the extra-European world safe for democracy, or at least free from 'foreign' conquest, was not very clearly appreciated; and the growing Radical-Labour movement, republican in outlook, was inclined to look forward with pleasure to the expected, if not inevitable, day when the British connection would be peacefully severed to the satisfaction of both parties. Australia was the land of the future, burning 'with the feverish energy of youth'; Australian nationalists were beginning to build up the 'Australian Tradition', repudiating or idealizing the convict past and attacking Great Britain for sustaining it. The tradition soon began to appear in her literature.

> But the Motherland, whose sons ye were!
> We know her, but light is our love of her,
> Small honour have we for the mother's name,
> Who stained our birth with the brand of shame.
> We were flesh of her flesh, and bone of her bone,
> We are lords of ourselves, and our land is our own.

This is the 'Voice of Australia',[1] and in the same way emerged the Eureka legend that transformed a minor riot into 'Freedom's Fight of Fifty-Four'.

> The bitter fight was ended,
> And with cruel coward-lust

[1] Published in the *Bulletin*, 23 September 1893.

They dragged our sacred banner
Through the Stockade's bloody dust.

Yet ere the year was over
Freedom rolled in like a flood;
They gave us all we asked for
When we asked for it in blood.

As in the United States, there was a passionate belief in freedom, and a passionate love of Australia as a land where freedom existed and could be maintained; in the same vein as the inscription on the Statue of Liberty in New York harbour, which did not yet appear so ironical as it does to-day, we read

Bright shall her banner be, stainless a mark to the nations,
(Not like their blood-sodden rags, with their mem'ries of war)
Telling of hope for the countless unborn generations
Marking a land that is Freedom's from shore to shore.'[1]

Australia was the land of the future.

We live but a day of thine ages, whose land in its infancy lies
With a history all blank in its pages, in the lap of the seas and the
skies;
Could we sleep, and in centuries waken, and view thee, the young-
est of lands,
The world, with the voice of thee shaken, the fruits of the years in
thy hands,

. . . . . .

Oh, shake off the shadows of failure, the heights for thy climbing
are steep!
Take arms for thy glory, Australia, and sow that the ages may
reap.[2]

These hopes for the future were reflected in a glorification of the present and a belief in the unique superiority of Australian society, and in resentment of any criticism of it, how-

[1] Ibid., 12 March 1892.
[2] Ibid., 8 April 1893.

ever moderate. For example, Trollope had pointed out that although it was 'almost impossible to speak too highly' of Victoria generally, yet it was 'not a perfect Elysium', for it lacked 'that refinement of manner and delicacy of sentiment which centuries give to an old country', and he went on to deprecate the prevailing over-glorification. 'Self-praise in the colonies is "called blowing"', he wrote, 'and I said to the colonists, "don't blow".' The Victorians however liked to 'blow'; they disliked the suggestion of any shortcomings; and when Trollope next returned to the colony they showed that they disliked it. But alongside this resentment of criticism and perhaps even part of it, was the expression of a great love for Australia. Almost for the first time there appeared an appreciation of the beauty of the bush, no longer compared unfavourably with the English countryside simply because it was different, but seen to have a peculiar charm of its own when looked at 'through clear Australian eyes, and not through bias-bleared English spectacles'.

'It is not in our cities and townships that the Australian attains full consciousness of his nationality,' wrote Collins in the 'bush philosophy' of *Such is Life*; 'it is in places like this ... where the monotonous variety of interminable scrub has a charm of its own.'

'Banjo' Patterson had the same outlook:

> For us the bush is never sad;
> Its myriad voices whisper low,
> In tones the bushmen only know,
> Its sympathy and welcome glad,

and the artists, first the Swiss Buvelot and then the natives, Julian Ashton, Tom Roberts, Charles Conder, Arthur Streeton, began to see its beauty and to paint what they saw to 'distil the mysticism of the Australian landscape'. Streeton's technique was simple, says Hancock, but 'it was sufficient to express upon canvas his direct enthusiastic vision of Australia's blue distances', and through him 'Australians discovered their country. . . . His landscapes have become

Australia, just as Perugino's skies are Umbria. His vision is part of Australian nationality.'

In this land, opportunities seemed boundless and resources illimitable. But there must be equal opportunity for all, without privilege, and each man must be free to use his particular talents to their full. This the 'bushman' would surely do; he was coming to be romanticized as the typical and highly praiseworthy Australian—lanky, wiry, rugged and sun-tanned, an individualist, enterprising, tough, always able to 'make do', the one 'powerful and unique type yet produced'.

'I acknowledge no aristocracy except one of service and self-sacrifice,' wrote Collins; 'human equality is as self-evident as human variety.' With this belief in equality came the idea of mateship,

> *The mateship born in barren lands*
> *Of toil and thirst and danger,*

an idea that became almost a religion in the poems of Henry Lawson and in the eyes of the working class whose worst enemy was the 'scab'; an idea which typified the spirit of the bush, even though the bush was no longer typical of Australia. But then this was just another of those romantic illusions so warmly held in this period of booming prosperity and wishful thinking.

Not that all radicals had their heads in the clouds; for alongside the dreams of the idealists was growing up another Labour movement, practical and hard-headed, based on the craft unions which had existed for over forty years and which were now rapidly growing in the boom. In the 'seventies were founded various Trades Halls and Trades and Labour Councils; in 1879 the first intercolonial union congress. The jealousies of the craft unions, the difficulties of communication, interstate jealousy and local variations in law and working conditions frustrated an over-ambitious scheme for federation approved in 1885, yet the fact that the *idea* had been accepted showed a growing consciousness of working-class unity which would be very apparent in 1890. Meanwhile, Parliamentary committees were being formed to press for legislation wanted by unionists and amendments to the law which extended the right to strike and gave strikers immunity from prosecution for conspiracy or intimidation. In Victoria, particularly close liaison between the Melbourne Trades Hall and the government led in that state at least to better regulation of factories and mines.

Of even greater significance was the extension of unionism to unskilled workers, coming 'as a new religion bringing salvation after years of tyranny'. W. G. Spence had revived the Amalgamated Miners' Association in Victoria in 1878, with the aim of uniting all miners—gold, silver, copper and coal—into one body; although he did not quite succeed in this, there were 25,000 members in the A.M.A. in 1886 when he went on to 'organize' the shearers. Here the difficulties were immense, for the shearers were scattered, but on the other hand in many cases their working conditions were bad. The squatter, according to Spence, could do what he liked. He fixed hours. He was the judge of what sheep were improperly shorn, and fixed the fine for bad work or bad conduct which might include swearing at a cantankerous sheep. He could impose fines for absence if the shearer were sick (or malingering). He provided the rations (and decided what should be paid for them). In short, in those days the 'boss' had the absolute power which so many employers condemn the union for wielding to-day; and though many masters were considerate, there is no doubt that some were not. Shearers' huts were primitive things, draughty, wet, insanitary, unfurnished:

> *Of fittings there are none for nobody cares*
> *To trouble a shearer with tables or chairs.*

By 1890 the Amalgamated Shearers' Union too boasted nearly 25,000 members with another 7,500 in a separate union in Queensland. Spence claimed that his policy was always conciliatory; he wanted agreements, not strikes. But there was no lack of strikes in the pastoral industry between 1886 and 1890 and no one could deny that a new power had arisen in the land.

The unions, except possibly in Queensland, had little idea of socialism. Karl Marx was practically unknown. Theoretical notions came more from John Stuart Mill or Henry George, then often thought of as the workers' Messiah. But theory was not important in a country adopting 'le socialisme sans doctrines'; what was important was the correction of abuses, and in this task Labour could go a long way in company with radical liberals, whose master, if anyone, was also Mill, and who also looked with favour on Henry George, even if (or perhaps because) they could not fully understand him. In any case both groups supported the extension of democracy, triennial parliaments, payment of members, the reform of Legislative Councils; both were ready to tax the wealthy landed classes; both were ready for the state to undertake public works and both were ready for the state to regulate social and industrial conditions, whether by factory legislation or otherwise. And nowhere was this co-operation easier than in attacking the Chinese, a policy which appealed to the growing Australian nationalism as well as to the economic interests of the working class.

In the days of the gold rush the miners had objected to Chinese on the diggings and a special residence tax had been imposed on them in Victoria; but despite occasional riots their presence was tolerated. In 1871 there were only some 25,000 in the country; but in the next ten years they again appeared to be a threat to the livelihood of the Australian working man, especially in cheap manufacturing establishments and as seamen on ships. The squalor and wretchedness of the Chinese were portrayed in vivid language, with denunciations of opium smoking and general immorality added. In 1888 a Melbourne trade-union journal even compared their appearance to that of 'a certain kind of animal which youngsters have a partiality for in the Zoological Gardens'. Here was 'White Australia' with a vengeance and

a Chinese spokesman was not slow to remark, after an outbreak of rioting, that if such things had occurred to Englishmen in China, 'every newspaper in Great Britain would
have been aflame with indignation; your envoy at Pekin
would have demanded prompt reparation . . . and the Em-
peror lectured on the barbarous and scandalous conduct of
those who insulted and maltreated peaceful and industrious
foreigners.' The result of the agitation was that all the
colonies passed anti-Chinese legislation, imposing heavy
fees on immigrants. The Chinese ambassador in London
protested and the Colonial Office explained its embarrass-
ment to the colonies. But the Australians were not impressed.
'Neither for Her Majesty's ships of war, neither for Her
Majesty's representative, nor for the Colonial Office, do we
intend to turn aside from our purpose,' declared Sir Henry
Parkes. To the radical republicans here was fresh cause for
breaking away from the Empire; to the more moderate, it
was just another case of the lack of sympathy shown to
Australia by Great Britain.

For even the most loyal frequently felt irritated with the
mother country when their growing nationalist feelings
were ignored. Gladstone's government had refused to con-
firm Queensland's annexation of New Guinea in 1883, with
the result that shortly afterwards the Germans occupied the
north of the island. Lord Salisbury seemed unconcerned that
the French were using New Caledonia as a penal settlement
or that they might annex the New Hebrides, until Alfred
Deakin indulged in some plain speaking when he attended
the first Colonial Conference at Queen Victoria's Jubilee in
1887. To some, British disinterestedness was a reason for
closer connection. Schemes of 'Imperial Federation' were
taken up. New South Wales sent a contingent to the Sudan
in 1885. Griffith in Queensland was glad to feel that the
'fleets of a great empire are ready to assist us'. Some closer
co-operation in defences was achieved by the naval agreements of 1887, even though they were not immediately ratified by all the colonies. Such ideas were helped by the con-

temporary revival of imperialist feeling in Britain. No longer were the colonies 'mill-stones round our necks'; rather thought *The Times,* 'with the colonies massed around us we can hold our own in the ranks of the world powers . . . without them we must sink to a position of a merely European kingdom . . . which entails slow but sure decay.' But the radicals were unimpressed. They suspected a trick whereby 'the Salisbury gang have conceived the idea of transferring the responsibility of defending the Empire from the Imperial to the Colonial Exchequers.' They had strongly opposed British intervention in the Sudan, 'the most disgraceful and unjustified campaign with which she has ever stained the pages of her history', asking, 'Is Patriotism a virtue in Englishmen yet a Crime in Sudanese?' They hated the traditions of the old world; they rejoiced that Australia 'is committed to no usages of petrified injustice; she is clogged by no fealty to shadowy idols enshrined by ignorance; she is cursed by no memories of fanaticism and persecution; she is innocent of hereditary national jealousies and free from the envy of sister states.' They disliked their ties with England and their lack of independence.

Both reactions were the natural results of the growing national feeling. Neither independence nor a strong voice in the Empire would have been possible without the great development of the preceding years, and, in turn, either could only be effectively achieved if the colonies were to federate. But in the meantime, whether in the celebrations of Queen Victoria's Jubilee or in their somewhat self-righteous patriotic superiority, both imperialists and radicals had forgotten that much of this development was unsound and that Australian prosperity was most insecurely founded. Extension of settlement, overseas borrowing, the growth of Labour, each carried with them some threat to the economy should there develop that 'hitherto undiscovered combination of circumstances', which was being so cheerfully ignored. In fact, the storm clouds which had been gathering so long were about to burst.

Chapter Eleven

THE STORM BREAKS

For nearly ten years Australian labourers, speculators, businessmen, politicians and nationalists revelled in their fool's paradise of the artificial prosperity created by overseas investment. Less than three million people borrowed nearly £200,000,000 during the boom, half through their governments, half privately. At first this had been justified; the country needed development. But when to stop, that was the question. The nationalist-isolationist *Bulletin* was one of the few critics of overseas borrowing; but it was not yet 'respectable', at least in financial circles. Indebtedness seemed infectious, and from the ease with which the money could be got men seemed to infer that they were being actually foolish if they did not get more. Caution in spending was thrown to the winds; railways were built for political reasons, whether the lines were potentially profitable or not, and in 1890 nearly half the interest on government loans, which had been borrowed for allegedly 'remunerative' works, was being paid out of taxation. Everywhere over-optimism led to over-expansion. Farms were bought and sheep and cattle were grazing in areas where the climate was risky and where costs were high. When the good seasons should end or prices should fall, there would be trouble.

South Australia was the first to suffer. Her land laws, favourable climate and lack of gold had long made this colony 'the granary of the continent'. Her wheat harvest equalled that of all the other colonies put together, and her farmers had not been backward in technique. But in the good seasons they had been tempted beyond 'Goyder's line', which marked the Surveyor General's opinion of the safe climatic boundary for wheat. The optimist had argued then that 'rain would follow the plough'; but it appeared that they had reasoned on unsound premises. From 1876 to 1904, not one crop reached ten bushels to the acre; eighteen crops were less than six bushels, including five successive years after 1881; for five successive years after 1896 yields were only four. The 'plough had outpaced the rain clouds', the soil was over-farmed; and slowly but steadily the price of wheat fell from 5s. 10d. to 3s. 8d. Pastoralists too suffered from the drought. Their tenure was insecure while governments were resuming their leases; they found it hard to get money for improvements; rabbits were coming in waves.

The colony was not helped by its over-eager assumption of responsibility for the Northern Territory. Up to 1850 various attempts had been made to establish trading posts in the north: Melville Island, Raffles Bay, and Port Essington alike had been established with high hopes but abandoned. But the successful expeditions and enthusiastic reports of McDouall Stuart and John McKinlay in 1861 and 1862 revived interest. South Australia won the territory from Queensland; a North Australian Company was floated and the government planned another settlement on the coast. This was not helped by the quarrels with the first administrator, and nearly five years' argument over the best site before Port Darwin was selected, but the failure that had been foretold twenty years before was indeed inevitable in an isolated land with uncertain rainfall and no labour. None the less the government went on to spend £4,000,000 on a settlement which after fifty years contained 3,000 people. In 1872 it built a telegraph to Darwin at a cost of £400,000, arguing that this would 'promote the occupation of large tracts in the interior'. But not even the ability to send messages at one shilling a word brought settlers. Nor did the discovery of gold at Pine Creek in 1871, when transport costs were so high and men would not stay. Three more plantations in the north failed between 1880 and 1890. A railway was pushed to Oodnadatta, stretching out nearly 700 miles in the desert to the middle of nowhere, but plans to import Indian coolies under the Northern Territory Immigration Act of 1882 broke down owing to the combined opposition of the Indian government, the eastern colonies in Australia and the financial crisis in Adelaide. South Australia was comparatively lucky. The drought brought heavy losses and the Commercial Bank of South Australia failed; but though many investors lost heavily, at least the results were not as disastrous as the later more spectacular crash in the east which had five years longer to mature.

Melbourne speculators were the most exuberant. In the late 'eighties Victoria escaped for a time the worst of the drought. Over £50,000,000 was borrowed by public and private creditors between 1885 and 1890. Railway construction gave plenty of employment; the 70,000 immigrants in these years raised the population to over a million. The housing boom stimulated speculation not only in country but also in suburban lands. Building societies purchased and subdivided suburban estates, they accepted payment on easy terms, and gave extensive credit even after the banks had begun to show signs of caution. City blocks changed hands for over £200 a foot; it was almost impossible to buy without being offered an advance on the purchase money next day. The hysteria was increased by so much speculation in the new Broken Hill and Mount Morgan mining shares on the Stock Exchange that the volume of business reached £6,000,000 a week in 1888, though there was no comparable increase in production to justify these extraordinarily inflated values.

Boom style extravagance was marked in contemporary building and decoration in the suburbs now being opened up by the new railways, and gas, cable trams and the other 'mod. cons.' of the era were being brought to the city dwellers. Their numbers had grown very rapidly—in New South Wales from 46 per cent of the total population in 1861 to 65 per cent in 1890, and in Victoria even more.

Manufactures had expanded tenfold, in the towns, to contribute one-seventh of the national income after 1881, instead of one-twentieth in 1861. It was in the towns that 'services' increased—especially those of professional men and government administration. It was in the towns that building took place on a grand scale; but this industry was inefficient and in any case it absorbed capital without increasing national income except by providing greater comfort (or luxury) for the inhabitants. This fact, the slow decline of the older goldfields and the settlement of both graziers and farmers on inferior lands all help to explain why national income per head did not increase significantly; but even with the help of British capital, to build the cities and to absorb so many immigrants *without a fall* in living standards were no mean achievements.

In the eighties the value of pastoral output ceased to expand, as droughts, rabbits and soil exhaustion reduced productivity and overseas prices collapsed. A sudden drop in wool from 12¼d. to 9¼d. a pound in 1886 made it hard for the grazier to carry the debt he had cheerfully incurred in easier circumstances; by 1889 banks and pastoral companies were holding many properties worth less than the sums advanced on them. Station owners, like the farmers only on a larger scale, were weighed down with their debts. No wonder that with falling prices and bad seasons they were worried about their costs; and these included the cost of labour. Not at once was there any attempt directly to reduce wages, but the pastoralists' slogan was 'freedom of contract', by which they meant the right to employ whomsoever they wished, whether unionists or not. After their triumphs of organization since 1885 the shearers especially, though not only they, looked on this as the first step in a plan to 'smash the unions', for it was a basic principle of the new unions that none but unionists should be employed. Such a principle of course was necessary for the success of their organization, since only by their presenting a united front to the employer could grievances be effectively remedied and working conditions improved. All should join the union. Sometimes methods of proselytism might be somewhat rough; but the usual appeal was to the Australian tradition of 'mateship' wherein the deadliest sin was 'scabbing', by the man who would let down his mates.[1]

The new unions were not intrinsically hostile to 'capital' as such. At this time the idea of a harmony of interests prevailed, not only among the skilled crafts unions, but among the miners and shearers as well. 'The policy of the union is conciliation,' declared Spence. He was always emphatic that strikes could be readily avoided by a round table conference between the two parties, for 'beneath the surface of labour disputes, the interests of capital and labour are identical'. But justice could only be achieved between equals; and the forces of labour and capital would only be equal if the men were fully unionized. Hence not only his insistence on the closed shop, but his belief in the moral value of unionism, declaring that, 'if altruism is the ideal of human brotherhood and high civilisation, the Trade Union is the first step towards it.' It followed that an attack on the unions would arouse in Spence an almost religious zeal in their defence, to sustain the more material and mundane motives of some of his fellows. And though unionism as a whole was not revolutionary there were some militant spirits.

In 1889 the Queensland Trades and Labour Council drew up a plan for an Australian Labour Federation to link all unions in a permanent body which would control their activities. Its state branch was formed at once. Here was perhaps a threatening sign of solidarity, especially when the political movement in Brisbane adopted a 'socialist objective'. The inspiration was that of William Lane, who had come to Brisbane from Bristol in 1883. Moved by the

[1] One sometimes wonders wherein this differs (except possibly in language) from the public-school tradition (English in origin) of not 'letting down' the side; but most Australian workers at all events (and many who write about them) like to think that there is something 'mystic, wonderful', not to say unique, about this idea of the kinship of the bush (and the working man).

poverty and distress of the slums, he preached the doctrine of a socialist 'co-operative commonwealth' which would remove such evils. This could be achieved by the workers if they stood solidly together, for 'it is socialism that is moving the world.' Others were not so explicit in their ideas as Lane; but undoubtedly there was an intellectual ferment among the workers. They desired a 'reconstruction of society', said Spence, and even if they did not quite know what this meant, at least 'the yeast of the new order was stirring mightily through the ranks of the masses.'

With these feelings, the unions, particularly the shearers, were struggling in 1890 to consolidate their recent gains, to force the employers not only to recognize them but cease employing non-unionists. Although in 1889 nearly ninety per cent of the stations 'shore union', the shearers wanted one hundred per cent. In May 1890 the Queensland pastoralists agreed to employ only union shearers; but this concession was made only after 'non-union' wool from Jondaryan station had been declared 'black' by the seamen and wharf labourers at Brisbane. Elated by this success, the shearers in New South Wales issued a manifesto on July 14 appealing for 'such a cordon of unionism around the Australian continent as will effectually prevent a bale of wool leaving unless shorn by Union shearers'. Meanwhile the pastoralists had formed an organization, though one 'with no aggressive policy; it is established purely for defensive and conciliatory purposes'. They refused to dismiss non-union shearers during the current season, but offered to employ only union labour in the future. It was alleged that this offer was not sincere and was only made to gain time; of such an accusation there can be no proof. At all events, it seemed clear to employers that in existing conditions they could not afford to continue making concessions to the men; they were determined to make a stand, whether or not this should involve the destruction of unionism. And this applied not only to graziers. 'We are determined to fight the seamen,' the chairman of the Steamship Owners' Association is reported to have said on July 29. 'We are a combined and compact body and I believe that never before has such an opportunity to test the respective strength of Labour and Capital arisen.' The president of the Sydney Trades and Labour Council felt the same way. Now was the time to stand firm. To the shearers it seemed that to accept non-unionists again after the Jondaryan affair would mean weakly surrendering a vital principle. They declared that the existence of the union was at stake. They too claimed to be defending their rights against aggression, and were ready to fight. But before hostilities broke out over wool they were precipitated by two other disputes on the water-front. In Melbourne, the Marine-officers' Association, newly formed to protest against their pay and conditions, wished to affiliate with the Trades Hall. The shipowners considered such a move would be 'subversive of discipline', but as the owners had refused all concessions until the officers had threatened to join the general union movement, the latter now insisted on their right to affiliate and left the ships. In Sydney the dismissal of a fireman from the S.S. *Corinna* accentuated ill feeling though it was not the cause of hostilities; for it was said that the dismissed man, a union official, had been victimized, although in this case the owners offered, if not to reinstate him at least to find him another job. But the details are perhaps irrelevant; what were involved were the principles of unionism and of freedom of contract, and as a matter of principle other unions and employers alike rallied in support. Perhaps both sides realized too that with the onset of depression this battle was the prelude to an attempt to lower the cost of labour.

Beginning as it did on the water-front, the struggle has been called the 'great maritime strike'. It was far more. By September 1890 50,000 men were involved. Of these half were shearers and a third miners who had come out in support. An intercolonial committee representing the greater part of the union movement took charge of the strike. But the odds were against the strikers. When the shearers 'came out', their demonstration of 'mateship' exposed them to prosecution for breach of contract, and forced them to ask for strike pay instead of contributing to the strikers' funds. Numbers of unemployed in Sydney and Melbourne provided an adequate pool of non-union, 'scab', labour. The governments of New South Wales and Victoria gave police protection to the 'volunteers'. In Sydney on September 19 the Riot Act was read and mounted troopers charged on Circular Quay, though exactly why is somewhat difficult to determine. In Melbourne, Alfred Deakin claimed that the extra police and military were called in not to attack the strikers, but 'to check the criminals carrying on their war against society'. Naturally the unions criticized this 'partisan' attitude, but by this time their defeat was in sight. Notwithstanding the subscription of nearly £50,000 in both Sydney and Melbourne to the strike funds, it was clear the unions had overtaxed their strength. They received some outside support, for example from Cardinal Moran in Sydney and Chief Justice Higinbotham in Melbourne, but on the whole press and public were hostile. They argued that the struggle had been caused by the tyranny of trade unionism even when the employers refused a request for a conference unless the principle of 'freedom of contract' were conceded in advance. Before the end of October the unions were forced to surrender, owing to the 'practically unlimited supply of unorganized labour and the exhaustion of funds'. Even in September it was said that a 'visitor to the Melbourne wharves could hardly know that anything is amiss'. On Guy Fawkes' day the last strikers agreed to return to work.

The employers were not slow to press home their advantage. In 1891 the Queensland pastoralists successfully asserted their right of 'freedom of contract', after a bitter struggle against the shearers' union which was now described as 'a closely knit band of criminals' and 'a force of armed banditti'. Armed police protected the 'free' labourers, but there was neither bloodshed nor revolution even though the strikers' camp flew the blue flag of Eureka. The pastoralists of New South Wales and Victoria were more conciliatory, but in 1892 the mining companies repudiated their agreement made in 1890 and were able to enforce 'freedom of contract' at Broken Hill. In despair William Lane set off in 1893 to establish a new socialist Utopia in Paraguay.

This project, like so many similar attempts in various parts of the world before, was a failure. But at least the party escaped the bank crash that followed in Australia; for capital having won its victory over labour was about to suffer a most humiliating disaster, bringing widespread misery to many of its middle class allies. At the time, many were ready and anxious to make the unions the scapegoat for the misfortunes that followed, in an attempt to conceal their own most foolish if not dishonest practices. But labour was not to blame, save perhaps that the notoriety which the struggle brought to Australia attracted attention to the unsound policies so long adopted by those public and private financiers who had built up a jerry-built paper structure as the basis of the country's economy. The utter defeat of labour should have brought confidence, if anything, to British investors; but what confidence could there be where every industry was so grossly over-capitalized? Already English private investment in Australia had fallen off; what if loans to governments were also to cease? Would not the experience of Baring Brothers, English bankers, in South America in 1890, suggest to overseas depositors the wisdom of withdrawing their money from the Australian banks? And, if so, could the banks meet their liabilities? Forty-one land and finance companies in Melbourne and Sydney with liabilities of £25,000,000 had failed in 1891 and 1892. Only four small banks collapsed in this period, yet it was obvious that many advances on city land were lost, that overdrafts to depressed primary producers were temporarily 'frozen hard' and that loans for urban housebuilding would not be repaid while the borrowers remained unemployed. To obtain funds some institutions continued to seek English deposits

by offering high rates of interest. They got more than
£4,000,000 in 1891 and another million even in 1892 to
raise the total to £40,000,000. But in January 1893 the important Federal Bank suspended payment; in April the
'pioneer in the land-mortgage business', the Commercial
Bank of Australia, did the same. Panic followed. Within a
month, there were eleven more suspensions. The 'run' was
made by local depositors, not the British. The latter have
since been unfairly blamed for the crisis, to satisfy at once
the critics of 'imperialist exploitation' and the self-righteous-
ness of local bankers.[1] At the same time it was the fear that
British depositors would want to withdraw their money (as
well they might) that made the banks unwilling to use all
their resources to allay the local panic.

In Victoria where the crisis was worst, the banks were not
helped by the government. In 1891 the Munro ministry had
passed the Voluntary Liquidation Act making it more difficult for the creditors of an insolvent institution to enforce
compulsory liquidation through the law courts. This
strengthened the hands of company directors, who were
often able to compel their creditors to agree to their locking
up their funds for long periods, a measure hardly likely to
instil confidence in bank depositors. The Real Estate Bank,
of which Munro himself was the 'head and front', soon suspended payment and the Premier retired to London as
Agent General. In January 1893 the conservative leader,
Patterson, took office; he showed no more knowledge of
finance than his predecessors. Remarking 'we are all floun-
dering', he declared a week's bank holiday in May when the
panic was approaching its height, a step which effectively
undermined what little confidence in the banking system
remained. All the Victorian banks save one were forced to

---

[1] One of the most famous of these was Henry Gyles Turner, manager of the
Commercial Bank of Australia, perhaps the most blameworthy of all for its
rash policy, whose *History of the Colony of Victoria* and *First Decade of the Commonwealth of Australia* are replete with the most severe attacks on his political
opponents.

reconstruct. In Sydney Sir George Dibbs showed more initiative in authorizing the issue of treasury notes and making bank notes temporarily legal tender. With these, the banks could satisfy depositors while the panic lasted. After this there was only one suspension in New South Wales—by the Commercial Banking Company—and this was entirely unnecessary and due only to the directors losing their heads. Even so in Australia as a whole twenty-two banks suspended payments; only ten remained open throughout.

The bank smash brought the greatest suffering to Victoria, adding considerably to that already caused by the trade depression and unemployment. It is hardly too much to say that it caused a kind of phobia for a generation (almost until the 'great depression' of 1930 caused another one). It certainly spelled the end of Melbourne's predominance as the financial centre of Australia, as her population drifted away and industry remained blighted. All financial and public leaders had shared in, if they had not contributed to, the speculative mania, which was based on a foolish optimism that refused to consider the relation between costs and the value of output. Financiers and politicians had failed in their duty when they ignored the fact that capital values had no meaning apart from annual net income.

Like Victoria, Tasmania suffered severely. After convict transportation had been stopped in 1852, the colony had sunk into a prolonged depression. British penal expenditure naturally ceased, and when it did so the colonists found that even the punishment of crime and importation of 'depravity' had their compensations. To make matters worse, the gold-fields in Victoria drew away both free settler and ex-convict; immigrants were few; even agriculture and grazing were more profitable on the mainland. Not until after 1871 was the first railway opened—the Western line from Launceston. Privately owned, it was soon unable to meet its obligations. A new generation of 'village Hampdens' refused to meet the special rates on their properties which they had agreed to pay in such an eventuality, and met attempts to distrain their goods and chattels with threats of violence. Eventually the government had to take over a line whose future losses could always be blamed on the inefficiency of public ownership; the local residents had obtained their railway before there was traffic enough even to pay its running expenses, and with it not only a considerable increase in the value of their land, but also the satisfaction of flattering themselves that they had successfully defended their liberty and property against intolerable oppression. However, the line did assist 'development' and so did the 'main line' from Hobart to Launceston—opened in 1876, also built by a private company and likewise later taken over by government because of its losses.

More important than development of this sort were the mineral discoveries—not the abortive search for gold which in the early 'seventies caused the flotation of ninety companies and the bankruptcy of eighty-eight, but the finding of the world's richest tin-mines by 'Philosopher' Smith, at Mount Bischoff in 1871. Transport was a problem in this wild, wet, cold and inhospitable region accessible only by pack-horse. The word 'unexplored' appears on the twentieth century map of the area only ten miles to the west, but a private railway (at first horse-drawn) was opened in 1878. The discovery of the tin led to further prospecting. The rich gold deposits at Beaconsfield were discovered in 1877, silver-lead at Mount Zeehan and gold at Mount Lyell in 1882 and copper at Mount Lyell in 1886. The upshot was prosperity and speculation both in real estate and in mining shares, and the government joined in with public works. But much of the expansion was not justified and by 1896 the writing was on the wall. The mines, though successful, were not producing any 'second Ballarat'; tariffs were closing the mainland market for agriculture products; the only bright spot was the help refrigeration was bringing to the fruit-grower. In 1891 the Bank of Van Diemen's Land, which had been making advances to over-optimistic mining ventures and whose balance-sheet was shown to be fraudulent, was forced into liquidation. The crisis then developed as on the mainland, intensified by the financial convulsions in Melbourne. Although none of the other banks suspended payment, the government could borrow neither in London nor locally; public works were perforce suspended; building came to a standstill and naturally mining development ceased. There was not only unemployment but widespread destitution, and as in Victoria the situation was not relieved until there had been a large exodus of population—largely to the goldfields of Western Australia.

New South Wales, more dependent on wool, reacting earlier to the price fall and bad seasons, and more gravely upset by labour troubles, escaped the worst of the banking troubles by seeing the red light in time; even so, the depression was severe, unemployment heavy and distress acute. In Queensland, as in the south, there had been over-borrowing to build railways which turned out unprofitable. There too, drought, falling prices and labour troubles combined to depress the pastoral industry, while the sugar growers were perturbed by falling prices and threats to their coloured labour supply. In 1885 the then liberal Premier, Samuel Griffith, had threatened to ban the importation of Kanakas after 1890, despite the view of Governor Sir Anthony Musgrove (and others) that sugar cane could not be successfully cultivated by white labour. But when the time came, conditions had changed. By a transformation so typical of contemporary Australian politics, but inexplicable by rational standards, Griffith was now in coalition with his former arch-antagonist, the conservative Sir Thomas McIlwraith; at the same time, the sugar industry was being revolutionized. Smallholders were replacing the large plantations, and central crushing mills, using white labour and efficient modern machinery, were replacing the old plantation manufacture; but this had not, as Griffith had hoped, removed the Kanakas from the canefields and, with prices falling, how could even the small farmer increase his labour

costs? Was it the 'malign influence' of McIlwraith, or the
'rough forces of facts and prices', or the renewed agitation
for the separation of North Queensland that made the ex-
liberal renew temporarily but indefinitely, the Polynesian
Labour Regulation Act in 1892? Perhaps it was the deepen-
ing depression and the fear of reducing any further the value
of properties mortgaged to the banks. At all events, although in 1893 the Queensland National Bank suspended
payments, it remained solvent; and since its principal depositors, apart from the Queensland government, were
British, its reconstruction involved no great hardship in the
colony. But the reduction in public works threw men out of
work and there was acute distress in Brisbane. Though more
'development' in the north would be desirable in time,
especially when the world meat market should expand, for
the moment zeal had outrun discretion, and indebtedness
was too heavy.

This accumulated debt, and the need to pay interest on it,
were among the difficulties confronting the 'separation
movement' which was seeking to divide the planters' tropical North Queensland from the more democratic south.
Through the 'eighties and 'nineties the agitation had continued and grown, but debt, drought, democracy in the
form of the Shearers' Union and the growing mining population, and the changing conditions of the sugar industry
gave the planters pause. They began to consider the suggestion of Joseph Chamberlain, in reply to their separation petition in 1895, that a Federal Government of Australia might
help them to solve their difficulties. Such a federation was
now a political possibility, and although it would probably
mean 'White Australia' it would at least bring a nation-wide
protected market for the products of the north. Meanwhile,
to the majority of Australians it was becoming more and
more apparent that the colonies needed to create some form
of federal union so that together they might be able to face
more successfully the problems of the future, and recover
from the difficulties of the immediate past.

Chapter Twelve

FEDERATION

It was probably the economic crisis of 1893 that gave the decisive spur to the Federation movement. The theoretical advantage of a federal union were as obvious to the far-seeing in 1850 or even 1890 as in 1900; but not until 1900 was theory put into practice. Although to begin the twentieth century with the foundation of the Commonwealth had a certain appeal to tidy minds, this was not the only reason for success. During the preceding fifty years the drawbacks of governing a continent divided into six independent colonies had gradually become apparent; but only gradually, and only to a few. Merchants and interstate travellers might curse the intercolonial customs barriers—particularly those on the River Murray—but merchants and interstate travellers were but a small proportion of the population. Sydney and Melbourne were only linked by rail in 1883, Melbourne and Adelaide in 1887 and Sydney and Brisbane in 1889; and the sea voyages were slow, uncomfortable, and unpleasant. Few, even, were the interstate visits of sportsmen, apart from cricketers; and these travelled without the attendant herd of commentators that seem to be such a necessary part of the game to-day. With their contemporary communications, Brisbane and Adelaide were farther apart than London and Canberra to-day; Perth seemed the *ultima Thule*; Sydney and Melbourne, though closer, were divided by a bitter rivalry.

United, the colonies could speak with a stronger voice on foreign affairs, and improve their defences. But did the colonies want to speak with a stronger voice on foreign affairs, or even to improve their defences? Isolation was as strong in Australia as in the United States of America, and in the happy days of Queen Victoria while the British navy was supreme there seemed little danger of foreign aggression in the remote Pacific. Admittedly there had been some little stir over the Germans in New Guinea, or the French in Tahiti or New Caledonia: this was but an evanescent excitement, and confined to a small group of the population. At the Colonial Conference in 1887, Alfred Deakin was impressed by 'the powerlessness of great, populous, wealthy and important communities to gain a hearing with a foreign power or even in the Imperial Parliament'; but on his return he found the Victorian Legislative Assembly hard to move. There was no feeling of urgency; instead widespread apathy and indifference during a period when most people were very prosperous and the leaders of the community were so busy speculating in land as to leave themselves little time to think of anything else.

The exclusion of Chinese labour from the colonies was a point of interest not only for the trade unions, but also for most of the middle classes, anxious to avoid the social problems inevitable in a community of mixed race and colour. But on this question all the colonies were already unanimous; all had passed similar legislation to preserve the purity of White Australia, and even in Queensland an act banning the recruitment of Kanakas after 1890 had been put on the statute book in 1885.

In short, up to 1890, Federation, though something to be idly talked about, and always a suitable subject for the peroration of an after-dinner speech, especially in Victoria, was not seriously discussed in Australia. A loose 'confederation' with a Federal Council meeting every alternate summer in Hobart (an attractive spot in January) was formed in 1885, but its legislative powers were very restricted and it had no executive power at all. It passed acts dealing with lighthouses and *bêche-de-mer* fisheries, but could not see they were carried out. New South Wales was never a member; South

Australia only from 1888 to 1890. But if its very existence was evidence of *some* desire for common action, its weaknesses show how limited that desire was, and how unwilling the colonies were to sacrifice their 'freedom of action'. Why then did opinion change?

At first the process was very slow. Sir Henry Parkes set the ball rolling in a famous speech at Tenterfield, in October 1889, when, with the recent report by General Edwards in mind, he particularly emphasized the urgency of federal defence, and called for a national convention to draft a federal constitution. After some difficulty a Premiers' Conference was held in Melbourne to discuss the matter, and agreed to Parkes's proposal. In March 1891, the convention met in Sydney and a draft constitution was drawn up for submission to the various local Parliaments. Rarely has there been a greater flop. In New South Wales it was violently attacked as unjust and likely to jeopardize her traditional free-trade policy. Was she, a teetotaller, to keep house with five drunkards? demanded Reid, soon to be leader of the Free Trade party. The protectionist leader of the Opposition, Dibbs, was equally hostile, and so was the veteran Sir John Robertson. The Labour party thought it undemocratic and militaristic. They were more interested in social reform. Even Sir Henry Parkes himself, while Premier, continually postponed Parliamentary debate on the proposals. The other colonies either did nothing or discussed the scheme in a desultory fashion. They were waiting for a lead from New South Wales and, lacking it, their interest waned. The whole project seemed to be stillborn.

But the excitements of the next three years, though temporarily diverting, had their effect on public opinion; by the end of 1894, even lukewarm political leaders realized that some action was necessary. The convention of 1891 had at least given a stimulus to propaganda by the enthusiasts. In Victoria, the Australian Natives' Association, a friendly society founded in 1871, took up the cause, and encouraged the writing and publishing of federalist literature. In New

South Wales, and particularly in the border districts, Federation Leagues sprang to life, supported particularly by those feeling the pinch of intercolonial duties. July 1893 saw the famous meeting at Corowa, in the Riverina. Here the usual grandiloquent but platitudinous resolutions were followed by a proposal that each colony should pass an enabling act to provide for the election by popular vote of representatives to a new convention; this body would then draw up another federal constitution which should be submitted to the people at a referendum. It was an appeal to the people, away from the politicians; it was a plan covering the whole process of constitution-making from first to last, and one simple enough to be readily appealed to in propaganda, and it was taken up at once by the Federation Leagues, which now included a newly founded body in Sydney itself.

Federal sentiment in Sydney was weakened by personal and party bitterness. The League itself was only founded after a somewhat acrimonious exchange of letters between Parkes and Edmund Barton, wherein each claimed to have done more than the other to further the cause, and moreover it was continually short of funds. It spent £94 1s. 5d. in 1893-4, but next year, when Deakin proposed to visit Sydney it had to levy special subscriptions to make it possible to hold a meeting at which he could speak! In Victoria, where federal sentiment was far stronger, Deakin refused to hold ministerial office after 1890 though asked to join every cabinet that was formed; he wished to devote his whole energies to the federal cause. But in Sydney it was always suspected, rightly or not, that Parkes was interested in Federation more as a means of getting himself back to the Premiership than for any other reason. Barton was undoubtedly genuine in his convictions, but as Attorney General in the Protectionist Dibbs ministry from 1891 to 1893 he antagonized Labour by prosecuting the union leaders of the Broken Hill strike in 1892, and made it more difficult for free-trade politicians to support the federal movement. All the same, when Reid became Premier, with labour support, after the election of July 1894, he took up the federal cause officially, and arranged for a Premiers' Conference to be held in January 1895 to discuss the passing of the enabling bills.

Why this change of front? Reid was a very astute politician who took careful note of public opinion. The Federation Leagues were active; but the public at large remained apathetic. At none of the subsequent Federal referenda did half the electorate vote; there was far less interest taken in the Federation than in local questions. League members were very largely business and professional men. Labour was suspicious that social reform was being side-tracked—what was there in Federation for the working man?—and Reid, despite his victory in 1894, still depended on labour support to retain power. At the elections, although the protectionists won not a single seat in Sydney, they remained very strong in the country. Perhaps the Premier was anxious to increase his support in the Riverina. Perhaps, apart from 'politics', he was beginning to see some of those other advantages of Federation which the enthusiasts were so tirelessly reiterating.

Since the failure of the 1891 convention, the financial crisis had ravaged eastern Australia. Would closer co-operation have made it easier to weather the storm? 'Federation is no panacea', said the *Pastoralists' Review* in 1893, 'but it would be of considerable assistance in our present difficulties.' The *Journal of the Institute of Bankers* thought that after Federation the colonies would be able to borrow on better terms. 'Securities resting on the asset of a United Australia could no longer be flouted by a pack of London brokers, or depreciated at the caprice of half-informed and not disinterested London papers, but would take their place among the best securities that could be offered in any part of the world.' Since the colonies were anxious both to resume borrowing and to reduce interest rates, this was an important consideration. Moreover, owing to their deficits in the depression, both Victoria and New South Wales in the teeth of

strong conservative opposition had imposed an income tax
for the first time. In both colonies this was achieved with
labour assistance; but in New South Wales, as well as being
a measure of radical social policy, it had further consequences. The protection of local industries had interested
relatively few members of the Protectionist party, for the
'protective' duties in force affected only a number of agricultural products, not manufactures—hence the strength of
the protectionists in the country. In the 'nineties the conflict
was primarily between those in favour of a higher or lower
revenue tariff, and the latter wanted an income tax on the
wealthy to compensate for lower duties paid by the poor.
This 'social' distinction was now established; and though
there were of course 'diehard' free traders, particularly in
Sydney itself, the fiscal conflict had to an extent died down,
and the free traders could join the federal movement. Even
though New South Wales would probably have to submit
to some tariffs, at least there would be intercolonial free
trade, and this would help to revive commerce after the
depression.

Apart from the fiscal question, improved communications were bringing the colonies closer together. The great
strikes of 1890 had shown that intercolonial federations of
employers and of working men existed; many trading companies were now operating in several colonies. Even in
Australia, quite apart from some anxiety about the French
in Tahiti or the Germans in New Guinea and Samoa, the
growing tensions of international affairs could be felt to
stress the need for better defences. All these things contributed to the growth of Australian, rather than colonial,
patriotism, flamboyant and exuberant, boastful perhaps because youthful; a feeling obvious in the press and in literature, especially the *Bulletin* and its literary school, in sport,
in commerce, indeed in every aspect of life; a demand for
the fuller recognition that a Federation could give. Thus the
campaign included appeals both to romantic sentiment and
hard-headed self-interest, and often the sentiment and self-

interest were closely connected. 'Gentlemen,' said one speaker in Tasmania,

'if you vote for the bill you will found a great and glorious nation under the bright Southern Cross, and meat will be cheaper, and you will live to see the Australian race dominate the Southern Seas, and your sons will reach a grand heritage of nationhood, and you will have a market for potatoes and apples, and if X does come back to power in Sydney he can never do you one pennyworth of harm.'[1]

In January 1895 the Premiers' Conference officially accepted the plan put forward by the Australian Natives' Association, and the fight was on in earnest. New South Wales, Victoria, South Australia and Tasmania passed acts providing for the popular election of ten delegates each to a convention, and the parliament of Western Australia agreed to nominate representatives. On March 4 1897 the elections were held and less than three weeks later the convention met at Adelaide. It included the five Premiers and two leaders of opposition, for the electors did not vote on party lines; those who appeared to be staunch federalists were chosen, and though a few subsequently opposed their own handiwork, none of the overt opponents of Federation were elected.

Agreed that the federal form should be adopted, was the central authority to be strong or weak? The thinly populated states, especially Western Australia, feared that they would be swamped by Victorians and New South Welshmen. They wanted the powers of the Commonwealth to be limited; and they wanted the states' house, the Senate where each state would have equal representation, to have the same powers as the House of Representatives which would be elected on the basis of population. On the former question they had their way. 'The powers, privileges, and territory of the several existing colonies shall remain intact,' it was resolved, except for 'such voluntary surrenders as may

---

[1] Quoted by R. S. Parker: *Historical Studies of Australia and New Zealand*, Nov. 1949, vol. iv, p. 20; (c.f. a criticism of this article, ibid., pp. 224–240).

be agreed on to secure uniformity of law and administration in matters of common concern'; of these, the most important were foreign affairs, defence, external and interstate trade and commerce, customs and excise, banking and currency, immigration and, destined to be of great importance, conciliation and arbitration in the case of industrial disputes extending beyond the limits of one state. To the states remained control of nearly all their domestic affairs—social services, health, education, labour and industry, agriculture, mines, lands, police, rivers and railways—the last the subject of a bitter dispute between New South Wales and Victoria, which was anxious to develop its Riverina trade. But even with the powers of the Commonwealth so limited, the smaller states were afraid. Could they not be unfairly taxed by the more populous states unless the Senate could reject or amend financial measures? Yes, they could; but to give the Senate such powers would be undemocratic, they were told; it would involve the rule of a minority; never could Victoria and New South Wales agree to allow the Senate to amend money bills. On this point there seemed utter deadlock; but a compromise was reached whereby the Senate might 'suggest amendments'. Even so the proposed constitution was attacked from both sides. Sir John Forrest, Premier of Western Australia, stood out to the last minute; the Labour party, particularly in New South Wales, criticized it as undemocratic, giving too much power to the less populous states, where the party was weaker.

The opposition in New South Wales was in fact a remarkably mixed bag. There was the so-called 'Geebung' party, whose 'consciences were never satisfied, unless they called their intercolonial neighbours a band of robbers'. There were the extreme free traders among the Sydney merchants, the 'Calico-Jimmy' politicians. There was a part of the Labour party which regarded Federation as a deep-laid plot by which the capitalists were planning to use the more conservative colonies to check social reform, and this view was justified to some extent by remarks such as that of the extreme conservative Bruce Smith, who argued that 'this growth upon the body politic can be removed for all time by the proposed Federation of the colonies,' or of Cardinal Moran who hoped that Federation would prove an antidote to Socialism. Even so the working class did not always follow its leaders. The labour nominees polled badly in the convention elections, and although seventeen labour members of parliament campaigned actively against Federation in the referendum, fifteen of their electorates gave a majority in favour. At the opposite extreme were the conservatives led by Dr. McLaurin, Legislative Councillor, Chancellor of Sydney University and chairman of the Bank of New South Wales, who thought the constitution too democratic with its adult franchise and elected second chamber. Moreover, despite the bitter debates of the past, there was no direct relation between free traders and protectionists, and the Federals and their opponents. Leaders (and rank and file) came from both groups. Some free traders, while afraid of a 'protected' Commonwealth, thought intercolonial free trade a sufficient compensation; others did not. Some protectionists thought on opposite lines and, looking forward to commonwealth protection for industry, were not afraid of intercolonial competition; but others were. Partly a difference of theory or outlook, it was also partly a question of what one wanted protected, and from whom. Consequently different border areas reacted differently. Northern New South Wales, with its eye on the Brisbane market, was inclined to vote 'yes'; southern Queensland and Brisbane, thinking of New South Wales competition, were strongly 'no'.

The 'outback' whether in New South Wales, Queensland or Western Australia was stongly 'federal'; in fact it was the 'outback' that carried the day in these colonies. Here seemed to be a chance to attack the vested interests in Sydney, Brisbane and Perth, which always managed to control all government and to diddle the countryman who regarded himself as the backbone of Australia. Anti-city feeling lies always close to the surface among primary producers; and the bushman felt more 'nationalist', more an Australian, in his opposition to the mutually squabbling and jealous capital cities. But in New South Wales, some country districts benefited by especially low rail freights to Sydney. Some of the less prosperous farmers, fearing interstate competition, hoped for the return of the local protection they had lost in 1896—especially against Victorian grains. (This would seem to be the principal reason for the high 'no' vote in the wheat areas.) The question of cost bulked large in the arguments of both sides. Federation would reduce New South Wales expenditure, said one. True, but the Commonwealth government would itself be extravagant, replied the other, and New South Wales as the wealthiest state would in effect be subsidizing the other colonies. Particular objection was raised to the 'Braddon blot' which provided that three-quarters of the federal customs and excise revenue should be returned to the states. This, for some reason often reiterated but never explained, was said to commit all Australia to a policy of high indirect taxation,[1] which is (correctly) believed to be unfavourable to the poor. In fact it provided a guarantee of revenue to the states, for which all state treasurers would now be extremely grateful as they make their annual pilgrimage to Canberra to ask for grants from the Commonwealth; but in 1898 it was thought unduly favourable to the small states. These were also said to be favoured by the fact that, should there be a deadlock on any measure between the two houses after a double dissolution, the final vote would be taken at a joint sitting by a three-fifths majority, thus giving undue power to the small states' 'over-representation' in the Senate.

Labour opposition in Sydney seized on these allegedly undemocratic features; for it was assumed the small states would be conservative, and why should the working man of

---

[1] Dr. H. V. Evatt, leader of the Federal Labor Party from 1951 to 1960, has repeated this argument with approval in his *Australian Labor Leader* (Sydney, 1940), pp. 98 ff., in relating W. A. Holman's objection to the clause; but his reasoning is as unconvincing now as Holman's was then.

Sydney either subsidize these reactionaries or allow them to block progressive legislation? Labour leaders in Melbourne were less critical. For Victorian industry, in its depression, was looking to the markets in the other colonies which interstate free trade would help to keep, markets where without Federation tariffs might at any time be imposed. If anything the duties payable in Victoria itself would be lowered by Federation, but to this only a group of farmers protected by the 'stock tax' and sugar duties objected. It was thought that Melbourne would gain considerably by becoming the Federal capital, but what would Sydney get out of it? Only the loss of much of the Riverina trade. Parochial jealousies were inflamed. Appeal was made to the innate prejudice of the multitude against change—a powerful force to be reckoned with by the federationists. Nor did Reid himself do much to scotch it in his 'report' at the Sydney Town Hall, where he spoke, he said, 'not as a partisan but as a judge'. He freely criticized the proposed constitution although he said he would vote for it. 'I cannot take up this bill with enthusiasm. I see serious blots in it; but I cannot become a deserter from the cause.' For this ambivalent attitude he was hailed as 'Yes-No' Reid; but as Premier of New South Wales he wanted to remain on the fence during the forthcoming state election, and it was his duty to point out what he thought were the burdens it would place on his colony. All the same, the result of the 1898 referendum was a small 'yes' majority in New South Wales, and an overwhelming victory in Victoria, Tasmania and South Australia.

Even so, there was still a great deal of apathy and opposition. The *Bulletin* deplored the 'height and depth and vastness of the popular indifference on the Federal question. Nine-tenths of the population takes no interest in the future Australian nation and nine-tenths of Australian politicians are equally indifferent.' Queensland and Western Australia were standing aloof; in the other four colonies less than half the electors had bothered to vote, so that the overall majority of two to one still meant that less than one-third of the electorate had actually voted 'yes', and most important, in New South Wales, the affirmative vote of 72,000 was 8,000 short of the minimum prescribed by the enabling act, so that technically the referendum was lost.

A further Premiers' Conference, now attended by Queensland, was held in Melbourne. Four amendments were made. The new capital was to be in New South Wales, though at least one hundred miles from Sydney. The 'deadlock' majority was reduced from the three-fifths to an 'absolute majority'. This was a victory of no great importance for 'democracy' seeing that such a vote has never been taken, but in 1901 the fear of 'big' versus 'little' states contests was a perfect nightmare to politicians who were unused to the working of a strict party system in their separate colonies and could not foresee it in the Commonwealth. The 'Braddon clause' was limited to ten years, but, finally, in its place the Commonwealth was empowered to make grants to the states, a provision which in time would completely reduce them to dependence on the Federal government.[1] These changes, added to another year's propaganda for the cause, were sufficient to carry the day. At the 1899 referendum, sixty per cent of the electorate voted, and seventy-two per cent of those voting or forty-three per cent of all electors approved the constitution. In the southern colonies the opposition was negligible, for South Australia improved its 'yes' vote from two to one to five to one, and Victoria and Tasmania voted fifteen to one. In New South Wales the figures were 107,000 to 83,000 (instead of 72,000 to 66,000); the narrowest squeak was in Queensland, which approved by only 38,000 to 31,000.

This was partly due to the lack of previous propaganda. In Queensland there had been no earlier referendum; there were few Federal Leagues; Griffith, a staunch advocate in 1891, had retired from politics to become Chief Justice. In addition the federal cause was bedevilled by the demand of

[1] See pp. 261 et seq.

the North Queenslanders to secede from the colony, irritated as they were by poor communications and apparent neglect of their interests and fearful of losing their supply of black labour. Refused outright separation or even a local 'state' federation in 1895, the northerners were looking to Australian federation as at least a partial escape from Brisbane. Even if it did mean the end of coloured labour, it would bring a continental free market for sugar, which would almost certainly be protected against imports. For northerners, defence and New Guinea were important; these questions would be better handled by a federal government. But in south Queensland farmers, merchants, manufacturers and workers were afraid of New South Wales competition under a system of intercolonial free trade; all the metropolitan electorates voted 'no', and so did the immediate hinterland of Brisbane and parts of the Darling Downs. The Labor party campaigned against the bill, though for reasons 'not very clear to themselves', according to one historian of the party. Judging from the figures, although the city workers may have been dubious, fearing unemployment, shearers and station hands despite the exhortations of the *Worker* must have voted 'yes', possibly by extending the doctrine of mateship, and possibly through seeing greater security in a federal 'White Australia'.[1]

Western Australia remained outside to the last moment. In the 'sixties it had provoked one of the earliest examples of federal feeling, the Anti-Transportation league, which was formed in the eastern colonies to protest against Western Australia's continued reception of transported British convicts. After this stopped in 1868 the development of the colony was slow. The north-west was still largely unexplored and attempts at settlement there were only moderately successful until the discovery and opening up of the Kimberleys in the 'eighties. Railway-building lagged, the educational system was backward, and not only had no serious attempt been made to solve the aboriginal problem but the

[1] See p. 181.

record of Western Australians in native affairs was so bad that the British government kept control over native administration for seven years after it granted responsible government in other matters in 1890. The population was then only about 50,000, but the sensational gold discoveries at Coolgardie in 1892 and Kalgoorlie on the 'Golden Mile', two years later, not only attracted miners from the east but encouraged agriculture as well.

In ten years the population grew to 180,000, but became fiercely divided into two groups, the farmers near Perth and in the south-east, and the miners who thought their interests were neglected by the government. They wanted telegraphs, railways and above all water supplies for the goldfields, and they even looked to Federation as a possible salvation. Sir John Forrest, the Premier, tried to hold the balance between miners and farmers. The telegraph and the railway were extended eastwards, and the ambitious goldfields water-supply project, involving a 350-mile pipeline from near Perth was begun; at the same time some of the agricultural areas of the colony were opened up by more railway-building and wheat production tripled. But many farmers looked with misgiving on the intercolonial free trade that Federation would bring, and feared that a national tariff on manufacturers would mean higher costs.

Forrest agreed. He feared that 'the West' would be swamped in Federation; he consented to hold a referendum on the matter only in response to the urgent prompting of the British Colonial Secretary, Joseph Chamberlain, while the delegates from the other colonies were actually in London to arrange for the Commonwealth of Australia Bill to be passed through the British Parliament. The colony was remote, a week's sea journey from Melbourne. Half her revenue came from the customs, largely from duties on imports from the other colonies. If that were taken away, it would be necessary to impose direct taxation! 'The people would not vote for Federation under the circumstances,' said one opponent, using the word 'people' when he meant 'wealthy'. But the government's hand was forced by pressure from the goldfields. It was not that they were the only newcomers to the colony, the so-called 't'othersiders', for there was also a large immigrant population in the farming areas that supported Forrest and strongly opposed Federation. But the miners were not interested in colonial protection; and they were the people most directly interested in the building of a transcontinental railway which they hoped Federation would bring. They were supported by big majorities throughout the 'outback' and up the north coast; they even threatened to separate from the rest of the colony so as to be able to join the Commonwealth. Eventually many of the opposition, realizing how disastrous it would be for 'the West' if the goldfields were to secede and join separately, became reconciled to their fate, and when the referendum was at last held it was carried by the surprisingly large majority of 45,000 votes to 20,000.

By this time the Commonwealth Constitution Act had been passed by the British Parliament, virtually without change. Chamberlain had wanted to permit appeals from the High Court to the Privy Council in constitutional cases, as well as on other subjects, but the Australian delegates argued that the constitution should always be interpreted in Australia. For a short time yet another deadlock seemed imminent, but in the end it was agreed that appeals could be made except where the dispute was over the constitutional powers *inter se* of State and Commonwealth, and so the last hurdle was cleared. On 1 January 1901 the new Commonwealth of Australia came into existence, a Commonwealth, it was hoped, which 'would dominate the Southern Seas, of which any man might be proud to be a citizen, and which would be a permanent glory to the British Empire'.

Chapter Thirteen

DEVELOPMENT RENEWED

In 1901 the newly formed Commonwealth was by no means a great or a prosperous dominion, but at least the long depression seemed to be lifting. Helped by the policies of the new government prosperity gradually returned, together with a revival of confidence both economic and political, which brought more immigrants and further development. Certainly, intercolonial jealousies were not banished overnight; the habit of 'thinking federally' took long to acquire and even now is not fully achieved. The very existence of the Federal capital at Canberra is a perpetual reminder of local rivalries. But the Federal government could and did do much to foster national feeling. Australia's small population and her continued dependence on Britain for defence obviously limited her freedom in the conduct of foreign affairs; but in their economic policies Australian governments were less inhibited, and from the first year of the Commonwealth appeared that attitude of 'economic nationalism', which has been almost unchallengeable dogma ever since.

Its most striking manifestation is in the policy of 'White Australia', now more euphemistically described as 'Immigration Restriction'. Hostility to coloured labour had existed throughout the nineteenth century—and not only in the minds of the 'workers'. The restriction of Chinese immigration was one of the few agreements achieved even before Federation. As early as 1840 Sir James Stephen had warned the Governor of New South Wales of the social dangers of admitting the Asiatic coolies that some of the squatters

wished to bring to the country; nor can any observer or
South Africa or the Southern States of the U.S.A. now fail
to rejoice that the colour problem at least is one which
Australia has never had to face. But the objection was far
more than one of colour. Xenophobia of all types has never
been far from the patriotic Australian who is[1] often almost
as ready to curse that 'Pommy bastard', his term of endear-
ment for the British migrant, as the foreigner of any colour.
If the legislators of 1901 objected to 'the nation of yesterday'
(China) and the 'servile nations of the world' (coloured),
they were also doubtful whether the Italian walking about
'with a knife in his hand and a razor in his pocket' was 'civilized in the ordinary sense'. The basis of this clap-trap was
economic, the fear of the hard work of the foreigner, of
sweated labour and of the undermining of the 'Australian
standard of living'. It was not 'the bad qualities but the good
qualities of these alien races that make them dangerous to
us', said Deakin, 'it is their inexhaustible energy . . . their
endurance and their low standard of living that make them
such competitors.' Consequently not only must cheap
'sweatable' labour be kept out of the country by the expedi-
ent of a dictation test which may be given to any immigrant,
English or other, in any European language ranging from
Irish to Magyar,[2] but the products of such labour must be
excluded too. Hence the need for tariff protection, which
was accepted as the national policy soon after Federation
despite some opposition from the surviving free traders of
New South Wales. 'The unanswerable argument for Protection' (it is the voice of Deakin again) 'is that if you want
to maintain a high standard among the workers of a community, so that these men may live the life of civilized be-
ings, then you must impose duties to protect them against

[1] Or perhaps one should say 'was', because it is possible he is becoming more
reasonable with greater experience, and as a more justified self-confidence in his
own abilities replaces the vainglorious boastings of the past.

[2] On one occasion an expert linguist was tested in Gaelic to make sure he
would fail, but the High Court held that this was not a living European
language.

the underpaid labour, the serf labour, the prison labour of foreign lands where less happy conditions prevail.'

This argument soon converted the Labor party which held the balance of political power in the Federal parliament, and in 1907 the idea of extending protection to labour by means of the tariff was explicitly provided for. Henceforth, Australian manufacturers would have to pay excise duties at the same rate as those on imports unless they paid wages and provided working conditions that were adjudged 'fair and reasonable'. This was the 'New Protection'; 'old' protection had only made 'good wages possible'; now they were to be made 'actual'. Naturally labour was pleased, and so were the more orthodox protectionists who regarded 'protection as a synonym for patriotism', a slogan which had great appeal to the temper of the times. So in 1908 disappeared the 'wishy-washy half-and-half tariff' that did nothing but raise revenue. In more ways than federating could Australia copy the United States of America.

None the less there was a snag. What were the 'fair and reasonable' wages and working conditions prescribed by the Excise Duties Act? They were to be certified by the President of the Arbitration Court, but as Mr. Justice Higgins, the gentleman concerned, complained, Parliament gave him no criteria for interpreting the phrase. Therefore it was hardly surprising that the Court began, as it has since continued, with a somewhat hit-or-miss method of adjudication. Perhaps this accords with another alleged Australian characteristic, indicated by the phrase, 'it'll do'; perhaps it indicates a preference of some democratic politicians for shelving responsibility. At all events, Mr. Higgins grasped the nettle firmly, and his first judgement, in the 'harvester' case, was epoch-making. It provided the basis of Australian wages for a generation, and it still constitutes a slogan to which unionists can appeal when feeling 'tetchy', though their reactions if such an appeal were taken seriously to-day would be interesting to observe. But in 1907 Mr. Justice Higgins was noted for his sympathy with the under-dog.

Had he not as a Victorian M.P. supported Protection, even in 1895, because he wanted to keep the people in 'good employment, in healthy conditions and working short hours'?[1] Had he not supported the establishment of the Commonwealth Arbitration Court from the conviction that 'if human life is to be used for the purpose of profit, it must not be used to its degradation?... Human life is the most valuable asset of any country, and our duty is to see that that life is not so employed that the health and vitality of the community are lowered'. To ensure this most desirable objective he decided that wages to be 'fair and reasonable' must be sufficient to 'satisfy the normal needs of the average employee regarded as a human being living in a civilized community'; and by a brilliant judicial *tour de force* he succeeded in translating all six question-begging indefinables into a figure of 7s. per day, since 6s. per day would only allow 3s. 7d. weekly for 'light, clothes, boots, furniture and utensils, rates, life insurance, savings, sickness and accidents, fares, unemployment, union fees, school requisites, holidays and amusements, tobacco, alcohol, religion and charity'— which obviously any 'reasonable' man would agree was insufficient. Henceforward this figure was the minimum he would prescribe in making any award in any industrial dispute that was brought before the Arbitration Court; and as more and more disputes were so brought, it gradually became the 'basis' of the Australian wage structure, which was modified in 1912 by 'certain curious and interesting figures, the result of much valuable research and calculation', which enabled him to measure changes in the 'cost-of-living'.

Although this remained the standard for Federal awards in industrial disputes, the policy of 'New Protection' was declared unconstitutional by the High Court. Established in 1903 as Australian court of appeal and interpreter of the constitution, in this latter function the High Court showed itself in the first years of its existence as the jealous watch-

[1] At that time, this meant 48 per week.

dog of the rights of the states. Australia was a 'federation'
not a 'union', and the 'essence and life' of the Federal constitution lay in the 'poise and balance' between Commonwealth and States. To the Federal government had been
given powers to legislate on certain subjects only; other subjects remained under state control. The power to levy excise
duties admittedly belonged to the Commonwealth; but
what if a duty was imposed for the purpose of regulating
industrial conditions—a matter which was reserved for the
states? The High Court held that in this case the duty was
invalid. Industrial conditions could not be regulated by the
Commonwealth in this way, and in a number of other cases
the High Court held Federal legislation unconstitutional.
The Trade Marks Act, prescribing that goods made by
trade-union labour only should carry the 'union label', was
held to be not legitimate legislation about trade marks, but
another illegitimate attempt to regulate industrial conditions
indirectly. The same reasoning was used when the Commonwealth attempted to control monopolies through its powers
over interstate trade and regarding 'corporations'. In 1911,
owing to their dissatisfaction with these decisions, the
Labor party tried to amend the constitution so as to give
more powers to the Federal government, but its proposals
were defeated at the necessary referendum, as so many similar proposals have been since. 'States-righters' are always
active and there is popular resistance to change. Opponents
of 'government interference' can be relied on to resist, just
as the political opponents of any government proposing a
referendum can be relied on to oppose it. Sometimes, indeed, even its supporters are lukewarm, as for example in
the 1911 campaign itself when the New South Wales labour
leaders were by no means enthusiastic about transferring any
powers to the Commonwealth where, they argued, the
'conservatives' were relatively stronger.

In fact, these conservatives had little say in Federal politics
before World War I. Up to 1909 the Labor party held the
balance of power in parliament, and was able to follow a

policy of 'support in return for concessions'. Deakin, the liberal-protectionist leader, deplored the 'three elevens in the field', but much of the voting strength of his 'middle party' came from Victoria, where not only was Protection the traditional policy, but 'liberalism' was more 'radical' than in most of the other colonies. The party was therefore, according to Deakin himself, able to ally itself with labour without loss of its independence or any sacrifice of its own policy. He deplored 'socialism', but the Labor party as such was hardly 'socialist' except in the eyes of its more rabid opponents, and Deakin realized the need for 'employing the machinery of the State to cope with the very great injuries which at present beset our social system'. This explains his support of compulsory arbitration in industrial disputes, as an assistance to the weaker party, his adoption of the 'New Protection', unconstitutional though it proved, and his introduction of a Federal scheme of Old Age Pensions in 1908. But gradually Labor became dissatisfied—'if the only idea of progress is Protection, it won't fill the bill,' said its leader. It withdrew support from Deakin, who then made his famous 'fusion' with the Free Trade party, relatively conservative and for some time engaged in a violent attack on that almost mythical creature the 'socialist tiger'. But the fusion was a failure. Stigmatized with that delightful originality which is such a feature of Australian politics as a 'Judas', Deakin himself admitted that behind him 'sat all his opponents since Federation' and at the elections of 1910 the Labor party won a large majority in its own right. Though its proposed constitutional amendments for the increase of Federal powers were defeated, the new Fisher ministry established a Commonwealth Bank, imposed a heavily progressive land tax with the avowed object of 'breaking-up' large estates, introduced a maternity allowance, popularly called the 'baby bonus', and extended by its Navigation Act the system of protection and the regulation of working conditions to Australian coastal shipping.

In all this the Federal government was but carrying on

where state governments left off. The Australian liberal had never been a diehard believer in *laissez-faire*, and if he ever seemed to be forgetting the need of the poorer sections of the community for help from the state, after 1890 at least the Labor party was there to jog his memory. Perhaps it is no coincidence that in Victoria where the liberals were most 'radical' labour was weakest politically. It was certainly not due to the weakness of Trade Unionism there, or the backwardness of manufactures. Liberals like Berry, Deakin, Higgins, Peacock, even Turner, had always been ready to support state action for the regulation and reform of abuses, action which not even the conservatism of the Legislative Councils was willing steadfastly to resist. It was a Liberal member of a Liberal cabinet who declared in 1894 that a man told to go to the bush to seek work 'was like one of those doves that Noah sent out of the ark and saw only a waste of waters. . . . We are our brothers' keeper, and the State as representing the corporate conscience and the corporate philanthropy owes a duty to those whom we have shut out from their natural opportunities. . . . I am glad to see that liberalism is striking its tents against any fixed belief in *laissez-faire*.' And so by a series of Acts, mostly modelled on those of England, though differing in each state, governments provided for employers' liability for accidents to workmen, regulated working conditions and limited hours in factories and workshops, in the mines and in the shearing sheds, in retail shops and on ships. Not that there were no critics to say that such legislation should have been passed sooner, or should have been more drastic, but certainly by the combined action of liberals and labour men a great deal of social legislation was on the statute books of the various states by 1910.

Of all this legislation the experiments in industrial arbitration were the most significant. In this field of social reform, Australasia, including New Zealand, was a pioneer, not in so far as the idea of outside arbitration or mediation in industrial disputes was concerned, but in giving this power to a state tribunal and making its award compulsory on the parties. During the strike of 1890 the unions had wanted a conference but the employers had refused. Deakin thought this 'arbitrary, unfair and a public calamity'; he greatly feared the effects of the 'disastrous' defeat the unions had suffered, and many impartial public men agreed. Could such a refusal be prevented in the future? Possibly, if arbitration were made compulsory and entrusted to the state. Labor was not at once convinced, especially about compulsion. It was still somewhat suspicious of the state. But the complete failure of the voluntary conciliation system introduced in New South Wales in 1891 converted it, and before 1900 in every state it was supporting, if not demanding, compulsory arbitration. Victoria adopted the Wages Board system, of the type later introduced in England by the Trades Boards Act of 1909; New South Wales and later the Commonwealth preferred the 'court' system of arbitration by a Judge. Only the representatives of 'organizations' could appear before the court, whose existence therefore directly encouraged the growth of unionism—a result unwelcome neither to the liberal-radical like Deakin who looked on the union as a necessary protection for the working man, nor naturally enough to the unions themselves.

Criticism was to be expected. Some employers and their political spokesmen preferred the 'board' system; some Labor representatives were reluctant to surrender the 'right to strike'; there was considerable confusion about the place and scope of 'conciliation' as opposed to 'arbitration'. Up to 1914 the arbitration idea was by no means universally accepted, apart from the many obvious defects so apparent in the early days of this 'great experiment'—the law's delays, its expense, and the legal technicalities and constitutional restrictions which created a 'veritable Serbonian bog' blocking the Commonwealth court especially. This tribunal could not deal with disputes in one state only, so sometimes an interstate dispute might be 'manufactured' to bring the case under Federal jurisdiction if it was hoped to get a more

favourable decision there than from a state authority. Inter-
court competition for business did not help to establish industrial peace. Workmen in the same factory might be employed under different, even conflicting, awards. The judges
were not 'experts' and often failed to understand the complex industrial processes they were trying to regulate. The
High Court, in its defence of State powers and rights, so
rigidly limited the jurisdiction of the Commonwealth Arbitration Court, as to threaten, according to its President, Mr.
Justice Higgins, a 'gradual paralysis of its functions'. Perhaps
he was biased. An enthusiastic supporter of the arbitration
system by which he was trying to create 'a new province of
law and order', he strongly resented the limitations on his
powers. Up to 1916 he could truly claim there had been no
strike against an award of his court, and he declared it was
'no more necessary for the workers to strike to obtain just
working conditions, than for a Chinaman to burn down his
house whenever he wanted roast pork'. Perhaps this was due
to Higgins's general sympathy with the worker and to his
view that it was the duty of the Court to 'act as a check on
the despotic power of the employer'. The state tribunals,
especially in New South Wales, were far less successful, and
from 1908 to 1914 the industrial history of Australia was
stormy. Rising prices created unrest; many unions, under
the influence of the newly arrived I.W.W. (Industrial
Workers of the World), once again asserted their preference
for 'direct action'; some ostrich-like employers were still unwilling to 'recognize' unionism, including notably the Brisbane Tramway Company with its American manager whose
intransigeance caused a general strike 'for the very principle
of Unionism' which almost paralysed the city in February
1912.

But the regulation of industry, whether by court or legislation, was but one aspect of what was described as 'socialisme sans doctrines', or alternatively that 'ill-defined blend of
radicalism, socialism and Trade Unionism, making up the
Progressive programme which aimed at securing a greater

share of comfort and opportunity for the great human mass'. As early as 1893 it had been alleged that, planted in Australia, 'the Englishmen to whom St. Simon and Fourier (would one now say Marx?) are names of derision, if they are even names, is rapidly creating a State Socialism . . . which surpasses its continental models'. State activity, and state assistance even to the staunchest individualists, could be found everywhere, and was ever expanding. It was not only that the state was asked to build railways or irrigation works requiring far greater resources of capital than private companies could provide; these 'utilities' were then required to grant favourable rates or to operate at a loss in order to help 'private enterprise' develop the country. Between 1886 and 1892 the Victorian government spent nearly £2,000,000 on the purchase of mining machinery for private companies. In 1891 a Victorian parliamentary committee, with a conservative squatter as chairman, recommended the paying of a bonus on black coal to encourage its production, remarking that 'it has proved almost impracticable to develop our coalfields by private enterprise . . . owing to a want of confidence that coal mining in Victoria can be made a successful undertaking'. It seemed quite in order for the state to step in and bear the loss, although in fact nothing was done for twenty years. The farmer always thought himself 'anti-socialist', but he believed in letting not his individualistic right hand know what his socialist left hand was doing (or taking). By 1900 he had succeeded in getting the state to help him to buy his land on the cheap, water it by irrigation, transport his crop at low rates by building uneconomic railways, protect his market by the tariff, provide him with cheap credit which he often refused to pay back, lend him money to help to destroy pests, like the rabbit or phylloxera, and help him to improve his technique by establishing agricultural colleges and research stations at the public expense; but of course he retained his liberty to attack 'experts' and decry 'new-fangled notions' whenever these institutions made any suggestions he disapproved of, or which involved any initial expense that the government might be reluctant to meet.

With all this help, and the further stimulus of rising world prices, it is not surprising that the farmer was able to recover from the depression of the 'nineties. In New South Wales, Carruthers, Minister of Lands under Reid, amended the land acts in 1895 to permit the virtual lending of land to genuine settlers at a nominal rent, thus letting the settler keep his own capital for making improvements. Later Closer Settlement Acts, modelled on that of Victoria in 1898, provided for the purchase of land by the government, and its re-sale on easy terms to farmers, who were further helped by receiving cheap credit from the State Savings or Agricultural Banks. Much public money was lost in this way. The land was bought too dear and the lots provided for settlers often in places too dry to be regularly profitable, like the Victorian Mallee. The settlers often had insufficient capital, and because a decent-sized property seemed 'undemocratic,' farms were nearly always too small for Australian conditions. The result was that sooner or later much of the farmer's indebtedness to the state had to be cancelled. But between 1891 and 1914 the area under crop rose from less than 850,000 acres to 3,400,000 acres in New South Wales, from two million to nearly four million acres in Victoria, and from almost nothing to over one million acres in Western Australia; the Australian wheat harvest of forty-eight million bushels in 1900 was over a hundred million in 1913; the yield was more than eleven bushels per acre, instead of eight and a half. South Australia was no longer 'the granary of the continent' with almost half its cultivated land as in 1880 (though in 1911 she had nearly three million acres under crop); but South Australian farmers were the first to listen to the 'experts' of Roseworthy College who were advising the use of superphosphate, known in England since the 'forties, and their example slowly spread to Victoria and New South Wales. The 'dry farming' technique of working fallow land extended the area of the wheat lands; even more important was the 'seed-breeding' of William Farrer, who after years of experimenting produced in 1902 a rust- and drought-resistant strain, named 'Federation', which, though since then much further improved, 'as dramatically as Macarthur's merinos laid the firm basis of a great exporting industry', helped as it was by the recent building of railways to the wheatlands.

Meanwhile refrigeration had made possible the export of butter, frozen meat and fruit. Butter production in Victoria, New South Wales and Queensland quadrupled between 1890 and 1914, to reach 100,000 tons, providing another profitable employment for the small farmer. In Tasmania, if he could not produce butter, he could and did grow apples. The frozen meat market gave a second string to the pastoralists' bow, especially in the wetter districts where the crossbred often throve better than the merino, and the profits from fat lambs gave welcome aid to the mixed farmer. But the pure merino took longer to recover from depression. Low wool prices, higher wages, heavy debts and the rabbit, a serious menace since the mid 'eighties, had compelled many outback graziers to surrender their leases in the early 'nineties. Then came the 'great drought', with eight successive years of subnormal rainfall, culminating in the Sahara year of 1902. In 1891 there were one hundred and six million sheep in Australia; in 1900, seventy million; in 1902, fifty-four million; and though the wool-clip fell less, it dropped from 640,000,000 to 410,000,000 pounds. Not until 1928 were there again a hundred million sheep in the country, but by 1914 thanks to subdivision, the better watering of paddocks from artesian wells, the more careful culling of the merino and the top-dressing of pastures the clip was back to 771,000,000 pounds from about ninety million sheep. The pastoralist had profited by his adversity, and could possibly reconcile himself to it with the reflection that a dry land, allowed by Nature to lie fallow periodically by drought, is necessary to grow the best merino wool in the world.

This rural recovery and expansion were accompanied by a similar process in industry, although in 1911 as in 1891 a third of Australian breadwinners were still employed in primary production. Industry was hit harder by the crash of 1891 and took longer to recover; there was no immediate technical development to encourage it, as in wheat growing and dairying. There had been some expansion, it is true, for the population had grown from three million to four and a half; but this was almost entirely by natural increase. Except to the Western Australian goldfields, immigration ceased, and in fact departures were greater than arrivals in Victoria, South Australia and Tasmania until 1905 (in Tasmania until 1940). Only after 1906 did the states begin to assist migrants again, at first in New South Wales; but despite vigorous advocacy of imperial migration by Alfred Deakin, and some rather lurid and misleading advertisements, it proved difficult to attract adults suitable for Australian rural life, and manufactures still played a relatively small part in the economy. They were chiefly confined to making commodities tied to primary production or satisfying the immediate needs of consumers—clothing, food and drink, machinery, wood-working, vehicles, saddlery and printing, but to this there was one striking exception in the rise of B.H.P.

The Broken Hill Proprietary Company, Limited, to give it its full name, was originally floated in 1885 to carry on mining operations on the Broken Hill silver-lead minefield. Its leases had been first pegged out in 1883 by a group of men employed on the Mount Gipps sheep station, on the 'broken hill' a few miles from what was then the centre of operations at Silverton. Two of the partners sold their shares before ore was found on the lease; another played euchre to decide the price he should be paid for half his share, which in three years was worth £640,000. But before the riches were won, the original syndicate formed a public company, putting up two thousand £20 shares for public subscription, and with this capital started operations. In six years, silver and lead worth £7,000,000 were recovered. After 1891 the company had its vicissitudes. A fall in the price of silver and lead caused the company to repudiate the wage agreement it had signed with the miners' union only a year before. A long lock-out followed, but the men were beaten and had to resume work on the company's terms. By 1896 a further 50,000,000 ounces of silver and 200,000 tons of lead had been mined, not to mention 20,000 ounces of gold. In 1897 it established its smelting works at Port Pirie on the coast; in 1902 it applied the newly discovered 'floatation' process to the treatment of the zinc sulphide now being mined in large quantities and turned a useless 'dump' into valuable mineral. Next it began to manufacture spelter at Port Pirie from the zinc concentrate produced at Broken Hill; then to build a sulphuric acid plant and to make super-phosphates; then to make its own coke for its smelters. All this obviously meant a substantial widening of its operations, so that when mining was halted in 1908 by another price fall and increasing costs of extraction as the mine was gradually being worked out, the company was by no means at the end of its tether. It tried to reduce wages, but Mr. Justice Higgins in the Commonwealth Arbitration Court refused to allow it, because the 'living wage must be kept sacrosanct. . . . If a man cannot maintain his enterprise without cutting down the wages which are proper to be paid to his employees, which are essential for their living, he had better abandon his enterprise; if shareholders are willing to stake their own money on a speculation they should not stake part of the employees' proper wage also. . . . There is no reason why the minimum wage should be cut down because of the present unproductive character of speculative property. . . . Dividends should not be distributed at the cost of the workmen's breakfast table—by reducing the food necessary for his wife and children.' Thus repulsed, the company shut down its mine until higher prices ruled again in 1911. But the wealth of the Proprietary mine was gone and the future of Broken Hill lay with other companies whose leases were not yet worked out; the future of the B.H.P. Company lay elsewhere—in iron and steel. In 1899 it had acquired leases at Iron Knob and Iron Monarch, two veritable hills of iron near Whyalla in South Australia, to supply iron as a flux for its lead smelters at Port Pirie. The ore was extraordinarily rich, seventy per cent metallic iron, so that when faced with the exhaustion of its mine at Broken Hill the company had a strong incentive, if it found other conditions favourable, to consider establishing a steel works. In 1911 it decided to do so.

Iron and steel were being made in Australia at this time (in fact an iron works had been opened as early as 1848) but the industry had never been profitable and in 1910 the firm of G. & C. Hoskins Ltd., which had bought the near bankrupt Eskbank Iron Works at Lithgow in 1908, was the only Australian producer. It was helped by the bounty of 12s. a ton which the Commonwealth Government agreed to pay in 1908 as part of its policy of high protection, and by a long-term contract with the state government of New South Wales which enabled the firm to expand its plant with an assured market, but it was handicapped by the high cost of freight to Sydney. The state Labor government, elected in 1910, was hostile, for Hoskins had been involved in industrial trouble and was strongly anti-labour politically, and the government was considering cancelling the contract and establishing a state steel works in accordance with its policy of nationalizing monopolies. An English expert, appointed by the government, advised that this should be done. He thought that if a steel works were established on the coast it would be profitable; it could be planned on a scale to supply all the iron and steel requirements of the Commonwealth and the cost of its products would compare favourably with the current price of British imports. The government had decided to go ahead, when B.H.P. announced that it too wanted to build a steel works and wanted help. B.H.P., like the New South Wales government, thought that steel production in Australia would be profitable; and unlike the government, it had very rich iron leases. It, too, wanted to establish its works near the Newcastle coalfield to minimize transport costs, since it then took about three tons of coal to make a ton of steel; but B.H.P. needed to acquire land on the water front and it wanted improved harbour facilities. The government, pressed by its desire to satisfy Newcastle and to establish a new industry in the state, conquered its theoretical objection to private monopoly and its preference for a state works, and agreed to the company's requests. Work began at Newcastle—dredging the channel, reclaiming land, building the blast furnace. Capital proved hard to raise, for the famous initiative of private enterprise was not conspicuously forthcoming. But the company had huge reserves accumulated from its mining profits; its directors, especially John Darling, invested large amounts of their private fortunes, the Commonwealth Bank, founded in 1912, underwrote a debenture issue that the private banks would not look at (it was 'not in accordance with the traditions of strict banking business'), and the work went on. In March 1915 the blast furnace was 'blown in'.

Thus the greatest single industrial advance of the early years of the Commonwealth was not in fact accomplished before the war. Since 1890, industry had not advanced relatively to agriculture, but in 1910 the Labor party, the party of the 'working man', swept the country, even though only two years before 'some years of barren opposition' had been predicted for it. Liberals were astounded—and horrified. Here was the 'red dragon' at large. Actually, it was not very red; how could it be, since it had obviously attracted the votes of many of the middle class? Its programme was not extreme, and differed little from the erstwhile liberals', for it had never tried to 'cry for the moon' but was willing to accept 'what was immediate and practical'. Herein lay at once its strength and its weakness—its strength because it could attract (and always has attracted) many middle-class votes; its weakness, because its political spokesmen, so dependent on these votes, have often been at odds with an industrial wing more ready to think only of the interests of one class which, however important, is only a minority in the community as a whole. Before 1900 every member of the Parliamentary party had agreed in the interests of unity to accept the decision of the majority of the party voting in 'caucus' on all important questions. This caucus control was denounced by its opponents (possibly jealous of the party discipline so conspicuously lacking in their own organizations) as destroying the 'liberty of the individual elector and the individual representative'; but though it did the latter, if anything it increased the power of the elector by making his member a mere delegate pledged under all circumstances to carry out the wishes of the party. But what were the wishes of the party? It was in interpreting these wishes that a widening cleavage appeared between the Members of Parliament and those outside, particularly union leaders. Members were often condemned as opportunists, out of touch with the rank and file, thinking of their salaries and privileges and only anxious to keep their seats. 'Once you allow the politician to boss the show,' declared the President of the 1907 Party Conference, 'he will give away everything to save himself.' This internal conflict has never been far from the surface, but it tends to be worse when the party is in power than when in opposition; for as cabinet ministers the political leaders have even greater need to remember their responsibilities to the whole country, while in opposition all can join in a common criticism of their opponents. By 1910 there had already been one fierce fight between politicians and 'the movement' in Queensland, and another was brewing in New South Wales, but the bitter antagonisms that were to bedevil the movement during and after the war, and in the fight for control by the powerful Australian Workers' Union, were still in the future. The ill-starred 'fusion' of 1909 left Labor as the principal party of progress; and what is more, it seemed the party expressing Australian national sentiment, and asserting the primacy of local interests as against those of Britain—though certainly never to the point of straining the elastic 'bonds of Empire'. Even in this respect it wanted to go little farther than Deakin had done at the Imperial Conference of 1907; but then Deakin had been 'captured'; and his nationalist as well as his progressive ideas seemed now to be controlled by his more conservative, more 'English', associates.

There was little feeling of 'working-class internationalism' in the Australian Labor party at this time. 'Australia for the Australians' was one slogan, and White Australia another; and though the seventh international Socialist Congress in 1907 might resolve that it was the duty of the working class everywhere to oppose wars, in 1903 the fighting platform of the Australian Labor party had included as one of its 'planks' the establishment of a citizen defence force, shortly after the youthful W. M. Hughes had declared in Parliament that it was the first duty of every man to defend his country, and that universal compulsory military service was the only democratic way of doing so. This 'democratic' argument, standing in contrast to the 'militarist' idea of a permanent 'class' army, won many supporters. Japan's victory over Russia in 1905 ushered in a spate of yellow peril propaganda. In 1908 the Labor party definitely committed itself to compulsory military training, while the conservatives still opposed it; and though the 'fusion' government, under Deakin's influence, did introduce compulsory service in 1909, it is probably true to say that the Labor party was the more enthusiastic about the scheme.

It was the same with the Navy. Though 'conservative imperialists' had been willing since 1887 to contribute towards the cost of the Royal Navy, radical nationalists wanted an Australian Navy. They repudiated the idea that the country was 'poor, forsaken, without administrative brains, courage, enterprise or intelligence, worthy only to drudge for the money . . . and to provide the lob-lolly boys, the slushers and the deck-swabbers'. Labor spokesmen strongly backed this demand and supported Deakin, on his return from the Imperial Conference of 1907, when he announced that Australia was to have such a fleet; and it was the Fisher Labor Government that in March 1909 ordered its first three ships. 'No community which is not charged with the ordinary business of its own defence', Mr. Gladstone had declared more than fifty years before, 'is really or can be in the full sense of the word a free community.' Now Australia was free and ready to assume at least some of the responsibilities of freedom; although, since without British sea power behind her, her local defences would have been but puny, it was only natural that Great Britain should continue to control the general foreign policy of the Empire. As time went on, and the dangers of war loomed nearer, Australian governments were more and more being informed, if not consulted, about foreign affairs at successive Imperial Conferences, and consulted as well as informed about Imperial defence.

For in the early years of the Commonwealth, the rabid and often anti-British Australian nationalism of the late nineteenth century was becoming more and more Imperial in sentiment. Not only did Britain back up Australian defences, she was Australia's best market, and the source of her best migrants. Deakin especially wanted to tighten the bonds of Empire; to create 'a unity of action, of sympathy and of aim' throughout the Empire, to establish Imperial preference in tariff policy and to bring out British migrants to fill Australia's 'vast open spaces'. By 1910 the Australian people and their governments were in another mood of optimistic expansion. Assisted migration was revived in all states and 200,000 migrants were attracted between 1911 and 1914. 'Closer settlement' schemes were advertised with the best and latest publicity stunts to attract settlers from Britain, like the Victorian pamphlet, *The Speedway to Rural Prosperity*, consisting, according to a later Royal Commission, of 'turgid panegyriecs of farming conditions, like a salesman's puffing generalities which most people have learned to discount when not uttered on behalf of governments'.

Even the Northern Territory was not entirely forgotten when the Commonwealth Government took over its administration in 1911. A commission of inquiry recommended railway building to help the stock raising for which the territory is best suited (every inquiry since then has reached the same conclusion); it thought there might be possibilities in mining. The government did little about railways (like every later government), but spent much money on experimental farms sixty miles from Darwin and on the Daly River; it offered free land and financial help to farmers who were prepared to ignore the pessimistic conclusions that the commission of inquiry had formed about tropical agriculture in the territory; it arranged with Vestey's to establish a meat works at Darwin to treat five hundred cattle a day, despite the fact that there were no suitable cattle in the district, and that the lack of proper rail and wharf facilities made it almost impossible to bring stock from the interior to the port, or subsequently to ship the meat to market. However, if the Commonwealth Government spent £10,000,000 on the territory between 1910 and 1929 in order to increase its poulation from 3,301 to 3,982 and its cattle from 500,000 to 800,000, at least it was rather more successful in introducing white settlers to the tropical Queensland coast. It put an end to the employment of coloured labour on the canefields by ordering the deportation of Kanakas and paying a substantial bounty on sugar produced by 'whites', and it imposed a heavy duty on cheap imported coloured-grown sugar. As a result the local crop doubled between 1900 and 1910, when over 26,000 were employed in the industry, and the Australian consumer was paying only one halfpenny a pound extra for implementing the White Australia policy.

Tropical Queensland is in fact one of the few parts of the world where white settlement at low altitudes has been a success, and where the white man has not depended on a large native population to work for him. Whether on the coastal canefields or in the cattle country of the interior, he has been healthy and prosperous; settlement has been only checked by the lack of rain in the interior. Northern Australia is virtually a huge cattle ranch, carrying about five beasts to the square mile, with a few mining camps scattered through it. Tropical agriculture is impossible over the divide and the heat and the dingoes make the land more suitable for cattle, which can run in widely fenced, or unfenced, country and travel long distances to water, than it is for sheep. On the Barkly Tableland, on Victoria River Downs and on the MacDonnell Ranges is good grazing country; unfortunately, without transport, the beasts must be driven long distances on the hoof, and they lose condition. Agitation for railway building has been continuous, but no line in this country would be profitable and governments have preferred to develop better areas first, for the far north can never be 'closely settled' by people of any race. It is not 'White Australia' that keeps it empty, but its climate. Nevertheless the Australian, boasting of illimitable resources which do not exist, tends to awaken feelings of envy in the crowded countries of Asia, and certainly the character of the north has posed problems for those responsible for its defence.

Before World War I, however, these problems hardly existed. Japan was an ally of Britain; the other peoples of Asia were not then a danger. The new Commonwealth preferred to try to overcome the disasters of the 'nineties by concentrating on the development of the south, the encouragement of industry as well as agriculture, the raising of the standard of living and the increase of her population by attracting British migrants; so that in 1914 she was able to proffer aid to the mother country on a scale that would have been scarcely dreamed of by those who organized the small contingents totalling some 16,000 men sent to the Boer War only fifteen years before.

Chapter Fourteen

THE FIRST WORLD WAR
AND AFTER

The outbreak of war between Great Britain and Germany in August 1914 took most Australians by surprise. In those days, as again later, they were somewhat indifferent to the affairs of Europe; even their government had little concern with foreign policy unless it concerned the south Pacific (which it rarely did) and few realized that more 'trouble in the Balkans' was going to produce the serious consequences that it did. At the moment political attention was centred on the Commonwealth election campaign. The anti-Labor government elected a year before with a majority of one in the House of Representatives had had much of its legislation blocked by the Labor dominated Senate; to break the deadlock, when its proposal to abolish 'preference to unionists' was twice rejected by the Upper House, it advised the Governor-General to dissolve both Houses. But, however bitter the party struggle, all were agreed on support for the war. Australia was legally committed, as part of the British Empire, but it was not a question of a mere legal commitment. The Labor leader, Andrew Fisher, who was to become Prime Minister after the election, truly expressed the feelings of the country when he made his famous promise to help to defend the Empire 'to the last man and the last shilling'. For a time patriotic sentiment reigned unchallenged.

The first step was to organize an expeditionary force—the first A.I.F. (Australian Imperial Force)—which by the beginning of 1916 consisted of five infantry divisions and three brigades of Light Horse. The first Australian division landed in Egypt to complete its training in December 1914. Four months later, on 25 April 1915, they went into action as part of the Australian and New Zealand Army Corps (the Anzacs), in support of the allied attack on the heart of the Turkish Empire—the Dardanelles and Constantinople—intended to establish easier communication with Russia and possibly open up a Balkan battle-front.

Unfortunately the landing was no surprise. Earlier naval bombardments had warned the enemy, and an assault, which in February would have been almost unresisted, was now unsuccessful despite the heroic efforts of the attacking troops. For eight months the struggle on Gallipoli peninsula went on. Further attacks in early May were again checked by the Turks, but two heavy Turkish counter-offensives also failed after heavy fighting which demonstrated the Anzac tenacity in defence as surely as the landings had shown their spirit in attack. In August the allies made another great effort, in the battle of Sari Bair, but the reinforcements they had received were insufficient to be decisive and once again the attack was a failure. After a period of inaction it was decided to withdraw from the peninsula, and in the winter the evacuation was successfully accomplished. The allied casualties of the campaign were 33,532 killed and 78,578 wounded; of these the Australians had 8,587 killed and 19,367 wounded.

The Anzac forces, after reorganization in Egypt, were divided. Four infantry divisions were transported to France, while the mounted troops joined General Murray's army in the Sinai peninsula. The former were concentrated near Amiens, ready to support the Anglo-French attack on the Somme. Towards the end of July they made their first attack, on Fromelles, where they penetrated the enemy line, but had to withdraw owing to lack of support. Following this however they succeeded in capturing and holding Pozières and, next month, Mouquet Farm, despite heavy enemy counter-attacks. In five weeks casualties amounted to some 25,000 men, losses which led to the holding of the first referendum on conscription for service. For a time the Anzacs held the line in the Ypres salient, but were back in the wind, the cold and the rain of the Somme for the winter.

After the German retreat to the Hindenburg line, in February-March 1917, the British hoped to capture Vimy Ridge, and in the April attack the Australians were in action against Bullecourt, which was captured though only after more than a month's heavy fighting. In June came the successful assault on Messines Ridge, followed in the autumn by the long and bloody attack on Passchendaele, in which the Australians added Polygon Wood and Brondseinde to their battle colours. In 1918, they suffered with the British in the last great German offensive, and at Villers-Bretonneux, later the site of the Australian war memorial in France, with the hard-pressed rearguards of the Fifth Army, they imposed the first check to the enemy's advance in that sector of the front. After three weeks the place was lost to renewed enemy attacks, but a counter-attack on the night of April 24–25, the anniversary of the Anzac landing, was brilliantly successful—perhaps the finest Australian feat of arms in France. Thereafter they were able to go over to the offensive—at first in a minor way along the Morlancourt ridge, which culminated in the capture of Hamel, and then in the major allied offensive in August, when they captured Mont St. Quentin and penetrated the Hindenburg Line.

In these attacks, the Australians were commonly used as 'shock troops'. 'There are certain divisions,' Haig's Chief of Staff had observed as early as 1916, 'which if given a thing to do, would do it. All the Australian divisions are in that category.' In the last offensive, although the Australian Army Corps represented less than ten per cent of the whole of the British divisions engaged on the Western Front, they captured twenty-three per cent of the guns and prisoners that were taken.

Meanwhile the Light Horse had played an equally brilliant role in Sinai and Palestine, when the British began their campaign there. For a year or more little was achieved, but on 31 October 1917 came Allenby's great attack on the Turkish Gaza-Beersheba line. The plan depended on turning the flank of the enemy defence. This was achieved by a magnificent charge by the Light Horse, under General Chauvel, which involved a two-mile gallop under shrapnel against trenches not fully reconnoitred. In the last half-mile they came under heavy machine-gun and rifle fire, but they galloped on unswervingly with bayonets fixed, until they were engaged in hand-to-hand fighting and swept into Beersheba town. Gaza was then evacuated by the Turks, and Jerusalem was captured in December. In 1918 the Allied advance went steadily on up the Jordan valley, until Damascus was entered on 1 October 1918, which virtually marked the end of the campaign.

The Australian Navy, as it fought in the war, consisted of one battle-cruiser, H.M.A.S. *Australia*, four light cruisers, two small cruisers and six destroyers, apart from smaller vessels. Its most spectacular achievement was the sinking of the German cruiser *Emden* by H.M.A.S. *Sydney*, near the Cocos islands, in November 1914, but ships of the R.A.N. played their part in the North Atlantic patrol, in the Mediterranean and the North Sea. An Australian Flying Corps was formed during the war, and served in France, and at the beginning of hostilities Australian forces captured the German colonies in New Guinea and the Bismarck Archipelago. Altogether, 417,000 men enlisted for service; 329,000 served overseas; 60,000 were killed or died as the result of war service, and the total casualties were 226,000, the highest casualty rate in any British force. In fact Australia lost more men than the U.S.A., as the Australian Prime Minister, W. M. Hughes, had occasion to remind President Wilson somewhat forcefully at the Versailles Peace Conference. Moreover, all this service was voluntary, for Australia never resorted to conscription. Yet it seems somewhat paradoxical that, despite the brilliant achievements and the great victories of the A.I.F. in France and elsewhere, it is the landing at Gallipoli, which ended in failure, that is annually commemorated in Australia, and is far better known there and more widely spoken of than the later more successful feats of arms.

The story of this 'baptism of fire' is now deeply ingrained in the mind of every Australian, and certainly it was the Gallipoli campaign that laid the foundations of the reputation of the A.I.F. as one of the most daring fighting forces in modern warfare. 'Anzac Day' was observed at least as late as 1975 with a feeling of almost religious reverence in Australia.[1] It was on this day, it is said, that Australia became a nation; the 'spirit of Anzac' is never to be forgotten, and to her earlier traditions of social progress was now added one of great military glory in the fashion of countries of the old world. No event in her history has been more widely or visibly commemorated than Australia's part in the war, and every town, village, church, school or club has its memorial and roll of honour to remind not only the present but future generations of the sacrifices made in the war. For it brought home the lesson that security was impossible without effort, that Australia could not remain aloof from the quarrels of a despised Europe, that warlike action is not the sole prerogative of continental autocracies but is, regrettably, often necessary to defend national liberty and independence.

The moving spirit was William Morris Hughes, who became Labor Prime Minister when Fisher retired towards the end of 1915. Born in Wales in 1864, Hughes arrived in Australia at the age of twenty. He worked at a variety of odd jobs before becoming secretary of the Waterside Workers' Union after the 1890 strike. In 1894 he entered New South Wales politics, and then in 1901 he was elected to the first parliament of the Commonwealth and was soon one of the leaders of the party. In many ways akin to his fellow countryman David Lloyd George in England, his zeal for social reform, his readiness for fiery attack on his opponents and his mastery of invective had long made him a controversial

---

[1] Although this 'reverence' appeared to evaporate when the hotels opened.

figure in Australian politics, but all through his political career he combined with his radical views a strongly nationalist fervour. He had always urged on his party colleagues the need for strengthening Australian defences and the need for compulsory military training. In his enthusiastic Australian nationalist-radicalism, he inherited the traditions

Mr. Hughes and Mr. Lloyd George enliven proceedings at the
Imperial War Cabinet.

of the *Bulletin*; but his nationalism was distrusted by the more 'orthodox' trade-union leaders, who were by no means anxious to permit their members' interests to be subordinated to war policy, and whose Irish ancestry, in many cases, contributed to a certain dislike of Great Britain.

In 1916 Hughes visited England. Here he received a tremendous welcome. His speeches, fully reported, were most moving and convincing expositions of patriotic sentiment. They were cabled to Australia; they were translated by an enthusiastic professor into Greek as being worthy of Demosthenes, and though this had little effect on public opinion, which was rather ignorant of Demosthenes, Hughes's oratory certainly added to his reputation in England. He attended sessions of the Imperial War Cabinet, where, according to tradition, he considerably enlivened proceedings by the exuberance of his insistent demands for greater action by the allies. More important, perhaps, he became convinced of the man-power difficulties of the Empire, and returned to Australia determined to follow the example of Great Britain and introduce conscription for military service. Already Universal Service Leagues were demanding such a policy and the principal newspapers were strongly in favour of it. The recruiting figures were naturally showing a decline, in the middle of 1916, after some 200,000 men had enlisted in the twelve months following the Gallipoli landing, but army statements asserting that 80,000 men were required in the next three months contrast oddly with the estimate of 5,400 a month made in 1918 by the Chief Justice, Sir Samuel Griffith, acting as a Royal Commissioner of Inquiry; 'ultimately found to be enormously in excess of the need', according to the official war historian, they were explicable only on the assumption that 'operations like those just concluded on the Somme would be a constant factor', although these were of a type to which 'the student will have difficulty in reconciling his intelligence'. The annual quota of 198,000 asked for by Mr. Hughes obviously could not be obtained by voluntary enlistment, but the Prime Minister gave an unfair picture of the position by pointing to the 16,000 enlistments of June, July and August 1916, and ignoring the 88,000 who had joined in the previous six months. Though there are many general arguments for conscription, it could not at this stage be justified by military necessity. The Labor party was officially hostile to the proposal, and in September expelled Mr. Hughes and his supporters. There was a large Labor majority in the Senate which would have rejected an outright conscription bill but as a compromise it was agreed to submit the question to a referendum to be held on 28 October 1916.

The conscription referendum campaign split the Labor party from top to bottom, and condemned it to years in the political wilderness. It was marked by the utmost bitterness, to which Mr. Hughes's vitriolic oratory added much. It seemed, says the official historian, that the Prime Minister thought that 'in breathing forth fire against his own enemies, he was assisting in the defeat of the enemies of the Allies.' Perhaps this abuse, echoed in the press, acted on the voters; perhaps some feeling of war weariness was appearing. At all events the proposal was defeated, and needless to say, the sound and fury did not help to maintain national unity or even to keep up voluntary recruiting. The A.I.F. voted for compulsion, but only by a majority of 13,000. In Victoria the leader of the 'no' vote was the Roman Catholic Coadjutor-Archbishop Daniel Mannix, who, with his strong Irish sympathies, had declared that in his opinion 'Australia had done her full share—I am inclined to say more than her full share—in this war,' and who argued that Australia should not be sacrificed politically and economically out of 'alleged loyalty to the Empire'. Dr. Mannix's stand gave plenty of scope to anti-Catholic and anti-Irish feeling, but his superior in Melbourne, Archbishop Carr, and all other members of the hierarchy, either supported conscription, or declared it a 'state matter', which the Church 'neither advocates nor opposes'. Victoria, where Dr. Mannix's campaign was naturally strongest, voted 'yes'; it was New South Wales whose 'no' majority of 178,000 was decisive, and there Archbishop Kelly had been an early and outspoken advocate of universal service.[1]

It was not the Catholic Church but the Labor party whose vote rejected conscription, and rejection was aided by the genuine repugnance to compulsion in a community whose liberal tradition was strong. Although unionists, like other sections of the community, had contributed their full quota of recruits, some labour leaders were beginning to

[1] The total figures for Australia were: 1,087,557 'yes'; 1,160,033 'no'. Victoria, Western Australia and Tasmania had 'yes' majorities.

ask, now that the country was being asked to send the 'last man' to the front, whether she was also contributing the 'last shilling'. The Federal government, following what were the orthodox economic views of the time, had shown itself very reluctant to impose heavy war taxation; but though orthodox (in 1914 if not in 1940) this policy did favour the wealthy rather than the poor. Up to June 1919 out of a total war expenditure of over £300,000,000, less than one-sixth was paid out of revenue; this was nearly all for interest payments. While Britain had multiplied her taxation nearly fourfold, to £13 6s. 6d. a head, Australia only increased hers by about fifty per cent, to £6 15s. 3d. per head. It was easy for Labor leaders to point critically to the war-time profits which were being made by some sections of the community. Commonwealth income tax was not introduced until 1915, and raised only £7,400,000 in 1917–18. War-time profits tax did not appear until 1917. The method of financing the war by loan tended to stimulate the inflationary tendencies always likely in such circumstances, and there was little effective price control (except on rents) until 1916, when prices were some forty per cent higher than at the outbreak of war. Real wages were falling; in 1915 they were fourteen per cent lower than in 1911, and in 1918 were still five per cent lower. To growing industrial unrest, the abortive rebellion in Dublin at Easter, 1916, added Irish nationalist ill feeling. One Queensland 'Home Rule' Minister openly declared that England was a country of 'cant, hypocrisy and humbug'. The New South Wales Labor party conference in 1916 was very critical, not so much of the war, but of the failure of the Labor governments to protect the interests of the poor. In these circumstances it was not surprising that the Labor movement decided to oppose conscription, although, since a number of Labor leaders broke with their party in consequence, it was still thought that the referendum would be successful. But apparently the 'no' forces, despite the press, were supplemented by many non-Labor votes, given silently by voters who kept their opinions to themselves.

After the defeat of the referendum, the expelled Labor men, led by Hughes, joined with their former opponents to form the new Nationalist party. At the general election in May 1917, this coalition swept the polls; but, despite this success, a second referendum on conscription was defeated more decisively than the first. During 1918, thanks to the bitterness of these campaigns, to the overbearing attitude of Mr. Hughes in dealing with his critics (including some of the states' governments), and to the appearance of war-weariness, recruiting declined further, as some Labor men, from being anti-conscription, were gradually becoming anti-war. The party was not communist or revolutionary; it had not yet accepted the so-called 'socialist objective' demanding the nationalization of the 'means of production, distribution and exchange'. It was a 'liberal bourgeois party' said Lenin in 1913. But the nationalist sentiment of 'Australia for Australians' could be used to criticize the hardships of a war said to be fought for the 'plutocrats of England' and not for Australian interests. American syndicalist influences from the I.W.W., though weak in the party, were not negligible; nor, after November 1917, was the effect of the Russian revolution. At the same time, the bitter quarrels over conscription were accompanied by the expulsion of the more moderate leaders, some of whom, in fact, had been unpopular with the rank and file for a number of years. The Labor government led by W. A. Holman in New South Wales had antagonized the powerful Australian Workers' Union over the question of land nationalization, when, so it was said, it 'brought itself into line with traitors'; it had failed to abolish the Legislative Council, or even to override its opposition to government bills by appointing party nominees; instead of establishing a state iron and steel works it had given special privileges to B.H.P.; it had failed to amend the law, in accordance with Labor policy, on workers' compensation, masters and servants, early closing of shops, mines, fair rents, the eight-hour day, shearers' accommodation or industrial arbitration; its leader had failed to support the Federal Labor government's proposals to amend the constitution by transferring more powers to the Commonwealth. In April 1916, the party conference passed a vote of censure on the Holman ministry, and though it subsequently refused to accept the Premier's resignation as party leader, that vote left a bitter atmosphere behind it. The party split in the middle of the year, therefore, was hardly surprising, nor was the consequent loss of political power. But this came at a time when the unionist backbone of the party was dissatisfied even with its own politicians, when industrial conditions were getting worse and when many conservatives were showing both in politics and in industry that they did not even yet fully accept the implications of unionism. On the excuse of the 'necessities of war', it seemed, a counter-attack on labour was to be launched, to which the only defence was industrial action.

As in the political sphere, New South Wales was the centre of conflict. There was a major upheaval in November 1916 in the coal mining industry, and in 1917 in the railways, a strike which quickly spread to miners, seamen, watersiders and other transport employees and which involved other states as well. Labor was defeated. Patriotic sentiment and the use of war-time regulations on the one side, lack of funds and poor leadership on the other, quickly ended the 'crisis'. But the defeat of the strikers, the anti-Labor political coalitions, and steadily rising prices did little to reduce the influence of those elements in the Labor party whose support of the war was becoming lukewarm. In June 1918 the triennial Interstate Labor Conference decided, subject to a referendum of party members, to assist recruiting only if it could be shown that the Allies were willing to make peace 'without annexations or indemnities', and that man-power was still available to meet Australia's own needs. Before the detailed party vote could be held the war was over, so the question became academic; but the resolution showed the trend of opinion, gave much scope for abuse by the con-

servative press, and highlighted two controversial aspects of
Mr. Hughes's policy.

At the Peace Conference the Prime Minister was the vigorous defender of Australian nationalism, strongly opposed to
the idealism of President Wilson. His success in getting what
he wanted is certainly a tribute to the vehemence of his
advocacy, if not to his farsightedness as a statesman, though
curiously most of his many critics allow their own nationalist
feelings to overcome their judgement in praising a policy
that turned out so badly. 'Whatever criticisms history will
pass on Mr. Hughes as war-time Prime Minister, it should
never fail to recognize the work he did for Australia at Versailles,' says Dr. Evatt, a bitter critic of Hughes's domestic
policies. Yet though Hughes certainly succeeded in getting
Australia on the 'diplomatic map'—an important consideration probably in the eyes of a man who so enjoyed the lime-
light in similar circumstances after the second world war—
his policy for all its 'jingoism' was curiously futile. He
wanted Australian control over the captured German Pacific
colonies south of the Equator, especially New Guinea,
despite the fact that this ran counter to the President's idea
of mandates. He got his way, for the C class mandate gave
Australia 'all the rights of ownership', but at the expense of
agreeing that Japan should occupy the German islands to the
north. The event showed that it was easier for Japan to
violate the terms of her mandate and fortify her islands than
for Australia to create strong defences in German (Northern)
New Guinea, and in spite of her virtual 'annexation' Australia was unable to resist the Japanese in the former German
colonies. Mr. Hughes's local imperialism was thus not an
outstanding success, even though it has never been proved
that an efficient 'League' and a full mandate system over
both Japanese and Australian acquisitions would have given
complete protection to Australia either. But Mr. Hughes
had little time for 'League' principles, though he agreed that
Australia should become a member. On the contrary he was
quite ready to tell President Wilson that 'in certain circum-

stances Australia would place herself in opposition to the opinion of the whole civilized world'. Thus he was able to persuade the British delegation to oppose a clause of 'racial equality' in the covenant of the League of Nations, and as the strenuous defender of White Australia was successful at least to that extent; but for one as sceptical as he of the whole League idea, the declaration in question would seem to have been hardly worth the fuss he made. In regard to reparations he was fighting for something more concrete; he wanted the maximum amount of compensation from Germany and appeared totally unconcerned with the question whether Germany could pay it. Here was a man dear to the heart of Clemenceau, the French Premier, especially when he dared to tell President Wilson that while the latter was 'a leader whose people had not borne the main suffering of the war', he, Mr. Hughes, represented 'sixty thousand dead'. He thought that 'every Australian who had placed a mortgage on his house to buy a war bond was as definitely entitled to reparation as was every Frenchman whose house had been burned by Germans'. He claimed £464,000,000 including £364,000,000 for actual war expenditure. The latter claim was struck out forthwith; of the remainder Australia was actually paid about £5,500,000.

Still there had been benefits from the war. Not least was the growth in prestige, and the effect of this, if not yet strongly marked in foreign relations, was at any rate noticeable in Imperial affairs. Even here, however, Australia showed no great haste to assert her independence of Great Britain in any formal way. Mr. Hughes distrusted any logical definition of what later became known as 'dominion status'. 'What is there that we cannot do?' he demanded, and the war, without any legal change, had made Great Britain more ready to listen to Australia's voice.

Apart from this, there had been material advance. Free from European competition, Australian manufacturing industries were able to expand by nearly a third, although in many cases this expansion led to a demand for higher tariff protection after the war. Most striking was the growth of the iron and steel industry, thanks to the opening of the B.H.P.'s steel works at Newcastle in 1915. During the war four additional open-hearth steel furnaces were built, as well as a second blast furnace. By 1918 nearly £3,000,000 had been spent on the Newcastle works. This naturally stimulated the mining of iron ore, and war needs doubled the output of zinc, lead and copper. A large electrolytic zinc works, using local hydro-electric power for the treating of zinc concentrates, was built at Risdon, in Tasmania—the first major industrial enterprise to be established in that state.

HORATIUS HOLDS THE BRIDGE

Mr. Hughes defends the White Australia policy against world opinion at Versailles 1919 (see p. 230).

But the war brought problems as well. In some industries labour became scarce. In the export industries, which implies the primary producers, marketing difficulties were acute. The wheat harvest of 1914 had been ruined by drought and was much less than what was needed in Australia. But next year, in an effort to recoup their losses, the farmers increased their acreage by over twenty-five per cent; the weather was good so both yield per acre and total yield (170,000,000 bushels instead of 25,000,000) were records. With many markets closed and shipping scarce, the various governments combined to buy the wheat and the banks agreed to make advances to the growers. Large-scale purchases were made by the British government and the arrangements were conspicuously successful save for the attacks on stored wheat by weevils and mice—thirteen tons of mice were destroyed in three days at eight Victorian railway sidings in 1917. The British government also bought, for the duration of the war, the whole available supply of beef and mutton from 1915, and the whole wool clip from 1916. But buying did not mean transporting, and as the war went on shipping became more and more scarce and expensive. Here Mr. Hughes again entered the ring. In 1916, after trying in vain to persuade the British Shipping Control Committee to make more ships available for Australia, he decided to carry out a long cherished desire of the Labour party and buy a government fleet. For £2,000,000 he purchased fifteen tramps, nine years old, but able to steam at a steady eight knots. They were extremely profitable, if not beautiful, for in two years their net earnings had exceeded their capital cost, despite the fact that the freights charged were lower than those of the private shipping companies. This was a striking example of the then Labour policy of establishing government economic enterprises to compete with those privately owned. Up to 1920, such institutions as the Commonwealth Bank and the State Savings Banks had offered alternative credit facilities to those of the private banks, and the New South Wales state brickworks, metal quarries, pipe and concrete works had considerable success in earning profits and in checking the prices charged by private enterprise. But, as with other war-time developments, the return to peace brought a reaction. There was a cry for less government interference in economic life, intensified by the heavy debts incurred by too much government borrowing for reconstruction, repatriation and soldier settlement, as victory and peace brought a renewal of that over-optimism which has occurred again and again in Australian history.

Chapter Fifteen

BETWEEN THE WARS

Looking back, the inter-war period seems a time of troubles for Australia. First came an unhealthy boom, then the misery of the depression. Recovery followed, but it was pitifully slow and seemed to be accompanied by a kind of spiritual malaise, wherein the values and virtues of pioneering society had disappeared, but had not yet been adequately replaced by those of a maturer form of civilized life. Possibly the boom and depression themselves helped to create a rather materialistic outlook while at the same time showing how inadequate it was; in the economic storm and stress there was too little opportunity to think of anything else—and yet the material base of society was very different from that of fifty or a hundred years before, when the bush had beckoned the adventurous and moulded their ideas. Australia was becoming an urban society; but temporarily, as was inevitable, a rather second-rate one, lacking some of the resources of those societies in the old world which consciously or not she was copying, while losing much of the individuality of her past. But in 1919 there were few misgivings about the future. Australia was a 'nation'; she had contributed in no mean way to the allied victory. 'Liberty is assured to us and to all men,' declared Mr. Hughes optimistically; Australians were free to 'build a new temple of their choice'.

Externally the 'new temple' differed little from the old. That is to say, Australia remained a member of the British Empire, accepted its change of name to British Commonwealth with little overt interest, talked much of Imperial interests but did relatively little to promote them when they conflicted with her own. Whatever might be the terms of the Balfour Declaration in 1926 or the Statute of Westminster in 1931, they had little effect on the actual conduct of Anglo-Australian relations. In practice, there had for long been no feeling of subordination, and no interference in internal affairs; the Commonwealth Parliament did not even adopt the Statute of Westminster until 1941. More important were questions of defence and foreign policy. Whatever might be the legal status of Australia, in fact it was Great Britain who bore the responsibility for defence and therefore must have the last word in policy. Certainly, Australians might think of 'contracting out' of some Imperial obligations, as at the time of the Chanak crisis with Turkey in 1922. Argument arose on the degree to which Australia might or might not actively participate in a war in which she was nominally a belligerent, but which sprang from a policy of which she did not approve. But was such a policy or such a war likely? With growing consultation between governments, and with both Australia and Britain allegedly basing their policies of the principles of the League of Nations covenant, such an eventuality seemed remote. The Dominions were not legally bound by the Locarno agreement in 1926; but at that time peace appeared reasonably secure. Ten years later, when war again seemed imminent, differences in policy between Britain and Australia were small, and at the Imperial Conference in 1937 the Australian government's memorandum noted that 'the League of Nations and the principles enshrined in the Covenant provided a focal point for a common Empire policy; . . . the declared policy of Britain and the Dominions, based on League principles . . . lessened the chance of any disruption, and facilitated a consistent and unified Empire foreign policy.' The magic formula 'collective security' seemed to destroy the possibility of disagreement between policies concerned with the defence of European interests or the localized interests of any other part of the Empire, and the general security of the Empire as a whole; for as Professor W. K. Hancock, himself an Australian, remarked, in his *Survey of British Commonwealth Relations*, some 'were willing to promise to the League what they would not promise to the Commonwealth, while the ardent imperialists realized that the larger obligation to the League could be made to include the more intimate obligation to the Commonwealth'. At the same time, while League principles received lip service from nearly all Australian political parties, the policy of 'appeasement' further strengthened relations between Britain and Australia. It was obvious that Britain was doing her utmost (some would say too much) to avoid war in Europe. This well suited the book of Australian isolationists. Australian public opinion was in general strongly in favour of the Munich agreement, and it is probable that any stronger British policy towards resisting aggression would have reawakened the old Australian ideas of remaining aloof from European quarrels and wars.

Of greater interest in Australia were the problems of Japan and the Far East. Here, even more than in Europe, the League of Nations appeared helpless. Japan had shown herself aggressive and had left the League. The U.S.A. was not a member. League intervention was certain to be ineffective and might well cause a spreading of war. Therefore nearly all Australians opposed any strong action against the Japanese if it could possibly be avoided. But the possibility of Japanese aggression 'south of China' did give rise to considerable anxiety about Australia's defences. The government placed its faith in 'Empire defence', of which the basis in this region was British sea power and the Singapore naval base, and which Australia could support by the co-operation of the Australian Navy and an efficient system of home defence. But many feared that it was dangerous to rely too much on British aid, for in an emergency even her naval strength might be committed to action in European waters. Therefore, it was argued, Australia should rely more on her own efforts, and in particular should develop her air force at the expense of her navy—a policy which gained much support from isolationist sentiment and from the air-minded. Others, while assuming that British naval assistance would be sent, urged the increase of land defences to resist an armed invasion until help arrived. This school included the leading spokesmen of the army. But in fact none of these policies was fully adopted. A sense of isolation, together with the desire for low taxation and increased social services, combined to check rearmament. Australians were unwilling, as yet, at least in peace-time, to undertake the responsibility of defending themselves, and during 1938–39 spent less than £17,000,000 on all three armed services.[1] Not all the Imperial declarations and statutes could alter the fact that Australia, though she might be 'free', was 'not equal' to the mother country; her safety in isolation still depended on the existence of the Royal Navy; her new stature in international affairs was little different from the old.

And if the independence in foreign policy was a thing of the future and if British help was needed in defence, in the economic sphere Imperial assistance was also welcome, though in this connection Australia could offer more in return. In the optimistic days after World War I, politicians, ignoring such a trival thing as the birth-rate, had spoken of a white population of the Empire of three hundred millions within a century; of these Australia with her so-called 'illimitable resources' was thought capable of absorbing quite a number. In 1922 the Empire Settlement Act, and in 1925 the '£34,000,000 agreement', provided for government loans to assist immigrants to come to Australia and to settle there. Planning only for some half million migrants in ten years, even these projects proved over-ambitious. In 1926 a Commission was established to consider and approve schemes of development; but they had considerable difficulty in finding any that were economically sound, and only

[1] This compares with £250,000,000 by Great Britain (excluding loan expenditure), £7,000,000 by Canada, £1,800,000 by South Africa, £2,700,000 by New Zealand.

about a quarter of the money agreed on was spent. All the same, over 300,000 immigrants arrived in Australia in the 'twenties of whom two-thirds were assisted. Meanwhile the old 'boom or bust' pattern was being repeated. More railways were built (4,000 miles of them), and irrigation works, electricity schemes, soldier settlement and closer settlement and 'improvements' of all kinds were carried out with the greatest enthusiasm with money borrowed from overseas. All went (comparatively) well while the prices of primary products remained high, though even by 1928, before the depression, half the money advanced to rural settlers had been written off as lost. The blocks of land were still too small to make a living, and the cost of land was so high that the farmer was at once saddled with a load of debt which he could pay off only in the most fortunate circumstances. And regrettably, circumstances were not fortunate. There were droughts, as there so often are in Australia; and when good seasons came along so did the depression, and the slump in prices destroyed any lingering hopes of prosperity.

True to Australian tradition, the primary producers had asked the various governments for assistance. Bounties and tariffs proliferated; not only locally, but in England as well. Even before the war Australian statesmen, like some of their colleagues from the other dominions, had been putting forward plans for Imperial preference, which they called Empire Free Trade if speaking to free-traders. Great Britain was not over-sympathetic. The British public, not wanting to pay more than was necessary for its imported foodstuffs, retaliated with the slogan of the 'free breakfast table'. After the war preference was granted on Dominion wine and dried fruits, which did not interfere with breakfast, and sugar, of which the untaxed imports from the Empire satisfied the consumer. Not until 1933 did Imperial preference blaze to its full glory, after the Ottawa conference. Then at last Britain extended her preferences to dairy products and meat, and in return Australia, having previously depreciated her currency for the benefit of local producers, lowered some of her tariffs to make her preferences more of a reality.

Tariff protection to Australian manufactures had been greatly raised in 1922, 1926 and 1928, and many were beginning to think that its costs were too high, especially the spokesmen for primary producers. But a committee of inquiry in 1929 found that what they termed the 'excess costs' of protection came to only about £36,000,000, of which £10,000,000 was on account of primary produce—sugar, butter and dried fruit; that the tariff had considerably diversified production; that Australia could not have supported its population at its existing standard of living without protection, and that, although it would be possible to expand the export industries under free trade, this would not offset the loss of manufactures deprived of tariff assistance. Before the Ottawa conference, although imports from Britain paid lower rates, even these were so high as to be virtually prohibitive in many cases. But the experiences of the depression made reductions possible. Up to 1930 wages in Australia were much higher than in Britain. Since 1907, when the famous 'Harvester' award had been made, the various wage-fixing tribunals had steadily raised nominal wages as the cost of living rose; real wages increased as the scope of their regulation was continuously widened, and at the same time hours were slowly being reduced and working conditions improved. But the wage cuts of the depression, together with the depreciation of the currency, made the English and Australian wage-levels roughly equivalent. The coal combine broke up and the price of coal collapsed. The pressure of the depression helped to stimulate efficiency, so that the industrial world was far more healthy in 1939 than a decade earlier, and the industrial advance of this period really laid the foundations of the later war economy. The great iron and steel firm of B.H.P., after struggling with difficulty through the 'twenties, became the cheapest steel producer in the world, thanks to its own very great efficiency, its plentiful supplies of very accessible high-quality iron ore and the fall in the price of coal. Cheap iron and steel was the basis of much other industrial advance. The clothing, textile, agricultural implements, food and drink industries had a long history but more important newcomers were chemicals, rubber, glass and electrical goods. By 1939 manufactures contributed nearly two-fifths of the annual value of production, almost double the proportion of 1911.

This was one of the gains of the depression. But the losses were catastrophic. Between 1928 and 1933, the wheat grower saw the price of his crop fall from about 5s. to 2s. 6d. a bushel; the price of wool dropped from about sixteen pence to eightpence per pound; in 1933 nearly one-third of the breadwinners of the country were unemployed. Most other groups suffered in much the same way. Not that Australia was unique in this respect. But the experience of the depression certainly burned deeply into the soul of the Australian public, instilling a determination that 'it shall not happen again'. True, it ended the unjustified, unquestioning optimism of the 'twenties; but it remains the bitterest memory of a generation, the memory of something brought about in the first place by world influences, but intensified by local conditions, by over-borrowing and unjustified extravagance.

For this, all political parties were to blame; but discussion of remedies aroused intense bitterness. The orthodox policy was to cut costs; then it was argued, primary producers could sell at a profit even with lower prices, industry would revive for the same reason and governments would balance their budgets. But the easiest costs to cut were wages, and to many this policy seemed like an attack on 'the Australian standard of living', a thing much cherished in the Australian tradition. Such a suspicion was not greatly allayed when conservatives, pleading sanctity of contract, argued that interest rates could not be reduced, notwithstanding the fact that lower prices had raised the value of money. The first efforts at reducing labour costs were bitterly contested. Awards of the arbitration court said to be 'unfavourable to labour', though involving in fact only small alterations to a few minor working conditions, caused serious strikes on the waterfront and in the timber industry. A more precipitate attempt of the coal owners to reduce wages in defiance of the court led to a lock-out in the northern coalfield of New South Wales which lasted fifteen months. It was the failure of the nationalist government's industrial policy which caused the sweeping victory of the Labor party at the Federal election of 1929. But even this government could at first get no other advice from the 'experts' than to reduce costs, particularly wages.

The first of these 'experts' were Sir Otto Niemeyer of the Bank of England, and Professor Gregory of the University of London. Their views did not enhance the reputation of English capitalists in Labor circles but they also ignored the fact that the 'deflation' they recommended would make the burden of debt, both public and private, quite unbearable and would bankrupt every financial institution in the country. Local economists soon began to realize the need for 'spreading the burden', both from the economic and the political point of view. Economically the loss of income was so great that recovery could only be achieved if all contributed something. At first the primary producers, the unemployed and some business men were the only sufferers. By the Premiers' Plan (alternatively called the Economists' Plan, or even the Copland Plan, depending on whether the speaker was a politician, an economist or Professor Copland) all Australians were to suffer a 10 per cent cut in 'real income', imposed through extra taxation and a reduction of both interest and wages. This was something which could be put before the electorate as fair and equitable. For the rest, the currency would be devalued to reduce the extent of internal adjustment necessary, and relief works would be undertaken for the unemployed.

This plan was adopted as a suitable compromise, and officially accepted by all parties. In fact both Labor and non-Labor governments alike failed to reduce their expenditure to the agreed extent, and many Labor leaders were particularly hostile. The public became suspicious of Labor's good faith, and the party itself was rent by internal feuds, of which the most violent was in New South Wales. Here the parliamentary party was allied to the so-called 'industrial section'. Led by the miners and railwaymen, this group had emerged towards the end of World War I in protest against the 'threadbare Fabianism' of the parliamentarians on the one hand, and the power of the conservative Australian Workers' Union' clique of reactionary intriguers and boodlers' in the Trade Union movement on the other, when 'union after union' was alleged to be dropping out of the A.L.P. To hold them and to offer a 'scheme of social reconstruction' after the party's defeat at the Federal elections of 1919, the Commonwealth Conference of 1921 adopted the 'Socialist objective', albeit with the proviso that private ownership of the instruments of production would not be abolished where it was being used 'in a socially useful manner and without exploitation'. A prolonged and bitter faction fight against the A.W.U.-dominated party executive followed. In New South Wales, the 'industrialists' won, helped by the parliamentary leader J. T. Lang, who in turn had had to seek their support against his critics. For almost a decade Lang was 'boss'. He consulted union leaders and rewarded them with jobs, and gained the enthusiastic support of the rank and file by his uninhibited efforts to implement labour policy at the expense of their 'class enemies'. 'Lang is right,' 'Lang is greater than Lenin,' were two of the popular slogans of the strongly left-wing group, which however remained independant of the official Communist party now making its appearance. Lang, as Premier after the Labor victory in the 1930 state elections, thus ruled the state at the behest of the more militant trades unions. The upshot showed what was likely to be the fate of the party ignoring the views of its other supporters, whose vote is so necessary for it to possess political power. Lang began with virulent abuse of 'Shylocks' and Professor 'Guggenheim' as he preferred to call Professor Gregory, and he went on in April 1931 to demand the repudiation of interest payments. A run on the State Savings Bank followed, helped by the heavy withdrawals to be expected in a time of depression. The Commonwealth Bank, partly for political reasons, refused to help, so the State institution was forced to suspend payments, though ultimately all depositors were paid in full. In the winter of 1931, Lang accepted the compromise of the Premiers' Plan (and his threats to interest payments had probably helped the Conservatives to realize that some reduction in rates was necessary) but he continued his left-wing programme in New South Wales as far as he could, reducing hours, amending the Industrial Arbitration Act in a manner favourable to the unions, extending family endowment and refusing to reduce allegedly 'extravagant' dole payments to the unemployed. Running into further financial difficulties as a result, early in 1932 he again refused to pay interest to overseas bondholders, and when the Commonwealth Government passed a 'garnishee' act, ordering the banks to pay over to it moneys held on state account, Lang retaliated by issuing a proclamation ordering all state revenues to be paid to the Treasury in cash, whether taxes, or the day's takings on the government railways and tramways. On this, the Governor, Sir Philip Game, intervened. He had already been in conflict with the Premier on the question of appointments to the nominee Legislative Council. For more than a year he had refused to 'swamp' this body, as Lang had wanted, and during that period the Council had acted as some check on the more extreme proposals of the government, having rejected, for example, a bill to reduce all public service salaries to a maximum of £500 a year, and having referred the amending arbitration act to a select committee. But early in 1932, to the dismay of conservatives, Sir Philip Game had yielded to Mr. Lang's pressure and the Council seemed as pliant as the Assembly. In May however the Governor, feeling sure of popular support, was ready to take direct action. Declaring that the Cabinet had, by its proclamation, ordered a direct breach of Commonwealth law, he dismissed the ministry, to the natural annoyance of Lang's supporters. Indeed Mr. Justice Evatt, as he then was, argued that such an action by the Governor was unconstitutional since the Premier could have been forced to obey the garnishee act by the ordinary process of law in the courts.

This was probably true, but such legalist reasoning ignores the fact that New South Wales was on the brink of serious disorder, to say the least. Lang had just forced through both houses, in all-night sittings, a bill to levy a tax, payable within a fortnight, of 10 per cent on the capital value of all mortgages. Intended as an attack on the banks, insurance companies and other financial institutions, this proposal marked the culmination of a violent term of office in which he had reduced Parliament to a mere rubber stamp. In their fear of greater extremes, not to mention a certain anxiety about rioting by the unemployed, the wealthier sections of the community had formed two organizations for the defence of their interests. The better known was the rather 'comic opera' New Guard, whose greatest exploit was when one of its members charged forth on horseback in front of the Premier to open the new Sydney Harbour Bridge. But though it had its ludicrous side, the New Guard, in the heyday of shirts of varying hues in Europe, was somewhat disturbing to the more normal political life of Sydney; and in the background, both in Sydney and in Melbourne, there were organizations more serious and possibly more formidable, prepared to resist, whether or not with the support of the state governments, any of the riots and uprisings which were expected in those stormy times. However the situation in Melbourne, with its moderate Labor and later coalition government, was never as serious as in Sydney, where it has been confidently asserted that had not the Governor dismissed Lang when he did, 'there would have been bloodshed in the streets'. At the ensuing election the Labor party was overwhelmingly defeated. At the end of 1930, of the seven Australian governments, six were Labor; but the confusion in the party, the split between its moderates and militants, between the A.W.U. and the 'industrial' unions as well as between the industrial and political wings, the defection of many of the moderate political leaders, the fear of a wild inflation or repudiation felt by the 'swinging' voter, all combined to destroy the party's political prospects, and by 1932 only one Labor administration remained in office. In the Commonwealth, defections from the party, both to right and to left, caused the government's defeat in the House of Representatives in November 1931; at the ensuing elections, a newly formed United Australia Party swept the polls, under the leadership of J. A. Lyons, a former Labor minister, who had resigned when E. G. Theodore, Labor Treasurer, had proposed a very mild (£18,000,000) expansion of credit by the Commonwealth Bank to finance a subsidy to the distressed wheat-farmers. The U.A.P., composed of the former Nationalists and right-wing Laborites, later on in coalition with the Country Party, retained office until the war. Caution and economy were its watchwords and government spending was kept at a minimum.

The result was a period which might well be termed the 'lost years'. After the disillusionment caused by the pricking of the bubble of the 'twenties and the suffering of the depression, development virtually ceased. It was not only that immigration ceased, that the birth-rate fell so low that demographers forecast an early fall in the population, and that low prices of primary products discouraged the further opening up of the country—which was perhaps wise, as farmers had too often settled in unsuitable areas—but that few improvements were made where they would have been profitable or were socially very desirable. City transport, slum clearance, education, public health, social services of all kinds came practically to a standstill. Hospitals and schools were not built. The universities were starved. The attempt of the Commonwealth Government to introduce a comprehensive scheme of national insurance was abandoned. Almost the only progress visible was in iron, steel and electricity, though even the advance of the latter in country districts was held up by the desire for economy; but cheap steel, cheap coal and currency depreciation enabled Australian manufacturers to compete with imports, despite the lower tariffs which followed the Ottawa agreements, so that by 1939 the economy was healthier than it had been ten years before, even though greater progress might have been stimulated in the later thirties.

But if economy was enforced in those spheres where the prospective beneficiaries had a vote, how much more was it imposed on those communities which Australian governments were ruling 'for their own good'—the natives of New Guinea and of Australia itself. British New Guinea (Papua) had come under Australian rule in 1906; German New Guinea was transferred, as a mandated territory, in 1919. Policy in Papua was dominated by Sir Hubert Murray, Lieutenant-Governor from 1908 until his death in 1940, and as a result two strands emerged. First, to the credit of Murray and the Australian government, it was accepted that the natives' interest must be paramount; that native labour must not be exploited, nor their lands transferred to white settlers on whose plantations they might in time be forced to work in order to live. The natives were completely uncivilized in the European sense; there were no local chiefs and little local government; inside the tribe, only the rule of the village elders. Head-hunting was common, cannibalism not unknown; the blood feud was widespread, as was belief in witchcraft and sorcery. Slowly Murray overcame these evils. He won the confidence of the natives. He extended the bounds of law and order, and slowly broke down the forces of superstition and private vengeance. The Royal Papuan Constabulary performed sterling service. Local natives were appointed as 'village constables' to represent the government, and village councils were established to associate the natives with the work of the administration. All these things were good; and if Murray's policy was little more than the establishment of a benevolent police rule, one must not underestimate the value of the benevolence, or of the extra-

ordinary reputation, almost the veneration, which it gained
for him among the natives and which was worth thousands
of lives in World War II. But at the same time, while Murray's humanity and love of 'his' people could scarcely have
been surpassed, he was perhaps too much the devotee of
'self-help', a difficult task for a primitive people. He wisely
opposed any violent attack on native customs (except those
involving murder and other crime); but he did little posi-
tively to assist the native. He prevented his exploitation by
commercial interests. He was anxious to encourage the
economic development of the territory so long as this did
not harm the people; but while he prevented their exploitation by commercial interests, and there was considerable
production of copra and rubber, his government had no
money and he refused to ask the Commonwealth for help.
Not until 1918 could he report that he hoped *probably* to be
able to do something *shortly* for native education. In 1938,
he was spending only £5,000 a year on this and £12,000
on native health—to meet the needs of 300,000 Papuans.
But the Commonwealth Government, despite the fuss
made about its annexation, was not interested in New
Guinea—either Papua or the mandated territory where conditions were much the same. It was a case of 'out of sight,
out of mind', especially when no votes were involved. There
is barely a reference in Parliamentary debates; there was
complete public ignorance and apathy. What welfare work
was done was left to the missionaries.

It was much the same with the Aborigines—whether under the control of the state governments of Western Australia and Queensland, or the Commonwealth in the
Northern Territory. True, the massacres of the early nineteenth century were no more; the natives driven away from
the fertile parts of the continent had become too few and too
diseased to need massacring; there were no more open conflicts between black and white of the type that between 1840
and 1880 led many writers to suggest (at least implicitly)
that the extermination of the Aborigine (like other 'pests')

might not be altogether a 'bad thing', and that the killing of up to a hundred natives in retaliation for the murder of one white family was both just and necessary. But there was apathy and neglect. The natives' hunting-grounds and their sacred places had been taken; diseases, brought by white men, ravaged unchecked. The activities of missions, though well meant, sometimes helped to destroy morale by undermining the mystique of the tribe and substituting in the Christian revelation something which too often the native could not understand. Although the growing knowledge of anthropology brought better treatment and better understanding towards the end of the nineteenth century, most whites, including their governments, thought their duty done in appointing Aboriginal Protection Boards to ensure that this 'dying race' should perish as comfortably as possible, as it was 'doomed by Providence to disappear before the progress of civilization'.

By 1938 the original Aboriginal population had been drastically reduced. There were then few more than 50,000 full-bloods (almost all in Western Australia, the Northern Territory and Queensland) and not many more of mixed blood, chiefly in New South Wales and Queensland. Government policy had then become slightly more positive, especially in the Northern Territory where political pressure from pastoral constituencies for cheap labour was less effective than in the states. But Western Australia, with the greatest number, was spending only 31s. on each of the natives, compared with £10 10s. od. for the education alone of its white children. Queensland expenditure was 75s. per native; her policy of reservations and missions was fairly successful, though paternalistic, but the Aborigines everywhere remained second-class citizens, badly educated outcasts in a society whose rulers had taken their lands. The Commonwealth Government, despite several pronouncements of a 'New Deal', had a dismal record of failure, and until the end of World War II had been as obstinate in refusing to do anything directly for the

Aborigine as it had been slow in developing the economic resources of the Northern Territory which it controlled. Here the Aborigine, as stockman and labourer, has an important part to play, and though detribalized, can be at least cared for. But the basis of Northern Territory development, which must be in cattle raising, implies better communications by road or rail, and neither the needs of the economy nor of defence could induce Canberra politicians to look towards this area in the 'thirties. Certainly it is wise to try to develop the more fertile, wetter and more temperate parts of the continent first, but in these years the anti-Labor government preferred to halt development almost everywhere.

For it has been one of the features of Australian politics since about 1910 that the Labor party has 'called the tune', leaving to their opponents little but a policy of opposition and resistance. 'Liberalism' had a vigorous record up to the first world war, and most of the Labor party programme was composed of 'liberal' policies. It was as early as 1901 that Australia was the country of *socialisme sans doctrines*, when the Labor party was still in its infancy and had never held office, and since it adopted the socialist objective in 1921 it has been as busy in trying to explain it away as in attempting to implement it. But though the Labor party never tried a policy of thorough-going nationalization, it continued the Australian liberal tradition of government interference in economic life, and even extended it somewhat, so that the 'role of the state' became one of the major matters of dispute between the parties. Labor governments felt little of the traditional distrust of the efficiency of 'public enterprise', for, escaping the corruption of the eighteenth-century British civil service which made government activity so suspect in the eyes of English radicals, Australia had experienced from its very foundation the need of government help in opening up the country, in the absence of private capital or capitalists ready to do so sufficiently rapidly. Brought up with this 'socialist' background, Australian radical thought was always ready to use government to supplement, and if need be to compete with, private enterprise. Government concerns could, by their competition, check the 'monopoly profits' of private capitalists, or alternatively earn them for the public. By 1920 there were government banks, ships, trawlers, butchers' shops, brickworks and dockyards as well as public utilities. Many of these, despite propaganda to the contrary, were financially very successful; but the non-Labour parties, alleging that they were competing unfairly with private enterprise, seized the opportunity of depression setbacks to dispose of many of them, on the ground that they were losing money (forgetting the number of private concerns that were doing the same, if not going bankrupt, at the time). These parties were willing to maintain, left-wing critics remarked rather bitterly, only those public enterprises, like railways, that private enterprise was unwilling or unable to take over, saddling their losses on to the community for the benefit of capitalists. Of course, such criticism was somewhat unfair. If losses of public utilities were sometimes borne by the 'nation', it was largely the more wealthy taxpayer who bore them. None the less the Conservative criticism was often wide of the mark too. For not only were many public concerns profitable and efficient, but the 'log-rolling' and the waste that frequently accompanied public administration, and were so rightly objected to, were more often associated with the major activities such as railways, irrigation and land settlement than with the smaller government trading ventures. Be that as it may, the Conservative governments of the 'thirties were determined to 'get out of business'; and the slowing down of government development policies resulted in fact, if not in intention, in the slowing down of development generally. Though economy was necessary after the extravagance of the depression, and though low world prices and low birth-rate tended to engender pessimism, with the advantage of hindsight it is certain, and even without that advantage it was often argued, that at least after about 1935, more active policies might, with advantage, have been removed. Ironically, the nominally dominant states of Victoria and New South Wales fared worst; for in Queensland the depression was less severe than elsewhere, South Australia, Western Australia and Tasmania were given special grants by the Commonwealth, in the west there was a marked revival of goldmining and in Tasmania the development of an important scheme for hydro-electrical generation.

It was commonly said that the Conservative policies of the 'thirties were dictated by industrial and financial interests, working through the United Australia party, which was formed in the depression to provide for the coalition between the moderate Labor leaders who 'came over' and the old Nationalists, the anti-Labor party dating from the conscription fights of 1916–17. If this is true, and there is much evidence to support it, it was obvious even by 1939 that the more progressive members of the party were resisting that control. The Federal Cabinet had an almost unceasing bout of resignations and reconstructions. The South Australian anti-Labor forces asserted their independence; and there was vigorous party criticism in Victoria and New South Wales. For Hancock's opinion given in 1930 remained true of Australian politics, that while 'there *do* exist strong conservative interests in Australia, they have been persistently baffled and thwarted in their attempts to express themselves in the parliamentary struggle'. Perhaps there was 'a resolute counter-attack against the radicals' in 1931–32; though momentarily successful amid the alarums of the depression, it could not last, but admittedly while it did last it fitted in with the prevailing mood.

For as a rule Australia's development has in the past been associated with rural development, and with the low ruling prices for primary products, whatever might have been done in the cities, there was certainly little incentive for advance in the country. The Country party itself was inclined to agree. This third part of the Australian political trinity had been formed during and after the first world war in protest against the apparent increasing dominance of the cities. Basically conservative (what farmers' party is not?), it has played an important part in non-Labor governments, in the Bruce–Page coalition from 1922 to 1929 and in support of Mr. Lyons and the various Conservative state ministries of the 'thirties; but in Victoria it has on occasions supported moderate Labor, and held office with Labor support. Like other parties, the Country party is a coalition, embracing large graziers, wheat-growers and dairy farmers, and at different times different sections get control and the conflicts between pastoralists and 'cocky' may be as great as that between capital and labour itself. Even 'protection' may be a bone of contention. The wool-grower so far, alone of primary producers, has been able to stand on his own feet; (in fact do not some economists still claim that all Australia is hanging on his back?). He wants little from government save low taxation and to be let alone. But most farmers want to get the shelter of the protective umbrella, alleging that they too are entitled to a 'fair price', and to 'Australian living standards'. In competition for their vote and the parliamentary support of the party, governments of different political hues have built a complex variety of marketing boards and committees in meat, wheat, barley, eggs, milk, butter, potatoes, fruit, sugar, tobacco, cotton and almost everything else, which fix prices, and often output, but care less about efficiency. Pushing these interests, the Country party claims it is only acting in self-defence against city merchants and trade unions and at times it may ally itself with either against the other; but usually its property-owning instinct is strong enough to keep it opposed to Labor, in return for concessions in policy and place from its city-bred Conservative allies. But the special interests of the farmer make him a particularly important part of the swinging vote, and both parties in consequence pay him an especial respect, defended, by rationalization, as a reward for his pioneering role, even though this was discarded more than a generation ago. This, in every class in Australia, was not

dead, but sleeping. In the years between the depression and
World War II, whether in politics or economics, in the
social services, in literature and culture, whether in the
material or intellectual environment the prevailing attitude
seemed one of 'safety first' rather than initiative, of security
and protection rather than progress and risk.

Perhaps it was typical that public interest was so strongly
centred on sport. The great 'Don' Bradman was at the
height of his career in the 'thirties, and the Melbourne Cup
annually attracted its 100,000-odd spectators. Why 'the
Cup' should so completely overshadow every other horse
race in Australia is something of a mystery, but it does; and
the first Tuesday in November, the day it is run, not only is
there a public holiday in Melbourne but, with the advent of
wireless, traffic halts throughout the country—even in
Sydney the trams pile up—as one and all find the nearest
radio to listen to the race. The most famous winner was
Phar Lap, 'a mountain of a horse', just over 17 hands, with
a heart that was curiously almost double the normal size,
and a galloping stride of over 25 feet. After winning stakes
amounting to over £66,000 he died in California in 1932,
whence his stuffed hide was brought to Melbourne and
given pride of place in the entrance to the Museum, his
skeleton was taken to New Zealand where he was bred,
and his heart was sent to be preserved in Canberra. Perhaps
this is indicative of the contemporary sense of values and
achievement in a time of intense economic depression and
frustration.

Chapter Sixteen

WORLD WAR II

The outbreak of the second world war found Australia once again, and like the United States of America later on, unprepared. Australians, like Americans, had grown up taking their security for granted, forgetful of its dependence on the British Navy. Their wholehearted share in World War I had driven home the hardships and the sacrifices that war involved. Though they would participate again if necessary, distance from European quarrels made them often doubt the necessity. Australians, like the peoples of the other Dominions and their governments, had backed appeasement to the hilt, a fact often overlooked by British critics of the Chamberlain policy. What did Hitler or Mussolini matter at this end of the world? Not much, so long as Great Britain could still, if need be, offer protection against Japan. Even though the mounting tensions of the twelve months after Munich were felt in the Commonwealth, the actual declaration of war came as a shock to many who still tended to think, in Mr. Chamberlain's phrase of a year before, of quarrels 'in a far-off country of which many had scarcely heard'. And, of course, mental unpreparedness was matched by physical unpreparedness, following years of disarmament and defence economy, despite the slightly increased expenditures of the past two years and Mr. Hughes's intensive recruiting campaign to strengthen the militia, which raised its numbers to 35,000.

However, the outbreak of war came also at a time when the country was beginning to recover from its great depression in a mental as well as a physical sense. The familiar pattern of 'boom and bust', followed by a long and difficult process of readjustment, had been played out and by 1939 the country seemed about to gather its strength for further advance. There was growing criticism of the conservative political regimes which had held political power since 1931 or 1932. There were stirrings in intellectual and cultural activity. There was renewed agitation for further social progress towards a 'welfare state', and a feeling that the time was ripe for further economic development. These feelings showed themselves in the Australian attitude to the war —the desire to play a part worthy of her history and traditions, but also the desire to assert her independence from too close overseas control; the urge to make an 'important contribution', but likewise the urge, greater than in 1914, towards 'equality of sacrifice', and the wish to try to ensure greater social security in the post-war world together with a higher standard of living for the 'average man'.

None the less Australian war policy emerged slowly and tentatively. At first, and so long as the 'phoney' war continued, it was a debatable point whether the country should send a second large expeditionary force overseas. What of the danger from Japan, a factor not present in 1914? Was not Australia's duty first to defend herself, and then to help the mother country economically? Here was a second important difference from 1914. Then, Australia could contribute little in the way of arms and munitions. Now she could do much. It was necessary now to think of the over-all 'war economy' in a way that had not been done in the past. Despite a proliferation of plans, the taking of a 'national register' and the existence of a 'war-book', organization moved slowly, with an inevitable amount of muddle. Criticisms of the government for doing too little were accompanied by criticisms of public apathy, which in turn was commonly said to be the result of uncertain policies, administrative fumblings and contradictory objectives. For more than a year, the country stumbled rather than rushed into the fray, though probably the public and press, forgetting the difficulties of a sudden violent change in a country's way of life, only appeared to be more eager and more vociferous than the government; for the latter was often compelled to mark time, not because of any lack of desire for action, but because of the manifold obstacles in the way. But gradually these obstacles were cleared, and even before the Japanese entered the war at the end of 1941 the achievement was impressive.

From the beginning Australia had taken an important part in the Empire Air Training Scheme, and before the end of 1939 the first units of the Second A.I.F. had sailed for the Middle East, where, soon reinforced, they played a prominent part in General Wavell's first successful North African offensive in January–March 1941, while ships of the Royal Australian Navy were active and successful in operations in the Mediterranean. In April, Australian forces were moved to Greece to help resist the German onslaught; there they fought for more than a month before being compelled to withdraw with the rest of the Allied armies. The Greek campaign was the occasion of the first major difference of opinion between the British and Australian governments on the conduct of the war. General Blamey, the Australian Commander-in-Chief, like General Freyberg of New Zealand, had not been consulted about the move; he had merely 'received instructions' to the tenor of which he was strongly opposed. The Australian government itself was misled, despite the presence of the Prime Minister, Mr. Menzies, in London. It was argued that Britain had not made good her assurances about air-support and equipment; suggestions were made, at least in the press, that the Australian troops had been sent on a fool's errand. Although for the moment such allegations were denied by the government, it seems certain that this experience influenced Australia's decisions about the use of her troops in 1942. Meanwhile, with regard to both Greece and the Syrian campaign, in June–July 1941, in the words of the official historian, 'decisions had been made without effective Australian participation'.

Dissatisfaction with the higher direction of the war led to further political disputes and finally to a change of government. The German-Italian counter-attack in North Africa had left Australian forces besieged in Tobruk. Here they gallantly held out for some eight months, but at last the question of their relief became insistent. Blamey argued, ostensibly on grounds of health alone, that they should be relieved. General Auchinleck, the British Commander-in-Chief in the Middle East, demurred, emphasized the dangers of such an operation and declared that it would delay the offensive he was preparing. Churchill backed him up, but Menzies and his colleagues supported Blamey. Acrimonious telegrams were exchanged, but the Australian government refused to budge and in September–October the bulk of the Australians were withdrawn, without the losses forecast by Auchinleck and at least implied by Churchill in his post-war memoirs. Meanwhile, in Australia, the Labor party was becoming increasingly apprehensive of Japanese aggression. It claimed that the A.I.F. was needed for the defence of Australia, and suggested that the British government was paying insufficient attention to the Far East. At the same time, it was widely argued that the Australian public were still 'apathetic'. Mr. Menzies, after his visit to Britain and America between February and May 1941, spoke in a national broadcast of the need for 'an unlimited war effort'. But once more interest seemed to lag. The government did little to follow up this appeal; it was too much involved in political difficulties of its own.

The general election of October 1940 had left the House of Representatives equally divided between the two major parties, with two independents holding the balance of power. Labor refused to join a 'National' government, but an all-party Advisory War Council was created. This received confidential information and associated the Opposition with major decisions of policy, and for a time the procedure worked well, giving the government virtual immunity from parliamentary criticism. But personal jealousies inside the government parties were so blatant and bitter, and the press of Sydney, in particular, though nominally pro-government, was so persistent in its criticism, that Ministers frequently had to spend more time coping with their own supporters than with carrying on the war. Some Labor members, notably Dr. Evatt and Mr. Ward, were anxious to press home their attacks. Mr. Menzies resigned in August largely because of the continual attacks made on him by his personal opponents in press and party, but in the recon-structed government the divisions remained. Finally in October the independents overthrew it, nominally on the Budget, but, in the words of one of them, 'because of desire to see responsible and stable government at this crucial time'. Labor took office with Mr. Curtin as Prime Minis-ter. There was no question of its support for the war, though the new government was perhaps less concerned with the Middle East and more concerned with Japan and the Pacific than its predecessor. But before it could make any voluntary change of policy, the Japanese struck on 7 Decem-ber 1941, and Australia was in such danger as she had never known before. Her only trained forces were overseas. At home, she had one armoured division without armour, and seven skeleton divisions of semi-equipped, untrained militia. There was a training organization for the R.A.A.F., but without operational planes. Her defence rested on Singapore plus possible British and American help.

The first two props soon fell away. One Australian divi-sion in Malaya was captured with the other British troops there, outmanœuvred by inferior numbers and air superior-ity. H.M.S. *Prince of Wales* and H.M.S. *Repulse* were sunk. Singapore fell. The Netherlands Indies were overrun. Java, Timor, Rabaul were captured in turn. In March 1942 New Guinea was invaded. By this time two of the three Australian divisions in the Middle East were being transferred to help the defence. It was intended that they should fight in Malaya or Java or Burma, but the Japanese had moved too fast. Mr. Churchill made a supreme effort to have them sent to Rangoon, where they might, he said, successfully resist the enemy. So they might, but Mr. Curtin, mindful of Greece, and Crete, and Malaya, was less confident, and insisted they return to Australia. In the meantime he recognized that in this crisis the country depended on the U.S.A., not on Great Britain.

'Without inhibitions of any kind, I make it quite clear that Australia looks to America, free of any pangs as to our traditional links or kinship with the United Kingdom. . . . We know that Australia can go and Britain can still hold on.'

Such plain speaking caused considerable fluttering in Imperialist dove-cotes (though it did but foreshadow the post-war A.N.Z.U.S. pact, from which Britain was to be excluded); but it marked the beginning of the close contact between American and Australian forces which continued in the Pacific until the end of the war.

By mid 1942 the acute danger was over. Reinforcements arrived from the United States and from the Australian troops in the Middle East; the training and equipment of the Australian militia improved. The naval-air battles of the Coral Sea in May and Midway in June secured the American command of the sea; in the Solomons, United States marines had begun the allied counter-attack. From July onwards there was bitter fighting in New Guinea as the Japanese pressed southwards on the Kokoda trail; and in August at Milne Bay on the eastern tip of the island, they struck again. But slowly the Australians and Americans regained their ground, and by the end of the year were back on the north coast. The last Japanese offensive came in January–February 1943, from Salamaua to Wau on the tablelands of south-eastern New Guinea; it too failed. Thereafter came a slow but steady advance, helped by air and sea superiority; but though one Japanese outpost after another was isolated, the enemy would always fight doggedly to the last ditch, regarding surrender and imprisonment as the deepest disgrace. In 1943, the ninth Australian division, the last in the Middle East, returned fresh from the honours it had won at El Alamein, and took its place on the New Guinea battlefields, and by the end of the year the strenuous campaign in the east of the island had been won. Then General MacArthur was able to begin his 'hops' along the coast, the size of the hop being limited generally by the tactical radius of land-based fighters, except when carriers were available. By the middle of 1944 the reconquest of the coast of New Guinea was complete, and the occupation of Morotai in September meant that the allies had advanced over 1,500 miles in little more than a year, cutting off nearly 200,000 Japanese troops. For the rest of the war bitter fighting continued in New Guinea while the enemy was gradually being mopped up, and culminated in the capture of Wewak in May 1945. The final campaign fought by Australian troops was the invasion of Borneo in June–July.

Ships of the Royal Australian Navy were early in the Mediterranean and Atlantic. They were actively engaged in the evacuation of Greece and Crete and on the 'Tobruk ferry run'. After Japan's entry into the war, they returned nearer home and took part in the Coral Sea battle, in the first allied attack on the Solomons and in a long series of amphibious operations in the South-west Pacific. Three cruisers, four destroyers and thirteen smaller vessels were lost during the war, but at the end of it Australian naval strength still included three cruisers, nine destroyers and fifty-three corvettes. The R.A.A.F. took part in the Empire air-training scheme, made 65,841 sorties against the enemy from the United Kingdom and fought over Europe, the Middle East, Malaya, North-west Australia, New Guinea and Borneo. In all Australia suffered 79,000 casualties in the three services out of 993,000 who enlisted from a population of about 7,300,000.[1]

Such a mobilization had its inevitable effects on the economy. Until the Japanese attack, few civilians had been

[1] Enlistments and casualties in each service were as follows: R.A.N. 49,000 and 3,000, R.A.A.F. 217,000 and 15,000, Army 727,000 and 61,000.

seriously inconvenienced by war-time shortages. The only commodity rationed was petrol, and it is a significant commentary on current ways of thought that even the introduction of petrol rationing after more than a year of war was bitterly opposed by the automobile interests (though naturally on the ground that economy in the unessential use of petrol would hurt the war effort). Apart from this, any minor inconveniences were more than offset by full employment and high earnings. With the coming of 'total war', the situation greatly changed, and from 1942 onwards civilians had to put up with more and more regulations and restrictions, as more and more shortages appeared. Clothing and most of the basic foodstuffs were rationed. The growing coal shortage brought restrictions in the use of gas and electricity, and in railway services. The delivery of household supplies almost ceased. Wages were 'pegged'; the control of employment extended. As in England, the unions of skilled workers accepted dilution schemes, and the use of female labour became more widespread. Building, except for war purposes, was banned, with the result that the war-time marriage boom and the steady growth in population brought with them an acute housing shortage. At the same time, with the development of munition production and other 'essential' industries, the economy assumed a shape undreamed of only a decade earlier.

World War I had affected industry chiefly by cutting off overseas supplies, and thus providing protection from competition—especially important to the infant steel industry. Apart from this, direct war production was almost confined to clothing for the troops. But in the second world war the munitions programme covered almost every major product except tanks. The manufacture of guns, merchant and naval vessels and aeroplanes in turn compelled Australia to make her own machine tools, and this caused an almost revolutionary development in the electrical, chemical and metallurgical industries and in precision engineering. At the same time, difficulties of shipping and marketing and the drain of manpower to the armed forces and munition industries seriously hampered primary production, which received a further setback from the disastrous drought of 1944-45. Losses in these years were serious; soil erosion almost created another 'dust-bowl' when the red pall was blown over the coastal cities, when the number of sheep fell by nearly thirty per cent and wheat had to be imported into the eastern states. Naturally such losses stimulated criticism of government controls and a 'blundering bureaucracy', but by and large economic regulations were accepted during the war with little more than the inevitable minor grumbling. Relations between the government and the business community were quite good, partly no doubt because, as in Britain, many 'controllers' and temporary civil servants were themselves business men, and because most people were ready to make sacrifices in the emergency. More troublesome were the relations between the Commonwealth Government and the states, despite vehement assertions of 'co-operation'; for the war if anything intensified the rivalry and conflict between the two which had existed ever since 1901.

In these disputes, the Commonwealth has always had the advantage. It is the 'national' government, and appeals to 'state rights' can often effectively be labelled 'provincialism', despite the objections to 'centralization' in a country as big as Australia. It is also the stronger financially. As early as 1903 we find Alfred Deakin writing that the 'plain implications of the constitution as a whole show that the people intended to make the Federal parliament the centre of their national government. The constitution left the States legally free but financially bound to the chariot wheels of the Commonwealth. Their need will be its opportunity. The less populous will be the first to succumb; those smitten by drought or similar misfortune will follow, and finally even the greatest and most prosperous will however reluctantly be brought to heel.' How true! Time proved that 'when two men ride on horseback, one rides behind'.

Before Federation the states depended for most of their revenue on customs and excise duties. When the Commonwealth was given control of the tariff, it was proposed that three-quarters of the revenue be given back to the states. Agreed—but only for ten years; then the states would have to look after themselves. When the ten years were nearly over, Deakin, then Prime Minister, offered to give the states a grant of 25s. per head of population. This was accepted; but Deakin's proposal to write the agreement into the constitution was defeated at a referendum, thanks to the opposition of the Labour party and those who opposed binding the Commonwealth. After World War I the grant continued; but the value of money was now less. In 1927 Mr. Bruce, the Prime Minister, threatened to withdraw it and so forced the states to accept the financial agreement of 1928, which this time was ratified by referendum as a constitutional amendment. By this the Commonwealth agreed to take over a large share of the state debt, and to pay as interest for fifty-eight years a sum equal to the *per capita* payment of 1926–27; but there was no provision for increased payments in the future, whereas in the past *per capita* payments had, of course, always increased as the population grew. The Commonwealth merely promised to contribute to the 'sinking funds' on future state loans. In return, the states lost their independence (some called it irresponsibility) as borrowers. The amount and terms of all government borrowing were to be decided on by the Loan Council, consisting of representatives of all Australian Treasurers—but with the Commonwealth having two votes and a casting vote.

How this agreement worked was shown in the depression. State governments wanting to raise loans for unemployment relief works could not do so without the consent of the Loan Council, which was dominated after 1931 by Conservatives opposed to such a policy. When the government of New South Wales proposed to repudiate its interest payments, the Commonwealth passed the Financial Agreement

Enforcement Act to 'garnishee' state revenue to pay the interest. Thus the Commonwealth insisted, despite New South Wales opposition, that interest payments should be a first charge on state revenue. To this extent the state lost control over its expenditure.

Even before the depression, the poorer states, Western Australia, Tasmania and South Australia, had become financially embarrassed. There were bitter complaints of the burdens of Federation, particularly of the cost of the high tariff protection of the manufacturing industries of the eastern states, and the high freights caused by the working of the Navigation Act, which reserved the coastal trade to Australian ships. Later Western Australia threatened secession, and in 1933 went so far as to present a petition to the Imperial Parliament asking for her independence. Commissions of Inquiry were appointed. They found the complaints, though exaggerated like all complaints, to a large extent justified. All three states were suffering from high taxation, necessarily imposed for works of development. In 1933 the Commonwealth Grants Commission was established—a permanent body to assist the 'mendicant states'. It decided to recommend grants on the basis of 'financial need', after considering the budget of the claimant. 'The grant should be sufficient to enable a state in difficulties to function at a standard not appreciably below that of other states.' Here was the idea of the Australian standard of living again—now applied to states. But it gave the Commission considerable scope to interfere with the domestic expenditure of the states, for 'he who pays the piper calls the tune' and 'beggars can't be choosers', although, be it said, the Commission has exercised its supervision with much wisdom and moderation.

Until 1942 the states at least raised their own direct taxation; now this 'privilege' was to be denied to them. The Commonwealth was anxious to levy the maximum possible income tax to meet war expenditure. But the states were 'competing' and their rates varied. The high tax levied in Queensland placed a practical limit on the rates the Commonwealth could impose; yet at this rate the Victorian tax-payer was thought to be getting off too lightly. The solution was found in 'uniform taxation'. The Commonwealth agreed to make 'grants' to the states, as it was legally entitled to do; for the time being, these grants were to be equal to the sums raised by state income tax, in each case. But—and here was the rub—it would do so only on condition that the states raised no income tax of their own. Consequently the major part of state revenue (as well as loans) came under Commonwealth control—and has remained there ever since. And obviously Commonwealth control over the major part of state revenue involves virtual Commonwealth control over the *total* amount of state expenditure, even if not yet over the way in which this sum is spent.

Even in their ordinary administration the states were suffering. Originally, the constitution had provided for a 'division of powers', transferring to Commonwealth control only a limited number of subjects. Commonwealth powers have been growing ever since. There has been no constitutional change.[1] Referenda proposing to give the Commonwealth increased powers have continually and consistently been rejected, ever since 1910. But practice, finance and interpretation by the High Court brought about great changes; and these were reinforced during the war. The 'defence' powers of the Commonwealth virtually overrode all others while hostilities were in progress; for in the days of 'total' war, even though the government had to 'satisfy the court that there is some connection between the legislation in question and the defence of the country', there were few regulations not 'incidental to the successful conduct of the war'. Control of prices, labour, capital, transport, press, police, sport—all these and more came under Commonwealth regulation. In fact, from 1942 to 1945 Australia was virtually under a unitary government.

[1] Except for an amendment, accepted in 1946, giving the Commonwealth power to spend money on social services, which confirmed existing practice rather than introduced any change.

Could the Commonwealth continue such regulation when the war was over? It was doubtful; so a referendum was held to transfer such powers for a limited period, during 'reconstruction'. It was defeated; and certain Commonwealth activities (such as price control) were declared illegal in peace-time. Even so many remained, for the High Court decided that 'defence preparation' was necessary even in peacetime, and for this reason the Commonwealth must be permitted, under its power (and duty), to make laws with respect to defence, to interfere to a considerable extent in, say, economic affairs, which would otherwise be outside its control. This has been especially the case during a 'cold war' in an atomic age.

Australia, like Britain, but unlike the United States, has no 'bill of rights' written into its constitution; hence governments can constitutionally restrict both personal and economic liberties if they so desire. But the federal system is sometimes unwittingly a check on government actions. In 1950 the High Court declared invalid the Federal act banning the Communist party; even in a 'cold war' this was not a proper measure for defence, and therefore it was outside the powers of the Commonwealth government. Though the Commonwealth can censor imports of both books and films, internal censorship is a matter for the states, so one sometimes finds the anomalous situation that a work banned as 'obscene' in one state is freely available in another. In the economic sphere, State and Federal governments alike are bound by the now notorious section 92 of the Commonwealth constitution to keep 'trade commerce and intercourse among the States . . . absolutely free'. The efforts to interpret these vague words, to determine what economic activities do, and what do not, involve transactions 'among the states' and to decide what is the significance of 'absolutely free' have been profitable to many lawyers, but have failed to produce any clear or precise meaning to the disputed phrase; but it has proved an effective obstacle to many government marketing schemes and to other interference in economic affairs.

Between 1900 and 1921 the High Court had used the so-called 'doctrine of implied prohibitions' to invalidate a considerable amount of Commonwealth legislation, on the ground that it was 'impliedly' prohibited by the constitution, considering the nature of a Federation, with its reciprocal rights between states and central government. In 1921 the Court, in a famous decision in the Engineers case, rejected this doctrine, although it was still ready to declare certain acts *ultra vires* because not within the constitutional powers of the Commonwealth; but generally the tide flowed strongly towards centralization, helped by war and by the increasing financial dependence of the states on the Commonwealth. During the forties the court became more active and twenty-eight laws were declared unconstitutional in whole or in part, compared with only thirty-nine between 1901 and 1940; but as a result of the 'intense judicial activity' of the period 'government policy was frustrated by judge-made doctrine rather than by clear constitutional restrictions', in the words of the Professor of Law at the Australian National University, and this 'to an extent not equalled since the Deakin period'.

But despite judicial rebuffs, notably to its attempts to give a monopoly to the government air-line and to nationalize the banking system, the post-war Labour government set the country firmly on the way to reconstruction. Its programme for rapid demobilization and for the rehabilitation training for ex-servicemen was a brilliant success. It consolidated its social security schemes with a constitutional amendment ensuring their validity, though it was left to its Liberal successors to implement a scheme for Pharmaceutical, Hospital and Medical Benefits in 1952. Before then, though the country was still worried by shortages of equipment and a large back-log of needs, the Chifley government in co-operation with the states, had undertaken substantial programmes of land settlement, housing, and public works, and revived assisted immigration on an unprecedented scale. It made Australia a member of the International Monetary Fund. It established a Stevedoring Industry Board, strengthened the Commonwealth Shipping Line, launched the Snowy Mountains Hydro-Electric scheme and in conjunction with New South Wales set up the Joint Coal Board to control and modernize the coal mines in that state. Thanks to the enterprise of private industry, and to the stimulus of the government's activities, by 1952 most war-time shortages seemed to have been met and the worst difficulties of 'reconstruction' to have been surmounted, albeit at the cost of substantial inflation and considerable industrial unrest.

Chapter Seventeen

POST-WAR ECONOMIC PROGRESS

Since the end of the war in 1945, Australian history has gone through two phases. The first, lasting about twenty-five years, was marked by full employment, rapid economic development and, within limits, a broad political consensus; the second | since | about | 1970 has seen increasing economic difficulties with slower development and more political tension.

At first, events in Australia reflected the moderately progressive views common throughout the 'Western' democracies at the time and endorsed by the large majority won by the Labor government at the 1946 elections. The primary emphasis was on 'full employment', to be achieved by the most efficient use of Australia's manpower for the further development of the nation's resources, and was to prevent the waste caused by idleness and unemployment in the past. Secondly, social services were to be extended to create a 'welfare state', and to raise as high as possible the standard of living of the working man. During the later years of the war, the government had been anxious about the possibility of heavy unemployment in a 'post-war depression'—natural enough in the minds of men with bitter memories of the years 1930 to 1933; at the same time, it recognized the dangers of a short boom, when the unsatisfied needs and accumulated savings of the war should be released. To meet these threats the Commonwealth had sought to amend the constitution to gain increased economic powers, but in this it failed. To meet the possibility of subsequent unemployment it drew up plans for public works on a large scale, including an ambitious scheme for the unification of railway gauges—a project periodically talked about and discarded for over half a century, though by 1970 at length completed as far as the main lines joining the state capital cities were concerned; but at the end of the war there was no sign of depression. On the contrary, huge works programmes, large-scale immigration, considerable investment by private companies, house-building and high wool prices brought about an inflationary boom of no mean order, from about 1948 to 1951 when it reached its peak. Certainly, there was a back-log of development that had to be made up; by rushing at it once again Australia repeated the mistakes of earlier booms in an atmosphere of cheerful, but somewhat excessive optimism, and the purchasing power of the pound fell to little more than a third of its pre-war level.

This boom, like the reconstruction which preceded it, was obstructed by constant industrial unrest, caused in part by the rapidly rising prices which it engendered, in part by long-standing grievances, in part by reaction to the war-time restrictions and shortages which were still so irritating, and in part by the good use made of these factors by militant (and sometimes Communist) trade union leaders. The unrest was greatest in certain key industries such as coal mining, shipping, railways and tramways, and the metal trades, and to a country that pinned its faith to a system of arbitration for settling industrial disputes (in which it was a pioneer) the continuous story of strikes was disturbing—not to mention being intensely inconvenient to the public. It seems possible that the militant control of some unions was gained after some dirty work in union elections, if one considers the remarkable changes that occurred when these elections were supervised by the arbitration court after 1948; at the same time it seems certain that many 'moderate' union leaders had been content to rest on their laurels, leaving to their more militant rivals a virtually unchallenged field for their efficient and superior organization, while a generation reared in the depression was very ready to make the most extravagant demands it could in days of prosperity. But by 1948 the reaction had begun, for Communist officials overplayed their hands. Moderate unionists showed a readiness to meet their challenge and the Liberal-Country party coalition government attempted to ban the Communist party in 1950 only when it was no longer in any way necessary.

Cynics have suggested that not entirely absent from the Liberals' motives in making this proposal was the desire to widen the division between radicals and moderates in the Labor party. In this the Liberals had some success, but in the referendum to amend the constitution, after the High Court had declared the Communist Party Dissolution Act invalid, divisions appeared in the Liberal ranks too; though officially the Liberals were in favour and the Labor party against, many of the former apparently lived up to their name in opposing their party and the proposal was rejected.

This had been one of the first major projects of the Liberal government elected in the reaction against Labor's proposal to nationalize the banking system. In 1945 the Central Banking Act had strengthened the hands of the Central Bank, brought it under closer government control and abolished the formerly semi-independent bank board. Rigorously conservative, with no positive policy or ideas, during the depression the board had successfully frustrated the Labor government's economic plans with the help of an anti-Labor majority in the Senate, and though it had since profited from experience and gained in wisdom, its demise was not widely regretted. But when the Labor Prime Minister, Mr. Chifley, who as a member of the Royal Commission on Banking of 1935–37 had been rightly impressed with the economic ignorance and narrowly bureaucratic outlook of the average branch bank manager, went on in 1947 to propose complete nationalization, public reaction was very different. Though Chifley was afraid that the High Court might declare some of the vital provisions of the 1945 act unconstitutional, and so weaken government control of the banking system if the private banks remained in existence, his opponents argued that the nationalization of the trading banks was the first step to a thoroughgoing socialist system which would destroy home and freedom. They repeated over and over again in advertisements how the private bankers had helped 'Bob Freeland', the typical Australian, to buy and furnish his house. Would the bureaucratic bank be so accommodating? The contrary was implied, if not asserted. Certainly the proposal was unpopular, and though in due course the Bank Nationalization Act was declared unconstitutional, it played its part in the defeat of the Labor government and the victory of their Liberal-Country party opponents, under the leadership of Robert Menzies,[1] in the elections of 1949.

The Country party had continued intact during and after the war, but the Liberals had formed a new organization in 1944, largely as a result of Labor's war-time electoral victories. Much progressive non-Labor opinion had disapproved of the negative attitude of the old finance-dominated United Australia party, and of the quarrels of many of its leaders. The politicians had recognized the need for an organization based on wider popular support, and even the die-hards could see the necessity of making some concessions to public opinion. Menzies called for a 'true revival of Liberal thought which would work for social justice and security, for national power and national progress and for the full development of the individual citizen though not through the dull and deadening process of socialism'. In creating a wider and more popular organization, Menzies and his assistants were successful, but could it 'launch out boldly, with new ideas and a constructive economic and social programme'? That remained to be seen. The party was anti-socialist and opposed to government regulation of industry; but in the boom of 1951–52 the Liberal cabinet was forced to reimpose many controls it

[1] R. G. Menzies, 1894–1978, in Victorian cabinet, 1932–34, in Federal cabinet, 1934–39, Prime Minister, 1939–41 and 1949–66, Knight of the Thistle, 1963, Lord Warden of Cinque Ports, 1965.

had previously lifted. Its budgetary policy was naturally more favourable to the higher income groups than was that of the Labor party, but the firm anti-inflationary policy it adopted in 1951 was far more sensible, if drastic, than anything that could be expected from the incoherent economic ideas and demagogic promises of the Labor party under Dr. Evatt, who had become its leader after Chifley's death that year.

The Liberals laid great stress on promoting national development, but since they were ready to impose a brake on the economy to reduce inflationary pressures, as in 1951 and 1961, when these seemed to be getting out of control, they were criticized for not sufficiently encouraging the country's economic growth. Such criticism was short-lived, and left the Prime Minister unmoved; indeed, like Louis Trevelyan in Trollope's novel, 'he knew he was right', and managed to persuade the electorate to agree. Rather lazy, complacent, arrogant though courageous, unwilling to suffer gladly either fools or critics in his own party, he saw during his term of office Australia's connexion with Britain weakened, despite his rabid royalism, the alliance with the U.S.A. strengthened, and until 1964 the defence forces run down. But it is hard to say that Labor in office would have acted very differently for, as in England, party differences were exaggerated by the faithful; basically, Liberal and Labor were at one, and only questions of degree, of speed and of emphasis divided them. Both were anti-Communist, nationalist, protectionist; both were in favour of restricting immigration from Asia and encouraging it from Europe. Labor's socialist objective was largely a paper one, and both parties favoured social services. Neither wished fundamentally to change the pattern of development which the country had pursued so far; and to this extent, both lacked initiative and startling new ideas.

In 1955 the Labor party split in two, the dissidents objecting that the official A.L.P. was too sympathetic to Communism, and opposing its demand that Australia should recognize 'Red China'. They formed the new Democratic Labor party, and drew their main strength from Roman Catholic elements in the existing party, especially in Victoria where they seemed to have the blessing of the aged Archbishop Mannix (d. 1963) and one of his Co-adjutors. Whether or not the A.L.P. was too closely connected with the Communists was a matter of opinion. In 1954, Petrov, an official of the Soviet Embassy at Canberra, 'defected'; a much-publicized inquiry into Communist activities which followed showed them to be singularly meagre, but the affair gave Menzies an excellent opportunity to blacken his opponents, and the somewhat eccentric behaviour of the Labor leader, Dr. Evatt, undoubtedly damaged his personal reputation and weakened his party. Certainly Evatt was no Communist. The Labor party consistently denied any Communist sympathies, let alone affiliations, and the Roman Catholic hierarchy in New South Wales specifically and repeatedly stated that loyal Catholics could support the A.L.P.; on the other hand the Labor executive in Victoria was much more 'left-wing' than that in New South Wales and it adopted a distinctly ambiguous attitude to what were known as 'unity tickets' or how-to-vote cards for union elections, which often contained the names of *both* Communists and Labor men. Labor's divisions meant that it could not provide a very effective opposition in Canberra, and though some critical rumblings from time to time emerged from Liberal back-benchers, they were not enough to worry the government seriously. Generally speaking the post-war Australian economy was prosperous. Between 1945 and 1970 real national income per head rose by nearly 50 per cent, a rate of growth about the same as in the U.S.A., though less than that in Switzerland, the Netherlands and the Scandinavian countries, and destined to be slower in the next decade.

Growth, critics said, might have been more rapid had more of Australia's national product been saved and invested, but between 1950 and 1970 about a quarter of it was used in this way. This was not significantly different from that in other developed economies, and the slower growth rate might as well be explained by the rapidly increasing population, which called for large-scale initial investment to satisfy its needs, and by the large number of children who were for the time being an economic burden, not an asset. This fact, plus the reluctance of governments to raise taxation, meant that the 'public sector' was chronically short of funds; but though far more could beneficially have been invested in schools, houses, hospitals, roads and public transport, if this had been done, doubtless many of those deploring the shortage of facilities for meeting community needs would have raised an outcry when asked to pay for providing them.

Probably more important was the lack of financial resources available to the states. Since the financial agreement ratified in 1928, all seven governments had agreed on a joint borrowing programme, but because the loans were underwritten by the Commonwealth Bank, the Commonwealth government had a strong voice in deciding the total to be raised. In 1942 the introduction of uniform taxation had deprived the states of income taxes as a source of revenue as effectively as the Commonwealth constitution had deprived them in 1901 of customs and excise duties and any chance of imposing purchase or sales taxes. Thus hog-tied financially they became dependent on Commonwealth grants to supplement the heterogeneous collection of stamp and probate duties, betting and land taxes, licences, lotteries and suchlike, which was all they could collect to meet their ever-growing deficits. In 1960–61 the states were dependent on the Commonwealth for *60 per cent* of their revenue, and though the former decided how this should be spent, they did not decide how much should be received.

In 1970–71 the Commonwealth agreed both to make more generous grants to the states, and that the latter, instead of the Commonwealth, should levy 'pay-roll' tax which, it was argued, was a 'growth tax' whose return would increase automatically as the economy expanded, and so would enable the states to meet more adequately their ever-growing expenses. But a decade later, despite promises of a 'new Federalism' made by the incoming Liberal Prime Minister, Malcolm Fraser, in 1975–76, nearly three-fifths of the states' expenditure was financed by grants from the Commonwealth. True the states had acquired a statutory right to about one-third of Commonwealth income tax revenue, but it was the Commonwealth government that decided what that revenue should be, and about two-fifths of the money granted was for a specified purpose, that is, one decided on by the Commonwealth. So, clearly, control of Australia's finances rested with the Commonwealth, and though this was defended on nationalist grounds, the spokesmen of the states remained dissatisfied, and one might well argue that for one authority to raise funds for another to spend is a bad system of public finance. Though the man in the street might care little what authority paid for education, health services, housing, transport, police and so forth, so long as these things were provided, it seemed to some people that Federalism was disappearing, if it had not already gone, especially when even in fields which were constitutionally of state concern the Commonwealth could, and did, increase its influence by special grants for particular purposes, of which it, and not the states, was the judge. Both Commonwealth politics and the Commonwealth public service came to appear more attractive to able men than those of the states, and those who had opposed formal increases in the constitutional powers of the Commonwealth in the past were more and more forced to turn to the Commonwealth government for help.

In the 'private' sector of the economy, highly protected as it was first by import restrictions and then by high customs duties, there was a tremendous industrial expansion. This was particularly noticeable in engineering, aluminium, building materials, fertilizers, textiles, cement, oil-refining, paper, motor-car manufacture, chemicals, rubber, plastics, all types of electrical and radio equipment, and in iron and steel. Here the giant Broken Hill Proprietary Co. Ltd quadrupled its steel production between 1950 and 1970, opened a new works at Kwinana, near Perth, a great boon to the prosperity of Western Australia, extended its operations at Whyalla in South Australia, and at Newcastle and Port Kembla, in New South Wales, so that despite occasional shortages steel imports seemed a thing of the past. Unfortunately, by 1982 this was to mean surplus capacity when the demand for steel slumped in a worldwide recession. It was the same in the automobile industry, where General Motors-Holdens, long accustomed to the assembling of motor bodies and the manufacture of many motor parts, after the war successfully undertook the manufacture of complete cars and utilities, and several other companies subsequently followed suit. Again, after twenty years' prosperity, over-capacity became apparent in the late 1970s, but before that manufactured products has made up between one-fifth and one-quarter of the country's exports. However, costs remained high, so the home market had to be protected, even though this led foreign producers to charge government spokesmen with hypocrisy when they objected to others taking protective measures against Australia's exports of primary produce.

Between 1951 and 1970 eight petrol refineries were built, which satisfied Australia's needs and were valuable from the point of view of national security. Since the search for oil in Australia and New Guinea at this time had yielded small results, spokesmen for the coal industry from time to time were able to criticize the increasing changeover from home-based coal to imported oil for fuel as possibly dangerous, but the discoveries of oil and 'natural gas' off the Victorian coast, plus the latter in South Australia, in due course reduced any such risk; by the mid-seventies, more than 70 per cent of the refineries' input came to be raised locally, and in 1980 the North West shelf natural gas project was launched. By 1964–65 coal and oil were roughly sharing the supply of the energy used in Australia, and during the 'sixties the coal industry's complaints declined as it found a very profitable export market in Japan; this helped to stimulate huge coal-mining development in central Queensland. By 1980 nearly 100 million tonnes were being mined annually, and exports, which had been negligible twenty-five years before, exceeded 40,000,000 tonnes, worth $1,630,000,000.

Australian investors provided most of the funds needed for this industrial development, but foreign companies, especially from Great Britain and the United States, also set up or extended plants here. During the 'fifties private companies invested foreign funds of on average $A200,000,000[1] a year, in the 'sixties more than three times as much, and in the thirty years after 1948 the total was nearly $A15,000 millions. Of all this, the greatest beneficiaries were mining and oil; about half the money came from the U.S.A. and Canada, and one-third from the United Kingdom. This certainly helped to speed up development, but it had its dangers. Some Labor spokesmen pointed to the high, even exorbitant, profits earned by some foreign companies—notably by the giant General Motors—though this was not a valid argument against foreign investment generally, and by 1982 such profits were, at least temporarily, only memories of the past. More serious was the argument that foreign interests were coming to control important sections of the economy, for by 1970 more than one-quarter of company assets were owned overseas, still more were under foreign control, and despite some restrictions, this movement continued during the 1970s. It was certainly true that any sudden interruption to the inflow of capital would seriously disturb the balance of payments and the prosperity of the country, but most informed financial opinion agreed that the benefits which foreign investment brought outweighed its possible disadvantages.

Since the war the man on the land has had mixed for-

[1] In 1966, decimal currency was introduced, with $A2 equal to the former A1, and $A1 equal to 8s. sterling; since then the value of the dollar has fluctuated between about 45p and 65p, or US$1.20 and 95c.

tunes. At first high prices, especially the wool boom during the Korean War, 1950–51, brought him unprecedented prosperity. During the rest of the 'fifties, the price index of Australian exports—wool, wheat, butter, meat, and sugar—dropped, while farmers' costs and industrial prices steadily rose, although increased output, thanks to research, better farming techniques, pasture improvement, myxomatosis, more mechanization, and greater use of pesticides, electricity and fertilizers partly offset the effects of low prices. However, though the real income of the average farmer was much higher than it had been before 1939, industrial incomes had risen even more, and partly as a result of what the majority thought were the hardships of country life, partly because of its inadequate returns, and partly because its hours of work were up to 25 per cent longer than in manufacturing, there was a steady drift from the land. The contribution of primary producers to the gross domestic product fell from about one-fifth as late as 1952 to about 6 per cent in the late 'seventies; only 7 per cent of the workforce were then employed on farms, instead of 28 per cent in 1933, and the rural population fell from more than a third of the total to about one-eighth, though by 1980 this movement was slowing down as unemployment increased in the cities. Certainly a bumper season and momentarily high prices in 1973–74 made it possible for the then Labor Prime Minister, Mr. Whitlam, to tell farmers they 'had never had it so good', when net farm income rose by 50 per cent, but this was a flash in the pan. In twenty years after 1962–63, the index of the ratio of the prices they received for their produce to those they had to pay for the goods and services they bought fell from 100 to 62, and in the non-material sphere, though better transport and television may have reduced isolation, social and cultural amenities, education and health services were not often up to metropolitan standards, so non-economic factors were not able to reverse a trend so strongly stimulated by movements in earnings and income.

Sheep grazing remained the most important single rural

industry, with the area under sown pastures increasing
nearly sixfold to just under 30,000,000 hectares (75,000,000
acres) and the average fleece increasing in weight by more
than 20 per cent (to 4·3 kilograms or 9·4 lbs) between 1950
and 1980. Though Australia still produced about one-third
of the world's wool, sheep numbers fell by about a quarter
in the 1970s (to about 130,000,000), thanks to the increasing
use of synthetic fibres, and since 1970 the Wool Commission
has supported prices by large-scale purchases, accumulating
stocks if necessary; but many graziers replaced their sheep
with cattle, and in the late 'seventies more than three times
as many beasts were slaughtered as before the war. Wheat
production rose similarly, though droughts cause considerable fluctuations from year to year, and a strained storage
capacity may be quickly replaced by a shortage of seed.
Sugar producers suffered less from the seasons than from
variations in foreign markets, particularly in the U.S.A., but
they too produced four times as much as before the war; the
dairy farmers, hit hardest by increasing labour costs, were
perhaps the least prosperous of the major producers, and
though they were able to improve the quality of their
cattle, they had to abandon farms in many less prosperous
areas.

Since more than half of Australia's primary produce is
exported—though this in the 'seventies made up only about
half of all exports, compared with four-fifths twenty years
earlier—the farmer's prosperity largely depends on overseas markets. The former pre-eminence of the United
Kingdom has gone, and in 1980 Japan (for wool), North
America (for meat and sugar), China and the U.S.S.R. (for
wheat), were Australia's more important customers, with
marketing being assisted by government agencies like the
Wheat Board, the Meat Board, the Wool Commission and
the Queensland Sugar Board.

During the 'sixties and 'seventies the mining industry
experienced a boom. Soon after the war, uranium was
opportunely discovered at Rum Jungle in the Northern
Territory, alongside a railway and the major north–south

transcontinental road, and provided valuable immediate wealth, as the government was able to negotiate an excellent long-term sales contract. In 1953 an Atomic Energy Commission was created to look after uranium mining and research and development in connexion with atomic energy for both industry and defence, and in 1958 it opened a research establishment at Lucas Heights near Sydney. Since then the increasing cost of nuclear power and growing opposition to it for environmental reasons, together with the greater use of hydro-electricity, the vastly increased output of coal and the opening of local oil wells, made its development in the near future less likely, though after a lengthy and intense political debate, uranium mining for export, halted for twenty years, was resumed on a large scale in the Alligator Rivers area in the extreme north of the Northern Territory. Apart from this, the spectacular development of copper-mining at Mount Isa in north-western Queensland, whose production was doubled by the Teutonic Bore mine in Western Australia in 1981, the exploitation of bauxite deposits in the Weipa region of Cape York Peninsula, near Gove in Arnhem Land, and near Bunbury in the south-west of Western Australia, and the discovery of high-grade nickel deposits at Kambalda and Windarra in Western Australia and Greenvale in North Queensland, greatly increased Australia's mineral output, just as the construction of alumina smelters at Bunbury, near Perth, at Weipa, at Gladstone in Queensland, Bell Bay near Launceston in Tasmania, near Geelong in Victoria, and Kurri Kurri in New South Wales brought giant industrial plants to new areas. Even more spectacular, however, were the iron-ore discoveries in the Hamersley Rangers in the Pilbara region of Western Australia, at Mount Tom Price, Mount Newman, Mount Goldsworthy and the Robe River, supplementing the deposits already being worked further north at Yampi Sound, which raised Australia's estimated iron-ore reserves from 368 million tonnes to 20,000 million! In 1980–81, iron-ore production was 92,000,000 tonnes, and of this 78,000,000 were exported, chiefly to Japan, though subsequently the economic recession reduced production, at least temporarily. With Australia then the largest bauxite producer in the world, second in iron, third in lead, and fourth in zinc and nickel, total mineral exports were worth about $A4,000 million having increased, in real terms, about twentyfold since 1950 and doubled in the 1960s; they then made up 30 per cent of all exports, partly replacing the ailing wool exports in the country's balance of payments, for the latter, which made up half the value of Australia's exports in the 'fifties, by then was accounting for less than a seventh.

These developments brought some settlement to the sparsely populated north and north-west, and even the central desert seemed to have its uses after 1947, when a Weapons Research Establishment was set up at Woomera, about 100 miles north-west of Port Augusta, South Australia. From here a guided missile range extended 1,200 miles, north-westerly, to the West Australian coast, over an area with perfect visibility, uninhabited and so sparsely vegetated that recovery of spent parts was easy. One of its early projects was connected with the Australian-designed Jindivik pilotless jet aircraft. For some time Woomera was used as a base for firing Australian and British rocket-boosted test vehicles, for the Sparta upper atmosphere and astronomical research programme in which the U.S. National Aeronautics and Space Administration took part, for the European Launcher Development Organization (E.L.D.O.), and for testing guided anti-aircraft weapons. Other settlements for space research and testing were established 500 miles farther west in Central Australia at Maralinga, on the edge of the Nullarbor Plain, in 1956, and at Talbarno in the north-west of Western Australia in 1959, and various tracking stations also helped the United States lunar space-flight programme. Since some of the tests included atomic explosions, the radioactive fall-out was serious; unfortunately this was not appreciated at the time.

Apart from this mining and defence, the government lagged in the programme for northern development which it had promised in 1949, so it was able to promise it again in 1963, again without great thought for its feasibility. All-weather roads for beef trains, liberal taxation concessions and good meat markets helped to revive the northern pastoral industry and attract American capital to it, but though white Australians could and did live in the tropics, not too many seemed anxious to, and those who did so wanted to be paid wages higher than they could earn in the south, and of course five or six times as high as those paid to tropical workers in Asia; so considering the cost of bringing roads and water to the Australian tropics and the difficulty of marketing tropical produce, investment (except for developments associated with mining), seemed to be more profitable in the more closely settled parts of the continent.

The greatest single public works project in the last forty years was the Snowy River Scheme in the wild mountainous region of the Australian Alps, planned to divert under the mountains part of the waters of the Snowy River, which hitherto had flooded tempestuously to the Victorian coast. By blasting tunnels through the Alps, the Snowy waters were made to flow into the Murrumbidgee and the Murray and to increase fivefold the amount of water available for irrigation; and since the headwaters of the Snowy were about 3,000 feet higher than those of the Murray, the water dropping from one to the other was used to generate electricity. Completed in 1974, its power, shared between Victoria and New South Wales, provides about one-fifth of Australia's generating capacity. Experts have hotly debated whether the scheme can also be justified for its contribution to irrigation; but however the cost be allocated, it has made available 8,300 million cubic metres for the Murray–Murrumbidgee system, increasing its capacity by about one-third and providing irrigation for about 1,000 square miles. This is only part of the large irrigation programme which has been undertaken since the war, which has roughly doubled the pre-war storage capacity. Unfortunately, in many cases, works were undertaken under political and emotional pressures without careful economic assessment, and the state has never even attempted to recover the capital costs and interest payments incurred in these schemes; though many projects in the south-east were reasonably justified, some were planned after little analysis of the economic aspects of water use, and the enormously expensive Ord River scheme in the north-west, undertaken for political reasons, has turned out, as economists forecast, an economic disaster.

While this development was going on, unemployment was negligible, and by 1970 real national income per head was 50 per cent greater than in 1945, though the growth rate was slower in the 1970s. Anyone who remembered pre-war conditions noticed a very marked change in the living standards of the people and an enormous increase in the consumption of what had once been thought of as luxuries. Ever since 1907, the Arbitration Court had been concerned to see that employers paid a living or basic wage —then £2 2s. 0d. per week. After 1937 it varied its conception of what was 'basic' in accordance with economic conditions. A 'prosperity loading' in that year was followed after the war by a reduction of standard hours to forty per week. By 1953 the basic wage had risen with the cost of living to over £12 per week, representing an increase of about 50 per cent in the 'real' basic wage since 1911, paid for a working week 20 per cent shorter. In that year the Arbitration Court specifically abandoned any reference to 'needs' in the fixing of wages. It assumed they were now satisfied, and adopted instead the criterion of what the economy could stand. As a result sometimes of strikes and sometimes of arbitration, wages continued to rise and conditions of work to improve. By 1981, wage-earners were earning, on the average, almost \$A300·00 a week; this meant that although prices had multiplied seven times since 1945,

average earnings had multiplied fifteen times, while the
working week had been reduced from forty-four hours to
forty, and employees were then receiving four weeks'
annual holiday with pay, as well as the unemployment and
sickness benefits, family allowances and long service leave
which had also increased real earnings since 1940.

These high and increasing labour costs called forth many
complaints from employers, and it was asserted in predict-
able quarters that in Australian industry there is too much
idleness, absenteeism and inefficient work. Certainly in
boom years the behaviour of labour may have left something to be desired in the eyes of perfectionists; but so, too,
did the behaviour of producers of all kinds when facing a
'seller's market', or so at least it seemed to the unprivileged
consumer. It had been argued that the increasing cost of
labour would ruin the country, but most company balance
sheets seemed the reverse of ruinous, and in 1950–51,
1959–60 and 1969–70 investors, including the English on
the last occasion, indulged in speculative booms which reflected little credit on their intelligence or foresight, though
naturally enough they were ready to blame anybody but
themselves when they burned their fingers.

Since the late 'seventies, unemployment has reappeared as
a serious problem, reaching 7 per cent of the workforce
(half a million people) in the early 'eighties. This is a waste
of resources which raises serious social problems, all the
greater because of the concentration of the workless among
the young, between 16 and 20 inclusive, of whom almost
one-fifth are looking for work. The fall in mineral prices
after 1980 deepened the recession, but the Commonwealth
government resisted calls for public works to stimulate the
economy and increase employment because of its fear of
increasing the rate of inflation. This had exceeded 15 per
cent a year in the mid-1970s, and as it remained steadily
around 10 per cent between 1978 and 1982, it seemed that
the Australian exporter was being inevitably priced out of
his overseas markets, despite a slow but steady devaluation

of the Australian dollar; however, many observers would argue that in addition to high wages, the difficulties of manufacturers arose from the inefficiency which followed from sheltering behind one of the highest tariff walls in the world.

But if Australia had its economic problems in 1982–3, it had by then a capital city, Canberra, of which it was very proud. Originally chosen to placate the jealous animosities of Sydney and Melbourne, its construction was delayed until after World War I. In 1927 the Federal Parliament moved there, but for years it had many critics. Designed by Walter Burley Griffin, it was said to be an absurd extravagance, placed in an inaccessible site. Pre-war governments showed little real interest in the place, but during the war the existence of three major administrative centres, 600 miles apart, in Sydney, Melbourne and Canberra, was a cause of such confusion, expense and fatigue, that it was obvious 'something' should be done. After 1945 Canberra grew rapidly, stimulated by the creation in 1958 of the National Capital Development Commission. With a population of 250,000, the seat of the Australian National University, Art Gallery and High Court, and with a new permanent Parliament House under construction, it bears little resemblance to the 'country town' of 1947, with only 17,000 people, nor does it any longer look, as Hancock put it in 1930, like 'a kind of suburban garden parcelled into plots by a network of paths which have no obvious beginning and no visible end'; Australia has successfully created an artificial capital city as an integrating force in a long-divided continent. 'Canberra is more than a city, it is an idea,' wrote one of the pioneers of federation many years ago. Today the idea has been realized.

Chapter Eighteen

CONTEMPORARY AUSTRALIA, ABROAD AND AT HOME

Until 1939 Australia's foreign policy, if it deserved such a name, consisted of following Great Britain. Occasionally she tried to influence the mother country, when her special interests were involved, but this was not often necessary. Both countries had a broad interest in the preservation of peace and the maintenance of a balance of power, and Britain was nearly as much concerned with east and south-east Asia as Australia was. The experiences of World War II aroused more interest in foreign affairs, but though better communications, the weakening of Great Britain and the more obvious spreading of international tensions outside Europe involved Australia more directly in world politics, she remained relatively powerless to influence them; as a result, her policy was confined to the minor role of trying to maintain good relations with near neighbours and to strengthen her ties with possible powerful allies, while discussion on foreign affairs seemed to be limited to repeating slogans like 'Communist menace', 'defence of democracy' or 'Resist imperialism', largely for reasons connected with domestic politics.

During the war, Australia's spokesmen had sometimes felt that their voices were insufficiently heeded in the councils of their allies, and Dr. H. V. Evatt, Minister for External Affairs in Labor governments from 1941 to 1949, a man who felt passionately that Australian foreign policy was important, and that intelligent Australian statesmen could exercise a beneficial influence in world affairs, wanted to try to gain a more significant international role for his country. In 1944 he negotiated a specific treaty of alliance with New Zealand. The next year, on a larger stage, he strongly supported the idea of establishing what he hoped would be an effective system of world security to replace the old League of Nations; he therefore took an energetic part in the various conferences which were held to draw up the Charter for the United Nations Organization, and on behalf of the small nations he led a vigorous fight to limit the 'veto' rights of the great powers. Nevertheless, despite the United Nations, and despite her wartime exertions, it seemed clear enough that in an emergency Australia still depended on the help of either Great Britain or the United States of America, and particularly the latter, to preserve the 'Australian way of life'.

Like the U.S.A., though not because of American persuasion, Australia was staunchly anti-Communist. She steadfastly refused to recognize the Communist government in China until 1972, even though welcoming China as a customer for wheat. She sent troops to Korea in 1950 and to fight the Communist rebellion in Malaya later in the decade. In 1951 she was able to induce the U.S.A. to join with Australia and New Zealand in the A.N.Z.U.S. pact, and in 1954 she joined the South-East Asian Treaty Organization; this involved no express military commitments, and never had the significance of N.A.T.O., but as time went on Australian defence forces largely adopted American types of equipment. However, the Australian–American relationship had its difficulties. The establishment in 1963 by the United States Navy of a communications station at Exmouth Gulf, near North West Cape, Western Australia, though defended by government spokesmen as something which would commit the U.S.A. both to help Australia and to maintain world peace, was criticized on the grounds that it would attract enemy attention in a nuclear war and that it involved some derogation of Australian sovereignty and independence—criticisms that were repeated in connexion with the base at Pine Creek near Alice Springs which became operational in 1970, with the establishment near Canberra of what is the largest facility of the U.S. Aeronautics and Space Administration outside the United States itself, and still more emphatically when the OMEGA submarine communications centre was opened in Gippsland, Victoria. Latent anti-Americanism, the product of jealousy and a dislike of the alleged 'Americanization' of the Australian way of life (often exaggerated by hasty generalizations about the cinema and television), was bolstered by the strong objections of many people to various aspects of United States policy. If Australia had encouraged American investment in her industries, she did not like the large profits earned by companies such as General Motors, particularly when they refused to allow their shares to be purchased on Australian stock exchanges, and so effectively excluded Australian equity capital; if the government raised public loans in New York, it strongly objected to the U.S.A. disposing of its wheat surplus cheaply in some normally Australian markets, to American tariffs on wool, to an apparently dictatorial policy on aviation rights, and to strict quotas imposed on the imports of Australian lead and copper.

But the difficulties which compelled Great Britain to reduce her commitment 'east of Suez', and what the government regarded as a threatening expansion by China in the middle 'sixties seemed to many to underline the need for closer relations with the U.S.A. Popular opinion was certainly divided over Vietnam, but the government appeared to have no doubt of the truth of a simple version of the 'domino' theory, and therefore was convinced that it should strongly support the United States. In 1964 Menzies' government persuaded the South Vietnamese to ask Australia for help so that it could send troops to fight the 'Communists' there, alongside U.S. forces, rather than nearer home. Menzies' successor as Prime Minister, Harold

Holt, proclaimed the popular slogan, 'All the way with L.B.J.', and after his death, John Gorton adapted the popular 'Waltzing Matilda' song to go 'waltzing' with those in power in Washington. For five years or so this policy was supported by the majority of the people and by most of the press, but in time it came to be questioned by many who claimed special knowledge of the problem, and so stimulated public debate on foreign policy and defence. Conscription for military service by ballot aroused some opposition, while the emergence of China as a major market for Australian wheat, and the effect on the farmer when the Chinese ceased to buy it, showed that unthinking anti-Communist crusading had economic disadvantages. All the same, such attitudes persisted, as became apparent when the U.S.S.R. sent troops into Afghanistan in 1980. Despite Russian purchases of wheat, the government of Malcolm Fraser cancelled a cultural exchange agreement with the Soviets, and tried to persuade Australian athletes to stay away from the Olympic games in Moscow. In this he failed, and denounced them as traitors, though by 1982, he had so far forgotten his irritation as to embrace the women among the evildoers who were fortunate enough to be successful at the Commonwealth Games held in Brisbane that year.

For at least twenty years after the war, Australia retained her traditional close relationship with Great Britain, where sentiment strongly reinforced considerations of trade and defence, especially in the case of the Prime Minister, Sir Robert Menzies. Britain had not signed the A.N.Z.U.S. pact in 1951, which was the first overt sign of the weakening of British ties, but on the other hand Australia maintained defence commitments in connexion with Malaya, and unhesitatingly supported Britain and France in their Suez adventure in 1956. Though this did not appear conducive to Australian interests, Menzies' largely self-determined policy had almost unanimous press backing and wide support throughout the community; despite the well-justified misgivings felt by many serious students of international affairs in Cabinet and Parliament as well as outside, many Australians, especially ex-servicemen who had been in Egypt in 1915 or 1940–41, showed that they still had a penchant for such drastic action, and it brought out the contempt felt for the United Nations in many quarters, and not least by Menzies himself.

As time went on this attitude changed. As Britain turned increasingly to Europe, trade with her drastically declined. The Australian population no longer thought of her as the 'mother country', and though the majority welcomed Elizabeth II as 'Queen of Australia', some republican sentiments began to appear. In her relations with Asian countries, Australia had a good image, thanks to her sympathy with the Indonesian resistance to Dutch rule in the old Netherlands' Indies; despite some traumas during the 'sixties when President Sukarno first agitated for Dutch New Guinea and later 'confronted' Malaysia and despite some popular criticism of the seizure of East Timor ten years later, successive governments have succeeded in maintaining good relations with their nearest foreign neighbour. Apart from this, Australia took an active part in the Colombo Plan, launched in 1951 to help the development of a number of Asian countries; in 1963 she became a full member of the United Nations Commission for Asia and the Far East, and in the early 'eighties was spending 0·6 per cent of the national income (about $660,000,000) on official assistance, nearly all in Asia and the South Pacific—a proportion which compares well enough with contributions from other countries.

For some years, relations were complicated by racial immigration restrictions, by Asian memories of 'white' imperialism, and by differing views on 'neutralism' and anti-Communism, but by 1970, the old 'White Australia policy' was a thing of the past. Asians entered the country freely as visitors, students and residents. Certainly Menzies appeared to regret the transformation of the Commonwealth that followed the independence of most of Britain's former colonies, and some Australians seemed little inclined to criticize either the South African Republic or Smith's regime in Rhodesia, but again the 'seventies saw a change. Successive governments have strongly opposed *apartheid*; sporting contests with the Republic were stopped, and Prime Minister Fraser played an important part in gaining recognition for Mr. Mugabe in Zimbabwe. Problems still exist because of Australia's reluctance to reduce the tariff barrier against imported Asian manufactures, though with the depressed economy and increasing unemployment of the early 'eighties, this policy had considerable support.

Until 1975, Australia was herself a 'colonial' power, holding the trusteeship of Papua New Guinea, with a population of 2,500,000, including 50,000 'non-indigenes', chiefly Australians. The government's objective was political independence for the territory, but while opinion in the United Nations, especially in Africa and Asia and among the Communist countries, was anxious to hasten its granting, the administration tried to steer a path between demands for political rights by the white settlers, who were necessary for the economic development of the country, and the need to protect the land and labour of the natives while preparing them to take over political power. But political development was severely handicapped by the lack of any common native language and the extremely small number of English-speaking natives—largely owing to the failure of the government to provide good secondary schools in the past. Even in 1966 there were only four in the territory. The University of Papua and New Guinea opened in 1967, but it was clear that it would be some years before it could produce a significant number of trained graduates, although to cope with the country's economic and political development the need for at least 200 a year was urgent. During the 1960s the majority of the legislative assembly came to be elected by indigenes, who also formed a majority in the Administrator's Council and represented their departments in the House, so that through a system of 'dyarchy', local control was introduced over such matters as primary and secondary education, health, the post office, town planning and land use, but since the Australian government retained responsibility for internal security, immigration, foreign trade, defence and the large-scale development plans, real power to determine policy seemed to remain in Canberra.

For many years financial aid to New Guinea, which had little political mileage, was limited by Treasury principles of public economy. In 1964 a mission from the International Bank for Reconstruction and Development reported rather gloomily that while substantial economic growth was possible, 'economic viability' would take several decades to achieve. It recommended a five-year development programme, with an immediate increase of about one-third in government expenditure, while suggesting that local sources would provide little more than a quarter of the revenue that was needed. The government agreed to spend more, and in the next ten years, economic progress was considerable, though hampered by the limitations of profitable markets for the territory's products such as copra and coffee. The development of the huge copper-mining project at Bougainville, where $A350,000,000 was invested to mine 30,000,000 tonnes of ore for the annual production of 150,000 tonnes of copper concentrates and 500,000 ounces of gold; unfortunately the operation aroused political difficulties involving objections to foreign investment (and allegations of exploitation), trouble over land use and the destruction of village sites and plantations, and the relationship of the Bougainville islanders to the people on the mainland. Some critics also feared that the economic success of the five-year plans might result not only in raising living standards and making the country 'viable', but also in leaving it dominated economically, for better or for worse, by 'foreigners' who seemed likely to control half the rural production and probably 90 per cent of business and industry. This might well have aroused local resentment, but this problem, like others, did not arouse much interest in Australia, where few people seemed to appreciate or be concerned by the affairs of their colony. However, independence was satisfactorily achieved with good-will on both sides, and subsequently, financial assistance to the new nation, including an untied budgetary grant, has been on a reasonably generous scale.

Less fortunate were the 160,000 Aboriginal Australians, of whom about one-third were full-bloods. As far as they were concerned, the prevalent attitude of most people was 'out of sight, out of mind', with a feeling of slight discomfort, when their problems were brought into mind. In some quarters, particularly in the north where blacks and whites were living side by side, there remained considerable racial antagonism, and despite the sympathy of the Commonwealth Minister, Paul Hasluck, little was done to improve their lot for some years after the war. In 1966, by a massive majority, Australians voted power to control Aboriginal affairs to the Commonwealth, which had the financial resources to help them, but the government, for once reluctant to interfere with the states, was slow to act. The subject was not an election winner, and in 1969 to an economy-minded government a grant of $A7,000,000 for Aboriginal health, education and housing services seemed quite enough, despite the Aborigines' infantile mortality rate (six times as great as that of the whites), and their need for special school facilities. In 1971 plaudits for Aboriginal tennis champion, Evonne Goolagong, seemed good publicity; showing on television the type of outback shack in which she grew up was denounced as bad taste.

At that time, the official goal was still assimilation, and though it was said of immigrants from Europe that 'no migrant is expected to disown his former cultural identity', the Aboriginal was expected to do just that. Considerable informal and sometimes officially induced segregation remained, and though the South Australian Anti-Discrimination Act of 1968 was an important step forward, neither it nor a later Commonwealth Act was very vigorously enforced. This was particularly important for those Aboriginals, about one-fifth of the total, who were living in overcrowded and sometimes insanitary conditions in the capital cities or in shanties on the outskirts of country towns, but all Aboriginals had to overcome not only prejudice but also the long tradition of paternalist control of their behaviour, especially on the reserves. Even though often imposed from the highest motives, this very substantially reduced Aboriginal freedom regarding their employment, amusements, leisure, mail, clothing and such like, and in the 1970s was particularly objectionable in Queensland, where about a fifth of them lived.

The discovery of minerals, on their reserves and near sacred sites which had been rarely interfered with previously because of the sparse settlement of the desert interior, brought up again the question of land rights, whose existence the British occupation had denied ever since 1788. The Land Rights (Northern Territory) Act, 1976, passed despite opposition from many land-holders and mining interests, established Aboriginal Land Councils to administer Aboriginal land, gave some protection to sacred sites, forbade mineral exploration without authority, and provided that mining royalties from Aboriginal land should be paid to an Aboriginal trust fund. Aboriginals were given freehold title to land in the reserves and were encouraged to acquire other Crown lands to which they could prove traditional attachment. On the other hand, they had no power to stop mining on the reserves. This was declared to be 'in the national interest', and despite the inevitable disturbance to the Aboriginal population of an influx of Europeans, such as had caused so much trouble in the rest of the Commonwealth in the past, two mining projects, which were virtually forced upon the Land Councils, showed the limits on their power. Apart from this, however, they made considerable gains. Though they did not become owners of Ayers Rock, because it is in a national park, nor of land around Darwin, whose town limits were artificially enlarged to equal four times the area of London in order to keep them out, they did gain freehold title to 27 per cent of the Northern Territory and 20 per cent of South Australia, with half as much again on leasehold. The agitation for land rights, following the agitation for wage equality, which was granted in 1968 after a lengthy struggle, stimulated a cultural revival among the Aboriginals. In 1973 the elected National Aboriginal Consultative Committee, followed by the elected National Aboriginal Conference in 1976, with a small executive chosen from it, provided official bodies to press their needs and claims, and it seems clear that they will not be as harassed and neglected as they have been in the past; but while prejudices remain strong among many in the white community and there is constant Treasury pressure to cut expenditure on Aboriginal welfare services, they will continue to find it necessary to agitate and to protest.

Australia is the product of the nineteenth and twentieth centuries. This is self-evident, but it is important for the explanation of many of her characteristics, her achievements and her failures. Her youth means that she has few, or no, ancient traditions, a state of being that contains both its drawbacks and its compensations. Certainly traditions are growing, and in many respects are nourished by inheritances from the old world; but many of these traditions are new, not old, and several generations of British immigrants have found that their ways are not the ways of Australia.

Socially, the most important feature is the absence of a wealthy leisured ruling class, bred in an aristocratic tradition, attending to public service as well as to private interest. Perhaps such a group exists nowhere except in the imagination of idealistic conservatives; certainly it does not exist in Australia. In the early days of the colony, power and social leadership were exercised by officials sent out from England, who, in many cases, began to settle on the land as squatters and pastoralists. But after the granting of responsible government, this group, though preserving much of its economic 'power', was never able or willing to carry on the burden of leadership in the community; one can search almost in vain for representatives of this class among those most important in Church and State, and Australia has no group comparable to the English 'landed gentry'.

One of the consequences is the strength of democracy. Popular constitutions were granted early in the country's history; thereafter, numbers were the state, for the opposing forces existing in an older country were lacking in Australia. The result, on the whole, has been an absence of special privileges and an emphasis on equality characterized by an ever-present willingness to use state power to help the 'ordinary man'. He should earn his own living, yes—up to 1939 the extent of the redistribution of national income by social services was extraordinarily small—but the state could and should help him to find his own feet. It should give him land, lend him money, and assure him a reasonable price for his produce or wage for his labour; it should provide public services like transport, water and power, often on easy terms; it should act as a perpetual protector of the interests of the under-dog.

Hence, many of the most characteristic features of Australian life reflect these interests. Free, secular and compulsory elementary education was early introduced and widely spread; higher education for a long time was backward and financially starved. In 1900, there were only three state secondary schools in Australia—all in New South Wales. As late as 1950, governments were spending less than £1 per head of population on secondary education, and total university expenditure was only about £3,000,000. Since then the situation has improved. The number of secondary enrolments has quadrupled, while the population only doubled. Government spending on education *per head* of population between 1946 and 1976 rose by about 50 per cent in real terms, though many schools remained seriously

overcrowded and understaffed, and, controversially, governments by then were giving financial aid to private (in fact,
largely Roman Catholic) schools. By this time about half
the fifteen- to nineteen-year-olds were being educated
full-time, compared with about 10 per cent between 1921
and 1947—but the proportion in the United States was
more than two-thirds.

As for tertiary education, on the initiative of Prime
Minister Menzies, the Commonwealth government appointed a committee of inquiry in 1957, headed by the
Chairman of the University Grants Committee in Great
Britain, Sir Keith Murray. Its report was most disquieting,
and won public support for action that Menzies himself
almost certainly already favoured. Both Commonwealth
and state governments made emergency grants to enable the
universities to extend and improve their buildings, equipment, libraries, staff and scholarships, all of which were inadequate, and a permanent Universities Commission was
set up to deal with the long-term development needed to
cope with an estimated doubling of student numbers in less
than a decade. By 1980 the nineteen universities open, instead of the six that were all that existed at the end of the
war, had 160,000 students, nearly fourteen times as many as
in 1939.

After 1978, amid complaints of extravagance and some
disenchantment, government grants and university funds
were cut in real terms. Shortages of equipment and the
abandonment of courses became more common. A number
of technical and teachers' colleges were closed. However,
fewer businessmen than a generation earlier regarded
'office-boy training' from the age of fifteen as a more important qualification than higher education, and in the
public service a similar attitude had appeared. Until 1940
university graduates in its clerical and administrative sections
were almost unknown. The regulation which required that
admission to the higher grades of the service should be by
examination was either not enforced or had been repealed

as a result of political pressure by the 'decent duffers', and in 1930 the Commonwealth Public Service Board regretted that 'the obligations of the Commonwealth in according a preference to returned soldiers . . . prevented the adoption of a system of limited recruitment from the Universities'. But when the number of ex-servicemen seeking public service employment declined, in order to compensate at least in part for 'the almost complete cessation of the appointment of junior clerks with good education standing since the war period', the Commonwealth in 1933 decided to take up to one-tenth of its clerical recruits from university graduates. Those who entered the service in this way rose rapidly; unfortunately, until World War II there were never sufficient applicants, for the public services, both Commonwealth and State, thanks to their indifferent traditions, were not regarded as providing very attractive careers and public administration was regarded as the province of the 'safe but mediocre'. If Australia had escaped from the evils of personal favouritism or the spoils system in its civil service by 1900, it retained those arising from the fear and dislike of appointing or promoting the individual of exceptional talent; but since the war most states have followed the example of the Commonwealth, and the university graduate is no longer a rare specimen in public appointments, though that is not to say that quite striking examples of maladministration do not emerge from time to time.

The Commonwealth Scientific and Industrial Research Organization, established in 1926, reorganized in 1949, and financed by the Federal government, has a fine record of successful research. At first its work was directed towards the problems of the man on the land, but in 1937 it extended its activities to assist manufacturing industry as well. Its early triumphs, in the 'twenties, included the discovery of the value of the *cactoblastis* insect to eat and destroy the prickly pear that had covered 25,000,000 hectares of Queensland, and investigating the value of eucalyptus wood for making pulp for paper. During the war it had many technological successes, and carried out important pioneer work in radar. In the early 'fifties, it successfully developed myxomatosis as a 'rabbit-killer', and so increased the country's sheep-carrying capacity by a third or more, and it also carried out successfully research on plants and plant fibres, soils, fodder conservation, animal health, wild life, entomology, meteorology and 'rain-making', anti-shrinkage and permanent creasing in wool textiles, industrial chemistry and various kinds of physics—radio, metallurgical, atmospheric, extra-terrestrial and atomic. Unfortunately as late as the mid-1970s, Australia was spending only about half as much of her gross national product on research as did the U.S.A. and even the United Kingdom—and though certainly this was better than during the 'sixties, when she had spent only a quarter, this meant that she was relying a great deal on the purchase of know-how from other countries.

As in many other 'Western' countries, increasing numbers of Australians have in recent years been becoming more concerned with the need to protect their forests, their fauna, and other features of their environment, not to mention the purity of the water they drink and the air they breathe. At first the conservationists' efforts were directed towards soil erosion, and after some initial opposition it proved possible to persuade the 'practical farmer' that soil-conservation practices were not merely another peculiar and troublesome fad of the theorist. Private organizations, like the Australian Conservation Foundation and the various state National Trusts, as well as some official bodies, struggled to arouse public opinion, and though they often seemed to make little progress against spokesmen for mining interests, the motor industry and 'developers', as well as many politicians, who were all vehement in pooh-poohing the warnings of nature-lovers and ecologists, eventually most states passed acts of some kind to protect the environment and to preserve historic places and wild life. But success has varied. Though National Parks have been extended in all states, in 1982 the Tasmanian government was supporting the plan of its Hydro-Electricity Commission to dam the Gordon River and so destroy part of the wilderness area which had been recommended for preservation to the World Heritage Commission; wood-chipping schemes were threatening forests in Victoria and New South Wales, and the Queensland government remained apparently indifferent to all pleas from conservationists. One of the greatest victories of the latter was to win the removal of lead from petrol from 1985, thanks mainly |to very bad smog in Sydney, but with increasing unemployment after 1979, the argument that jobs were more important than aesthetics or conservation seemed to carry greater weight than before with many people.

However, a concern with non-material things spread a little more widely in the post-war community. For too long, lacking the support of either government or private patrons, culture had tended to stagnate. A few might deplore the export of the country's best brains; but it was not a matter of major public interest or concern. This was probably not due to any inherently greater philistinism among the Australian nation than others; it was due in part to history and environment. How could the ordinary Australian appreciate the artistic or intellectual heritage of mankind when he had no means of seeing it, and little means of learning of it? He could see very few examples of great art or architecture. He had few great buildings or historical monuments to remind him of the heritage of the past even in the older cities, and most country towns were rather drab. But better communications, increasing travel, more leisure and better education all contributed to what the 'intellectual' must regard as an improvement, and the replacement in Sydney of the Harbour Bridge by the Jan Utzon-designed Opera House as the showpiece for the visitor (not to mention the original decision to build it) indicated that to some extent at least community values were changing.

For generations 'average' Australians tended to think in

terms of 'adequate comfort and reasonable convenience'. To quote Hancock again, they sought 'average satisfactions for average people—an excellent aim which becomes delusive only when it is pretended that the average is "divine". They have said, "Seek ye first a high standard of comfort, and the Kingdom of God shall be added unto you." What they have really wanted is the high standard of comfort. Perhaps Tocqueville was right when he reflected that no democratic nation "will cultivate the arts whose object is to adorn it".' To the intellectual this was all very regrettable; but it was not all that could be said, and if disgruntled critics deplore the fact that the newspapers do not reach the standard of *The Times* in London or New York, that the theatre does not rival the London stage, nor the opera that of Vienna, this only shows that some critics are at times extraordinarily stupid. Naturally Australia has produced fewer great authors than England and fewer great artists than, say, France, but book sales per head remain the highest in the world. The National Gallery in Melbourne was long the best in the British Commonwealth outside Great Britain, and its splendid rebuilding stimulated similar development in Sydney, Brisbane and Adelaide, while the opening of the extremely well-funded Australian National Gallery in Canberra in 1982 provided for Australians the opportunity to see another collection that rivals all but the very best in Europe and the United States. The extremely successful biennial Adelaide festival of the Arts brings many distinguished performers to the country, and the smaller annual festival in Perth, like the extensive government grants, particularly those made through the Commonwealth Council for the Arts (considerably greater per head than in the United Kingdom), show that governments, taxpayers and voters are aware that the arts cost money and are willing to support them. Recent novelists like Henry Handel Richardson, Eleanor Dark, Kylie Tennant, Norman Lindsay and Patrick White, and painters such as Sidney Nolan, Russell Drysdale, Fred Williams and Arthur Boyd have won international repute. If in the past, too, musical composers were rarities, Peter Sculthorpe and Dorian Le Gallienne have enriched the contemporary scene, and thanks to the Australian Broadcasting Commission, established in 1932, six major symphony orchestras (proportionately more in number than in London, even if not fully equal in quality), assisted by a large array of visiting celebrity artists and conductors, have since then constantly played to capacity houses in the capitals and the more important provincial centres.

The foundation of the Elizabethan Theatre Trust in 1954 as a permanent memorial of the first royal visit marked the successful culmination of many past ineffectual attempts to establish a national theatre movement. Supported by the Commonwealth and all the State governments as well as by a successful public appeal, stimulated by the ideas of the then British Council representative in Australia and by the energy and drive of that much-attacked bureaucrat, the Governor of the Commonwealth Bank, the Trust hoped, by reviving a living theatre in Australia, to encourage Australian actors, singers, dancers and writers, and to stop the flow of talented artists overseas, which had so much impoverished Australian cultural life in the past.[1] It has helped to keep up a constant supply of excellent modern and classical drama; it has established an opera company of about the same standard as that of Sadler's Wells in London and a ballet company which, like the Sydney and Melbourne symphony orchestras, has toured successfully overseas; and it has provided theatrical, ballet and operatic seasons in country centres and the smaller State capitals, usually neglected by commercial theatre in the past. As time went on not all its early promise was fulfilled, and intellectually more exciting work was done by an increasing number of independent theatrical

[1] Not all Englishmen recognize Australian artists in London; to mention only a few—Peter Finch, Robert Helpmann, Judith Anderson, Joan Hammond, Joan Sutherland, Kenneth Neate, William Herbert, Sir William McKie, Leo McKern, Sylvia Fisher. In 1960 a quarter of the Sadler's Wells opera company were Australians.

groups which, despite their exiguous budgets, managed to achieve great success. All this, like the boom in painting and sculpture, showed clearly enough that Australia was not a cultural desert, while those with less demanding tastes welcomed the arrival of television in 1956, with colour in 1975. As in the United Kingdom, and as with radio broadcasting, this is a mixture of about a hundred commercial and 'national' (non-advertising) channels; licence fees were abolished in 1974, and viewers now almost certainly exceed 90 per cent of the population.

As in so many countries, the ordinary man, while he does not entirely neglect the pleasure of the mind, usually prefers the pleasures of the body, especially when so many aids to these are so bountifully provided—the sun, the surf, the clear blue sky, the beaches and the bush—and more leisure time has become available as working hours have become fewer, not to mention the fact that technology makes them less arduous. What he lacks in 'culture' the Australian makes up for in devotion to sport. By this is meant not gambling alone, reputed to be the great national pastime (though not outdoing British football pools), but outdoor activity generally. Sport of all kinds has had a long history in Australia. The first recorded cricket match was played in 1826; football, as 'an amusement of the military', goes back to 1829; while horse racing and rowing contests are reported in Macquarie's time. One feature, helped by climate, space and a high standard of living, is the extent to which games of all sorts are played and not merely watched (although, to be sure, the crowds at football and horse-racing are criticized). The prevalence of public golf courses is exceeded only in Scotland, and public tennis courts are equally common. Both these games are relatively cheap and can be (and were) played by the youth (and many of the middle-aged) of all classes. All this helps to explain why a country with such a small population has had such a phenomenal record in international sporting contests—tennis, cricket, football, golf and athletics.

Australia is one of the very few countries to have competed in every Olympiad since they were revived in 1896. She has won the Davis Cup in tennis twenty times since 1905 (including six in partnership with New Zealand), being one of the four successful nations with Great Britain, France and the United States of America. She has produced twelve Wimbledon tennis champions (male and female). Her golfers are well known and successful in tournaments in the United Kingdom, the U.S.A., and Asia, and her oarsmen have built up a deserved reputation in their international contests. Rugby footballers continue to register successes against New Zealand and Great Britain, despite the fact that they are drawn almost exclusively from the two states of New South Wales and Queensland, in which this particular game is widely played. Elsewhere Australians have played their own game, developed first in Melbourne in the 1860s, a fast, spectacular game with eighteen a side, whose chief peculiarity to others (including most New South Welshmen) is the lack of an off-side rule, which permits forward passing, normally achieved by high marking (the catching of the ball in a flying leap), for which a free kick is awarded. Since the war, European immigrants have made soccer more popular too, and every year it increases the number of its teams and supporters.

Cricket is played throughout the land in all social strata, though except for a Test Match against England it does not draw the crowds that flock to football ground or racetrack (there are too many alternative attractions on an Australian summer afternoon—especially the beach). The first Australian team toured England in 1878, and four years later the memorable Australian victory at the Oval prompted the lament that England's cricket was dead, and that only its 'Ashes' remained to be carried to Australia. Since then, the fight for the 'Ashes' has been regularly and keenly carried on, with the advantage slightly in Australia's favour, especially during the period of the dominance of Sir Donald Bradman, which followed the famous 'body-line' series in Australia in 1932–33. This affair arose from the Australian allegations that English fast bowlers, in particular Larwood, were attacking not the batsman's wicket, but his body. Tempers ran high, and the matter threatened to cause Anglo-Australian ill feeling, but since then contests have resumed a more equable course, as have those against the West Indies, India, Pakistan, New Zealand and, until 1971, South Africa.

The record achieved by so small a population is itself an eloquent testimony to its love of sport. During two world wars, the excellent physique of Australians was also shown by the medical descriptions of the armed forces, though recently the rising standard of living has led on the one hand to complaints of over-eating, lack of exercise and general unfitness and on the other to an increasing passion for jogging and gymnasia. Overall the Australian is largely (some would say too largely) an outdoor individual, a sun-worshipper; having his god to worship, he proceeds to worship it. Not without importance to his intellectual development are the absence of the long winter evenings of Great Britain, and the presence of a climate which attracts him out of doors in practically every season of the year.

Perhaps the contemporary may over-estimate the importance of the sun in the past; for judging from his homes, the nineteenth-century Australian used to shun it, building his house to face south, and surrounding it with wide verandas. In the country, hotter, less well-off for cooling devices and often short of water, this habit still survives. But in the cities, where more than four-fifths of Australians reside, the typical 'solar planning' welcomes sunshine with large sheets of glass to provide warmth—a combination of acclimatization (noticeable, too, in dress and the attitude to the hat) and the disappearance of both the domestic servants and the cheap fuel that used to maintain perennial fires in the rather dank and shaded atmosphere of older buildings. Apart from this, the Australian has always been anxious to live in a house of his own, a five-roomed cottage, surrounded by a small garden. This he should own, not rent; flats are damnable things—un-Australian, calculated to destroy family life. One result has been the immense spread of suburbia. This was natural enough in the days when even the larger cities were apparently intended to contain vast open spaces, but it came to add considerably to the problems of transport when for every two people in the country, including children, there was in 1980 one motor vehicle. And these automobiles incidentally caused the death of 100,000 people between 1945 and 1980 (three times as many as were killed in World War II and the highest accident rate in any country) despite a substantial reduction in the casualty rate after seat belts were made compulsory in 1970 —a move in which Australia led the world.

A second result of home ownership has been the creation of a nation of small property owners, very commonly owing money on mortgage, but largely free from landlord-tenant antagonism. This social structure, together with the high general standard of living, has always been a moderating influence in left-wing politics, and an important influence countering doctrinaire ideas of socialism (which are suspect in any case as 'theoretical'). Generally the Australian people remain satisfied with the existing, basically capitalist, economy, and although they want considerable government intervention to control what are thought to be the abuses of capitalism, to supplement its weaknesses and to protect the under-dog, the atmosphere of post-war prosperity has allayed such criticism of it as was occasionally heard before 1939, at least until the appearance of quite heavy unemployment in 1982. This public indifference has seemed more regrettable to enthusaists who have tried to organize demonstrations against such things as the Vietnam war, *apartheid* in South Africa, the treatment of the Aborigines in Australia, or the use of nuclear weapons. Inflamed by the first two, between 1969 and 1971, demonstrations and 'student unrest' were more apparent than before, but compared with the U.S.A. or France they appeared very small beer. On the whole, the Australian public is more concerned with sport, crime and fashions than with political questions, and 'civil liberties' have often been attacked in the interests of 'law and order', national security, and apparently even administrative convenience, without arousing much significant popular protest; for although the Australian objects to being 'pushed around' he is not always over-considerate of minorities, nor as concerned with their rights as the more influential 'liberal lobby' in the United Kingdom or the U.S.A.

But the relative calm of Australian politics was rudely broken by the dismissal of the Whitlam Labor government by Governor-General Sir John Kerr on 11 November 1975, a date which many people have since remembered for this event rather than for the Armistice of 1918. The Labor party, elected on a 'reform' programme in 1972, had achieved much in withdrawing from the Vietnam war, establishing a health service, extending social benefits, assisting the arts, and caring for Aboriginals, among other things, but as time went on, it encountered increasing financial and economic problems, and its somewhat inept negotiations for obtaining a loan from Arabian oil sources, which had been leaked during the year, weakened public confidence in its abilities. It had never controlled the Senate, the upper house, but in 1975, the power of the Opposition there was largely due to the refusal of the state parliaments in New South Wales and Queensland to observe the convention that when filling casual senatorial vacancies arising from death or resignation, which was their constitutional duty, they should choose the nominee of the political party to which the former Senator had belonged. For some time, the Senate had been becoming increasingly intransigent on general legislation, but not until October did it decide to hold up a Supply Bill and thus make it impossible for the government legally to meet its financial commitments, including the salaries of the public service. Refusing to pass the Bill except on the condition that the government hold an immediate election, which the Opposition fully expected to win, it virtually claimed the right to force a government to the polls, even though the latter had a majority in the House of Representatives, and Kerr's dismissal of Whitlam in a sense involved the acceptance of the claim. Legally there seems little doubt that the Governor-General had the power to act in this way; politically the new ministry's overwhelming electoral victory might be thought to have confirmed his action—but the cost was intense political bitterness, directed not only at the new Prime Minister, Malcolm Fraser, but also at the Governor-General himself and at the powers of his office. The idea that a ministry possessing the confidence of the lower house could be thus removed was startling; the claim of the Senate to use its power to hold up Supply Bills to force an election was reminiscent of the crisis at Westminster in 1909, and the fact that the Chief Justice, Sir Garfield Barwick, a former Liberal minister, had given advice to the Governor-General in support of his action aroused further criticism in view of the belief that the judiciary should not be involved in actions upon which they might later have to give legal judgment. Since 1975, Senators have said they would not hold up supply again, but there is no certainty that they will never do so, all the more since Malcolm Fraser, at that time leader of the Opposition, had made such a promise earlier in the year before deciding to change his mind, apparently when his party's electoral prospects looked hopeful. Even by 1982 this affair had not been forgotten, and despite a successful rescue operation in the Governor-General's office by Kerr's successor, Sir Zelman Cowan, Fraser remained a politician deeply mistrusted by many people.

But generally speaking, this basically egalitarian society, devoid of persecuted minorities, has not fostered extremist politics, and though some conservative groups have been ready at times to denounce the unorthodox or eccentric as 'un-Australian', as a rule this has not been important, and the new strains introduced into this 94 per cent British community by the large numbers of non-British migrants since the war—especially Polish, Italian, Greek, Yugoslav and recently Asian, including 50,000 refugees between 1978 and 1980—may have brought greater variety into the life of the community. But in a hitherto insular and isolated community, the effect of their arrival was exaggerated at the time. Judging from the experience of the U.S.A. in the past, and Australia in the last few years, it seemed likely that the second generation would be almost completely assimilated. It was said that they would relieve the labour shortage; in fact their need for housing and public service accentuated it very severely, and helped to raise the price of land and the cost of education, transport, gas, water and electricity. However, while some with large families and no special skills were economically depressed, others brought a welcome improvement in cooking, some stimulus to music and culture, some broadening of the mind of the average citizen, and raised the population to 15,000,000.

Since 1950, crime figures have shown a tendency to rise, as in so many other parts of the world. Several factors have been blamed, with or without justification. It is the fault of the migrants, argue some, although statistics show they are not disproportionately responsible. Parental discipline is too slack, youth too much indulged and society too permissive, say others, and the evil influence of comics, television, films and magazines have had their critics in Australia as elsewhere, although increasing 'white-collar' crime, tax evasion and drug trafficking cannot readily be blamed on such things. The police forces are not helped by their being seriously undermanned and underpaid, though certainly by 1982, the various governments concerned were tackling the problem more seriously than before.

It has been commonly asserted that there has been a decline in religion, and therefore, according to the argument, in ethical standards, in Australia in common with most of the rest of Christendom. Officially (that is, according to the census returns), more than a third of the population belong to the Church of England, about one-fifth are Roman Catholics, just under one-tenth are Methodists, and almost the same are Presbyterians. Of the Anglicans especially, many do little more for their Church than fill in the census form and get married according to its rites, for, as in England, Anglicanism possesses a certain social flavour which is lacking in other denominations. All the denominations have their merely passive adherents, many of whom make up for their non-attendance at church by the bitterness with which they wage sectarian warfare, most marked in the anti-Romanism of the extreme Protestants, including 'low-church' Anglicans, but the Churches have never had the same hold in Australia as in older communities, where they have been helped by ancient traditions, beautiful parish churches and rich endowments. There has almost certainly been a growth of materialism in the twentieth century, though whether this means there has also been a growth of selfishness and dishonesty is a question that will be endlessly debated without being ever decided; however, remembering the evils for which militant clericalism has been responsible in various parts of the world in the past (and the present), it would be difficult to assert that the decline in religion has been accompanied by any very grievous consequences in public or private life, especially when one recalls the perennial pessimism of the *laudator temporis acti*, and the probability that at least as far as human nature is concerned, there is nothing new under the sun.

Basically this may be true, but in the last century and a half, the mass of the Australian people have become literate, which was not the case before. Able to read and to write, they want and are able to exercise political power and to achieve economic advancement. Much that is said to be unique in Australian history or peculiar to the Australian environment and character is the result only of this achievement in a society where the opposing forces of privilege, reinforced by tradition, are lacking. This is the century of the common man, and perhaps in Australia he attained his goal earlier than in many other countries. Here he has created his society, which is perhaps less dedicated to the 'gospel of work' than others, but is one where the popular attitude 'She'll do' reflects the wisdom of economists in adjusting marginal cost to marginal return.

The Australian states a hundred years ago were among the most democratic communities in the world, with both manhood suffrage and vote by ballot in most of them, and they were among the earliest to show that radical democracy could work without destroying society. Without a 'governing class', they have on the whole been well governed; they have been the pioneers of much social reform, particularly in the realm of industrial relations; they created and have successfully worked a federal system of government, which has difficulties not always appreciated by those lacking experience of it; at the same time, while developing their local nationalism, they have played their part in working out that unique structure, the (British) Commonwealth. Though Australia has its faults for the intellectual to sneer at and the would-be privileged to criticize, yet in pursuing the greatest good for the greatest number the community has to a great extent achieved its objective. Helped by the world-wide technical advances made during the whole of its history (is not its society in a sense the creation of nineteenth-century world capitalism?), the Australian nation has been fortunate in the time of its birth and its growth. In the future it may have to face threats both to its security and to its prosperity, threats which may tax the wisdom and test the resilience of the 'common man'; but up to the present he has come through his tests with flying colours, and while doing so has left the 'uncommon man' freedom to complain, and offered him at least sufficient power and wealth to retain such of his services as have proved necessary for the preservation and the development of society.

FURTHER READING

A New History of Australia, ed. F. K. Crowley, published in Melbourne in 1974, is now the best large single-volume history of Australia. It has a very full bibliography, and has since been supported by F. K. Crowley (ed.), *A Documentary History of Australia 1788–1900* (Melb., 1980), following his *Modern Australia in Documents* (1901–70), 2 vols. (Melb., 1973). C. M. H. Clark, *A History of Australia*, 5 vols. (Melb., 1962) is a compendious study but reflects the idiosyncracies of its author. Some other recent important books are:

GENERAL

Michael Cannan, *An Australian Camera, 1851–1914* (Newton Abbott and Melb., 1973)

K. S. Inglis, *The Australian Colonists, an Exploration of Social History, 1788–1870* (Melb., 1974)

Russel Ward, *A Nation for a Continent, a history of Australia 1901–1975* (Melb., 1977)

ABORIGINALS

Geoffrey Blainey, *The Triumph of the Nomads* (Melb., 1975)

Richard Broome, *Aboriginal Australians—the Black Response to White Dominance, 1788–1980* (Sydney, 1982)

BIOGRAPHICAL

L. F. Fitzhardinge, *The Little Digger, a Political Biography of William Morris Hughes* (Sydney, 1979)

A. W. Martin, *Henry Parkes* (Melb., 1980)

A. T. Yarwood, *Samuel Marsden, the Great Survivor* (Melb., 1977)

ECONOMIC

A. G. L. Shaw, *The Economic Development of Australia* (7th edn, rev., Melb., 1980)

W. A. Sinclair, *The Process of Economic Development in Australia* (Melb., 1976)

FURTHER READING

ENVIRONMENTAL

J. M. Powell, *Environmental Management in Australia, 1788–1914* (Melb., 1976)

FOUNDATION

Ged Martin (ed.), *The Founding of Australia—the argument about Australia's origins* (Sydney, 1978)

FOREIGN RELATIONS

T. B. Millar, *Australia in Peace and War: External Relations 1788–1977* (Canberra, 1978)

POLITICAL

Don Aitkin, *Stability and Change in Australian Politics* (Canberra, 1977)

P. Loveday, A. W. Martin and R. S. Parker, *The Emergence of the Australian Party System* (Sydney, 1977)

SOCIOLOGICAL

R. W. Connell and T. H. Irving, *Class Structure in Australian History* (Melb., 1980)

URBANIZATION

G. Davison, *The Rise and Fall of Marvellous Melbourne* (Melb., 1978)

Max Neutze, *Urban Development in Australia* (Sydney, 1977)

P. Spearritt, *Sydney since the Twenties* (Sydney, 1978)

WESTERN AUSTRALIA

C. T. Stannage (ed.), *A New History of Western Australia* (Perth, 1981)

WOMEN'S HISTORY

Elizabeth Windschuttle (ed.), *Women, Class and History—Feminist Perspectives on Australia, 1788–1978* (Sydney, 1980)

INDEX

Aboriginals, 17, 20ff., 108, 137, 194–5, 246–8, 293–4, 306–7

Adelaide, 69, 170, 182, 188, 301

Africa, 24, 36, 291; *see also* South Africa

agriculture
development to 1850, 38–9, 41–2, 46ff., 52–3, 95
development, 1850–1900, 130–2, 140, 156
development since 1900, 207–8, 231–2, 239, 251, 278–9
machinery in, 156, 278
see also wheat, New South Wales, Queensland, South Australia and Victoria

A.I.F., first, 218ff., 225

A.I.F., second, 255–6, 258–9

air transport, 26

Angas, G. F., 120

anti-Americanism, 288

anti-British feelings, 160ff., 166–7, 215, 225–6, 241, 290

anti-discrimination, 293–4

Anzac, 219, 222

A.N.Z.U.S., 258, 287, 289

arbitration, industrial, 199–204, 210, 239–40, 269, 283

architecture, 170, 300, 305

art, 162–3, 300ff., 307

artesian water, 19, 25, 208

Arthur, Lieut.-Gov. George, 107ff., 117

Asia, 20, 290, 296; *see also* immigration

assigned servants, *see* convicts

atomic energy, 280

Australia Felix, 19, 67, 119, 143

Australian Agricultural Company, 65, 75

Australian Broadcasting Commission, 302; *see also* radio

Australian character, 295, 301, 303, 307, 308ff.

Australian Colonies Government Act, 1850, 127

Australian Patriotic Association, 92–3

authors, 160ff., 301–2

automobiles, 276, 299, 306

A.W.U., 213, 227, 244

Ayer's Rock, 294

Ballarat, 124–5

ballot, 129

banks and banking, 138ff., 153, 170–1, 175–7, 179–81, 243, 270–1; *see also* Commonwealth Bank

bank smash, 1893, 177–8

Banks, Sir Joseph, 37, 63

Barkly Tableland, 19, 217

Barton, Sir Edmund, 185

basic wage, 199–200, 210, 283

Bass, George, 62

Bathurst (city), 58, 64, 68, 124

Bathurst, Earl, 45, 98

Batman, John, 65, 68, 118

Baudin, Nicholas, 105

bauxite, 280–1

Bentham, Jeremy, 35

Berry, Graham, 157–8, 203

B.H.P. Co. Ltd, 209ff., 227, 231, 238, 276

Bigge, J. T., 58–60, 64, 74, 89, 90, 107, 109

birds, 27–8, 80

Blamey, Sir Thomas, 255–6

Blaxland, Gregory, 51, 64

Bligh, William, 53–4, 56–7, 62, 89–90

Blue Mountains, 58, 61, 64, 68

Boer War, 217

booms, 138, 152ff., 168, 170, 233, 237, 269, 271, 275, 279, 284

Botany Bay, 33, 36–7, 44, 62

Bourke, Sir Richard, 68, 87, 90, 98–9, 107, 118–19, 133

Bowen, Sir George, 138, 158–9

Braddon clause, 191, 193

Bradman, Sir Donald, 252, 304

Brisbane, 69, 181, 190, 194, 205, 289

British Commonwealth, 234–5, 290, 311

British investment in Australia, 75, 152, 171, 176, 277

Broken Hill, 70–1, 153, 170, 176, 185, 202

Bruce, S. M., 251, 262

Bulletin, the, 159, 167–8, 175, 187, 192, 223

Burke, O'Hara, 72

bush, 18, 27, 80–1, 162ff., 190, 303

bushfires, 26–7

bushrangers, 107–8, 148–9

cactoblastis, 27, 298

Canada, 27, 29, 277, 279

Canberra, 65, 197, 285

capital and investment, 48–50, 152–3, 168, 170–1, 269, 273–4, 282–3, 292; *see also* British investment

Carpentaria, Gulf of, 17, 20, 61, 63, 69, 72

casualties, war-time, 221, 230, 259

Catholic, *see* Roman Catholic

cattle, 154, 216–17, 248, 279, 282

Cecil, Lord Robert, *see* Lord Salisbury

Chamberlain, Joseph, 181, 195–6

Chifley, J. B., 270–2

China, 33, 36, 166, 279, 287–9

Chinese, 19, 36, 124, 165–6, 183, 197; *see also* immigration

Chisholm, Caroline, 94–5

Churchill, Sir Winston, 256–7

Church of England, 98–9, 147, 310

cities and urbanization, 28–9, 101, 123, 135, 170, 305–6

civil service, 297–8

climate, 17ff., 25ff., 48, 58, 101, 120, 140, 156, 168–9, 208, 305; *see also* droughts, floods

closer settlement, 215, 237

Closer Settlement Acts, 207

coal, 59, 62, 153, 206, 238, 240, 267, 276–7, 280

Cobb & Co., 149

Collins, David, 106

Collins, Tom, 162–3

Colombo Plan, 290

Colonial Office, London, 23, 119, 155, 159, 166

Commonwealth Bank, 202, 212, 232, 242, 270–1, 274

Commonwealth constitution, 188–9, 191, 193, 196, 200–1, 261–6, 268, 270–1, 293

Commonwealth Grants Commission, 263

Commonwealth shipping, 232

communications, 25, 28, 149, 187, 195, 216–17, 300

communism, 227, 241, 265, 269–70, 272–3, 286–9

conscription, 224, 289

conservation, 299

convicts

    assigned servants, 44, 76, 78–9, 92, 112–13

    convict types, 96–7, 110–11

    difficulties of, 44, 49

    exiles, 114–15

    in Great Britain, 34–5, 58, 96–7

    in penal settlements, 110

    in Van Diemen's Land, 108ff.

    in Western Australia, 116

    juveniles, 112

    progress of, 45, 51, 57–8

    reformation of, 46, 98

    servants to squatters, 74–9, 83–4, 96, 115

    under Phillip, 39ff.

    see also transportation

Cook, Capt. James, 17, 21–2, 32–3, 36, 38, 63

Cooper's Creek, 69, 71

copper, 121, 179, 280, 288, 292

Country Party, 244, 250–1, 270–1
Cox, William, 49, 51
Cowen, Sir Zelman, 308
cricket, 101, 303–5
crime
    Australian, 309
    English, 34, 45, 56, 97, 110–13
Crown land, 23, 130, 294
C.S.I.R.O., 298–9
culture, 100ff., 162–3, 300ff.
Curtin, John, 257–8
customs, see tariff

dairying, 208, 238, 251, 278–9
Dampier, William, 20, 63
Dark, Eleanor, 57, 301
Darling Downs, 68–9, 121
Darling River, 18, 66–8, 70
Darling, Sir Charles, 144
Darling, Sir Ralph, 66, 68, 91, 99
Davey, Col. 'Tom', 106
Darwin, 169, 216, 295
Deakin, Alfred, 152, 166, 174, 183,
    185, 198, 202–4, 209, 213–15
defence, 160, 184, 214–15, 223, 234–6,
    254–9, 264–5, 272, 281, 287–9
democracy, 88, 104, 126, 128–9, 132,
    142–3, 296, 311
Democratic Labor Party, 273
Denison, Sir William, 116, 130, 144
depressions, economic, 82, 84, 94,
    120, 131, 178ff., 238ff., 268, 284
deserts, 17, 24ff., 28, 70–2, 281
Dibbs, Sir George, 178, 184–5
'diggers', 76, 123ff., 159; see also
    A.I.F.
droughts, 18, 38, 49, 66, 71–3, 82–4,
    140, 169–71, 179, 208, 261
dummying, 140
Dutch, 17, 20, 31, 63, 290

East India Company, 32–3, 37, 59, 120
economic growth, 58, 75, 87, 124,
    151ff., 207–8, 273ff.
education, 98–100, 146–7, 296ff.
egalitarianism, 156, 163
Egypt, 219, 290
Eldershaw, M. B., 26–9

electricity, 231, 260
Elizabeth II, Queen, 290
emancipists, 42–51, 57–8, 60, 90–3
Empire settlement, 236
eucalyptus, 26–7, 78
Eureka, 126, 131
Evatt, H. V., 191, 229, 243, 257, 272,
    273, 286–7
exports, 59, 75, 154, 208, 237–8, 276,
    279, 281, 284
Eyre, E. J., 70
Eyre, Lake, 19, 71–2

family allowances, 284
Farrer, William, 208
Fawkner, John Pascoe, 118
Federation, 129, 181, Chap. 12
    passim, 261ff., 274–5, 311
financial agreement, 262, 274
financial crises, 70, 139, 170, 175,
    239–42
First Fleet, 37–8
Fisher, Andrew, 202, 215, 218
Fitzroy, Sir Charles, 114
flax, 42, 59, 105
Flinders, Matthew, 61–3
floods, 46, 49, 53; see also climate
football, 303–4
Forbes, Mr Justice, 89, 91
foreign policy, 166, 182–3, 187, 215,
    229, 234–6, 253, 286ff.
forests, 26–7, 299–300
Forrest, Sir John, 189, 195
France, 43, 61, 105, 166, 183, 187,
    219, 221, 230, 289
Fraser, Malcolm, 275, 289, 291
free trade, 145–6, 238, 265; see also
    interstate free trade

Gallipoli, 219, 221–2
gambling, 102, 303
Game, Sir Philip, 242
Gardiner, Frank, 148
gas, 170, 260, 276
Gawler, Governor, 120
General Motor-Holdens (G.M.H.),
    276, 277, 288
George, Henry, 165

Germany and German colonies, 166,
    183, 187, 221, 229, 230
Gipps, Sir George, 85
gold, 76, Chap. 8, 152–3, 169, 178–9,
    195, 292
golf, 303
Goolagong, Evonne (Mrs Cawley),
    293
Gorton, John, 289
Governor's powers, 88ff., 144–5, 242,
    308
Goyder's line, 168
Great Britain, see United Kingdom
Greenway, Francis, 57
Grey, Earl, 129–30
Grey, Sir George, 120
Griffin, Walter Burley, 283
Griffith, Sir Samuel, 180, 193, 224

Hancock, Sir Keith (W.K.), 29, 136,
    162, 235, 250, 300
harbours, 29
Harrison, James, 154
Harvester Judgement, 199
Hawkesbury River, 46, 49, 53, 61
Henty family, 68, 118
Higgins, Mr Justice, 199–200, 203,
    205, 210
High Court of Australia, 200–1, 205,
    264–5, 270
Higinbotham, George, 143–4, 175
Hobart, 101, 111, 116, 183
Holt, Harold, 289
Holman, W. A., 191n., 227–8
horse-racing, 101, 252, 278, 303
Hotham, Sir Charles, 126
hours of work, 238, 283–4
housing, 101, 135, 260, 269, 305, 309
Howard, John, 35
Hughes, W. M., 214, 221–32, 253
Hume and Hovell, 65, 118
Hunter, Capt. John, 23, 54, 62
hydro-electricity, 231, 267, 282

immigration
    Asian, 81, 92, 133, 165–6, 170, 197,
        272, 309

assisted, 81, 84, 94, 103–4, 132–4,
    209, 215, 236–7, 269, 309
opposition to, 132–4, 159, 198
restriction, 165, 180, 183, 194,
    197ff., 213, 215, 230–1, 233–4,
    236–7, 258, 290
to Queensland, 138, 155
to Victoria, 123–4, 170–1
Imperial preference, 215, 237
income tax, 187, 226, 263, 274
India, 17, 55–6, 270, 305
Indonesia, 290
Industrial Workers of the World
    (I.W.W.), 205, 227
inflation, 267, 269, 272, 283–4
interstate free trade, 129–30, 182, 187,
    192, 265
investment, see capital and investment
Irish, 86, 98–9, 225–6
iron and steel, 209ff., 238, 244, 260,
    276
iron mining, 280–1
irrigation, 152, 276, 282–3

Japan, 33, 214, 217, 229, 235, 252–3,
    257–9, 277, 279, 281
Jevons, W. S., 135–6
Jindivik aircraft, 281
Johnston, Major George, 56
juvenile delinquency, 111, 309

Kalgoorlie, 195
Kanakas, 155, 180–1, 183, 216
Kelly, Ned, 149
Kerr, Sir John, 307–8
Kimberleys, 19–20, 194
King George's Sound, 63, 70, 117
King, Philip Gidley, 52–3, 105
Korean war, 278, 287
Kosciusko, Mt, 68

labour movement
    beginnings, 91, 123, 160, 163
    growth of, 151, 172, 176
    in politics, generally, 203, 248, 266,
        272–3
    in politics, re Federation, 184,
        191–2, 262

in politics, Federal, 199, 201–2,
212–14, 224, 232, 240, 244, 248,
257, 266, 270–1, 273, 307–8
in politics, N.S.W., 211–13, 226–7,
241ff.
mateship in, 163, 171, 174
nationalism in, 213–15, 227
socialism in, 172, 202, 213, 227,
247–8, 266
and trade unions: nineteenth-
century, 163–5, 171–5, 185;
since Federation, 205, 213, 228,
241ff.
and World War I, 224ff.
and World War II, 256–8
labour costs, 83, 155, 239, 284
labour shortage, 81, 83, 96, 132, 135,
140, 231, 309
Lalor, Peter, 126
land grants, 46, 50–2, 60, 65, 75, 93,
103, 117
land leases, 85, 130–2, 138–9
land policy, 85, 93–4, 103–4, 130–2,
139–40, 142, 150
land rights, 294–5
land sales, 85, 94, 119–20, 131–2, 138,
140, 142–3, 207
Lane, William, 172–3, 176
Lang, John Thomas, 240ff.
Lang, Rev. John Dunmore, 82,
99–101
La Pérouse, 43, 105
La Trobe, C. J., 125, 130
Lawson, Henry, 159, 163
lead, 153, 179, 209, 267, 281, 288
League of Nations, 230, 234–5, 287
Legislative Council, N.S.W., 84, 89,
92–5, 104, 114, 125, 128, 242
Legislative Council, Victoria, 144,
157–8
liberalism, 157, 202–3, 212, 248,
270ff., 307
literature, 159–63, 301–2
Lord, Simeon, 51, 59, 102

Macarthur, James, 93, 101
Macarthur, John, 51–6, 58, 60, 74, 154
McCulloch, Sir James, 143–4

McKay, H. V., 156
Macquarie harbour, 107, 110
Macquarie, Lachlan, 46–50, 56–9, 90,
106
Malaya, 121, 287, 289–90
Mannix, Most Rev. Daniel, 225, 273
manufactures, 59, 123, 134, 143, 171,
209, 231, 238–9, 244, 260, 275–6
maritime strike, 1890, 173ff.
Marsden, Samuel, 51, 53, 90
Marx, Karl, 165, 205
Masters and Servants Act, 92, 102
mateship, 163ff., 171, 174
Matra, James, 33, 36–7
meat, 154, 208, 237, 279
Melbourne, 65, 68, 118, 124, 134–5,
156, 170, 176, 178, 243, 252, 285,
302–3
in financial crisis, 1893, 170, 174, 178
Melville Island, 121, 169
Menzies, R. G., 255–7, 271ff., 288,
289–90, 297
Mill, John Stuart, 143, 165
mining, 28, 179, 215, 277, 279ff., 294,
299; *see also* specific minerals
Mitchell, Sir Thomas, 19, 67–9, 119
Moran, Cardinal, 174–5, 190
Moreton Bay, 69, 121
Mort, T. S., 154
Mount Bischoff, 179
Mount Isa, 280
Mount Lyell, 179
Mount Morgan, 153, 170
Mount Zechan, 179
Munich Agreement, 1938, 235, 253
Munro, James, 177
Murray River, 26, 65, 67, 69, 282
Murray, Sir Hubert, 245–6
Murrumbidgee River, 65–6
music, 101, 302, 309
Myall Creek, 24
myxomatosis, 278, 299

national income, 171, 273, 283, 296
national parks, 299
nationalism, 147, 151, 159ff., 165, 168,
187, 190, 213–14, 223, 227, 229,
266, 290

Navy, 214, 221ff., 235, 259
New Caledonia, 166, 183
Newcastle, 59, 211, 231, 276
New England, 69, 76, 85
New Guard, 243
New Guinea, 25, 33, 62, 166, 183,
    187, 194, 221, 229, 245–6, 257–9,
    276, 291–3
New Protection, 199–202
New South Wales
    agitation for self-government, 83–4,
        91, 127–8
    agriculture, 47–50, 95, 207–8
    Bigge's report on, 58ff.
    conscription campaign, 225ff.
    early government of, 54–8, 88–91
    exploration in, 61–5, 68–9
    Federation movement, 129–37,
        183–93
    forests, 300
    gold in, 123–4, 140
    immigration to, 96, 124, 133
    in depression, 1890–3, 178, 180
    in depression, 1930–3, 241–3
    politics, 141–2, 144–5, 225, 241,
        273
    public works, 151
    railways, 134, 143, 151
    relations with Commonwealth,
        241–2, 262–3
    squatting in, 76ff., 84–5, 131
    wool-growing in, 51–3, 60, 74, 84,
        132, 141
    see also bushrangers, education,
        labour movement, land policy,
        railways, religion, Sydney, tariffs
New South Wales Corps, 55–6
New Zealand, 17, 29, 31–3, 287,
    304–5
nickel, 280–1
Norfolk Island, 42, 105, 110
North Australia, 19, 280–2
Northern Territory, 71, 169–70,
    216–17, 246–8, 280, 294
North West Cape, 287

officers', trading, 38, 40, 42, 47, 50–2,
    54, 56

oil and petrol, 276, 280, 300
Old Age Pensions, 202
Olympic games, 289, 304
Ord River, 283
Ottawa trade agreements, 237–8, 245
Oxley, John, 64, 66, 68–9

Pacific Ocean and exploration, 31–3,
    183
Papua, see New Guinea
Paraguay, 176
Parkes, Sir Henry, 146–8, 166, 184–5
pastoral industry
    artesian water for, 25, 208
    cattle, 78, 154, 216–17, 248, 279
    costs, 83ff., 170–1, 279
    depression in, 1842, 84; 1890,
        170–1; 1930, 239; 1979, 279
    in South Australia, 120
    in Van Diemen's Land, 74
    in Victoria, 118–19, 131, 142
    progress and difficulties, 51–3,
        Chap. 5, 141, 153, 171, 208, 239,
        279, 288
    see also droughts, Queensland,
        shearers, sheep, squatters, wool
payment of members of Parliament,
    157
Peel, Thomas, 117
penal settlements, 69, 107, 110
penitentiaries, 35–6, 113
Perth, 195, 276, 280, 301
Petrov, 273
Phillip, Capt. Arthur, R.N., 30,
    37–42, 50, 61
Pigot, Lord, 54
Pine Creek, 169, 288
Pinjarra, 23, 117
Pitt, William, 43
Point Puer, 112
police, 125–6, 175, 309
political prisoners, 96–7
Polynesian Protection and Regulation
    Acts, 155, 181
population
    Aboriginal, 21, 24, 108, 247, 293
    Australian, 136, 159, 244, 259, 309
    Chinese, 165

New South Wales, 41–2, 95
Northern Territory, 216
Queensland, 137
South Australia, 121
Victoria, 119, 124, 131
Western Australia, 117, 195
Port Arthur, 110
Port Essington, 69, 121, 169
Port Phillip, 63, 65, 106
Port Phillip district, 76, 118–19, 130
Port Pirie, 210–11
Portland, 68, 118
Premier's Plan, 240
press, 89, 91, 102, 112, 256, 301
prickly pear, 27, 298
primary production, 244, 250, 278;
    see also agriculture, pastoral
    industry, dairying, sugar, wheat,
    wool
probation system, 113
protection, see tariffs
public enterprise, 122, 206, 232,
    248–9, 274
public service, 275, 297–8
public works
    Australia, 168, 237, 268–9, 282
    New South Wales, 59, 151
    Queensland, 138–9, 181
    South Australia, 120
    Victoria, 152

Queensland, 18–20
    Aboriginals, 20, 137, 246–7, 294
    agriculture, 138, 154–5, 180, 216–17
    development, 137–40, 216–17, 277,
        280
    exploration, 69, 71
    Federation, 190, 192–4
    financial crises, 138–9, 179–80
    labour movement, 172, 175, 205
    land policy, 132, 138–9
    mining, 153, 277, 280
    pastoral industry, 154–5, 175, 217
    see also Brisbane, Kanakas, sugar,
        White Australia policy

rabbits, 169–70, 208, 299
racing, see horse-racing

radar, 299
radicals, 86, 115, 126, 141–2, 157,
    165, 203, 299
radio, 303
Raffles Bay, 117, 121, 169
railways, 28, 130, 149, 168, 182, 217,
    237, 269; see also under each
    state
rainfall, see climate
Redfern, Dr William, 51, 57
refrigeration, 154, 179, 208
Reid, Sir George, 184–6, 192
religion, 98, 147, 309–10
representative government, 90–2, 103
republicanism, 126, 162, 290
responsible government, 116, 126–7,
    296
Ridley stripper, 156
Riverina, 76, 185–6, 189, 192
river transport, 26
rivers, problem of, 64–7
roads, 95, 149, 282
Robertson, Sir John, 131–2, 184
Robinson, G. A., 108
rockets, 281
Roman Catholics, 86, 98–9, 147–8,
    225, 273, 297, 310
rum, 47–8, 50
Rum Jungle, 279

Salisbury, Marquis of, 125, 166
Second Fleet, 41
secularism, 147
selectors, 132, 140–2, 159
self-government, 91ff., 127ff., 144ff.
Senate, 188–9, 307
settlers, free, 42, 46–7, 50, 65, 75
shearers, 164ff., 170–4
sheep, 52–3, 78, 119, 141, 208, 279
shipping, 232
slumps, see depressions
Snowy Mountains Hydro-Electric
    Scheme, 267, 282
socialism, 172, 202, 205–6, 227, 232,
    240, 248, 271, 306
South Africa, 17, 29, 52, 305
South Australia
    agriculture, 132, 168–9, 207

South Australia—*continued*
anti-discrimination, 293
depression, 168–9
exploration, 69–71, 168–70
Federation, 184, 193
foundation, 119ff.
grants to, 250, 263
self-government, 129, 141
see also public works, religion,
Whyalla, Woomera
Spence, W. G., 163–4, 172
spinifex, 19, 26
sport, 100–1, 303ff.
squatters
in New South Wales, 130–2, and
Chap. 5 *passim*
in Queensland, 138–9
in Victoria, 131, 140
political position, 86, 104, 128, 142,
157, 295–6
successes, 88, 121–2
standard of living, 29, 101–2, 134–5,
156, 200, 210, 238, 283, 306
Statute of Westminster, 234
steel, *see* iron and steel
Streeton, Sir Arthur, 162
strikes, 92, 173ff., 205, 228–9, 239–40,
269
Stuart, McDouall, 72, 169
Sturt, Charles, 66–7, 69–73, 101, 119
Sudan, 166–7
Suez, 288–9
sugar, 60, 154–5, 180–1, 216, 238, 279
Sukarno, 290
Swan River, 75, 116–17, 120
Sydney
amusements in, 100–1, 300, 301
convicts at, 44–5, 58, 90, 115
Federal movement in, 185–6,
190–1, 285
foundation of, 30, 37–8
harbour and bridge, 30, 243, 300
larrikinism and crime in, 58, 90,
102, 148
living conditions in, 45, 58, 94,
101, 134–6, 300
manufactures, 59
opera house, 300

press, 89, 102, 257
religion and education in, 98–9, 147
unrest in, 174, 243
Sydney, Lord, 36–7
Syme, David, 143

tariffs and protection
Commonwealth, 202, 211, 231,
238, 245, 251, 275, 284, 291
demand for, 95, 134, 143, 185,
198–9
Imperial preference, 215, 237–8
intercolonial, 127, 129–30, 145–6,
182, 187, 190
opposition to, 146, 184
see also interstate free trade, new
protection, Victoria
Tasman, Abel, 31
Tasmania
Aboriginals, 17, 20, 108, 118
constitution, 116, 129
depressions in, 178–80, 250, 262, 263
Federation, 188, 193, 262
fruit-growing, 208
hydro-electricity, 231, 299–300
land policy, 132
mining, 153, 179
railways, 178–9
tariff, 130, 145
see also Van Diemen's Land
taxation, 85, 125, 157, 187, 226, 309
uniform, 263–4, 274–5
Taylor, Professor Griffith, 25
telegraphs, 149, 152, 169
television, 303, 309
Tench, Watkin, 23
tennis, 303–4
theatre, 100, 302
Timor, 290
tin, 179
Tobruk, 255, 259
Tolpuddle Martyrs, 96
Torrens, Lake, 70–1
trade, with U.K., 32–7, 59, 74, 120,
215, 237, 290; *see also* exports
trade unions, 91, 163ff., 170–5, 205,
241, 269; *see also* labour
movement

transport and communications, 26,
   29, 95, 150, 179, 182; *see also*
   railways and roads
transportation of convicts, 35ff.,
   43–6, 93, 96, 103–4, 108ff.
Trollope, Anthony, 156, 162

unemployment, 94, 134–5, 150, 174,
   178, 180, 239–40, 268, 278, 284,
   300
uniform taxation, 263–4, 274–5
United Kingdom government
   attitude to Aboriginals, 23, 195;
      Kanakas, 155; responsible
      government, 124, 144ff., 158–9;
      settlement in Australia, 36–7,
      42–3, 106; squatters, 76, 85;
      White Australia policy, 155, 166,
      230
   defence policy, 235, 254–5, 288
   foreign policy, 166, 183, 215,
      234–5, 256, 286, 288–9
   investment, 75, 152, 171, 176, 277
   land policy, 85, 103–4, 128
   penal policy, 34–5, 46, 96–7
   research in, 299
   see also capital and investment,
      Imperial preference, trade,
      transportation, World War I
      and World War II
United Nations, 266, 287, 290–1
United States of America
   colonial revolution, 128
   compared with Australia, 17, 25,
      27–9, 122, 133, 151, 160–1, 183,
      198, 273, 299, 306–7
   convict transportation to, 35
   defence, 281, 287–8
   foreign policy, 160, 183, 229–30,
      235, 288
   investment, 277
   land policy, 131
   space programme, 281, 287–8
   trade, 279, 288
   see also World War I and World
      War II
universities, 147, 297
uranium, 279–80

urban development, *see* cities
U.S.S.R., 279, 289
Utzon, Jan, 300

Van Diemen's Land
   exploration, 31, 62–3, 105
   settlement, 74, 106–7, 115–16, 118,
      130
   transportation to, 96, 107ff., 116,
      125
   see also Tasmania
Vaughan, Archbishop, 148
Versailles, Peace Conference and
   Treaty, 1919, 221, 229
Victoria
   agriculture, 130–2, 207
   bank smash, 1893, 176–8
   bushranging, 149
   Chinese in, 165
   conscription campaign, 1917, 225
   Country Party, 251
   education, 147
   exploration, 65, 67, 72
   Federation, 184, 189, 191–3
   foundation of, 117–18
   gold in, 124ff.
   irrigation in, 152
   land policy, 130–2, 207, 215
   pastoral industry, 81–3, 141
   political disputes, 141–6, 157–9
   protection and tariff, 143–5, 157
   radicalism, 143–6, 157–9, 203
   railways, 134, 143, 152, 170
   trade unions, 164, 174
   wages and Wages Boards, 134, 204
   see also labour movement, religion,
      Melbourne
Vietnam, 288, 306–7
voyages of discovery, 31ff.

wages, 83, 102, 124, 134, 200, 226,
   238–40, 283–4
Wages Boards, 204, 210
Wakefield, Edward Gibbon, 93–4,
   96, 119, 221
Wentworth, D'Arcy, 51, 57
Wentworth, W. C., 60, 64, 87, 90–4,
   97, 101, 127–9, 146

Western Australia
  Aboriginals, 23, 246–7
  defence establishments in, 276,
    280–1
  discovery and exploration, 17,
    19–20, 63, 70
  Federation, 195–6
  grants to, 250, 263
  mining, 194, 276, 280–1
  railways, 195–6
  settlement and development,
    116–17, 132, 194–6
  transportation to, 96, 118
whaling and sealing, 59, 107
Whately, Archbishop, 113
wheat, 47, 49, 95, 155–6, 207–8, 231,
    239, 278–9

White Australia policy, *see*
    immigration restriction
Whitlam, E. G., 278, 307–8
Wilson, President Woodrow, 221,
    229–30
wool, 52–3, 74–5, 84, 171, 208, 239,
    278–9, 281, 288
Woomera, 281
World War I, 218ff.
  and U.K., 223–4
  and U.S.A., 221
  see also Hughes, A.I.F., Anzac
World War II, 253ff.
  and U.K., 255ff.
  and U.S.A., 256, 258

Zimbabwe, 291
zinc, 281